CW00954359

THE FIGHTING
PADRE

THE FIGHTING PADRE

Letters from the Trenches 1915–1918 of Pat Leonard DSO

Edited by

John Leonard and
Philip Leonard-Johnson

Pen & Sword
MILITARY

First published in Great Britain in 2010 by
Pen & Sword Military
an imprint of
Pen & Sword Books Ltd
47 Church Street
Barnsley
South Yorkshire
S70 2AS

ISBN: 978-1-84884-159-8

A CIP catalogue record for this book is
available from the British Library.

Typeset in 11/13pt Sabon by
Concept, Huddersfield, West Yorkshire

Printed and bound in England by
the MPG Books Group

Pen & Sword Books Ltd incorporates the Imprints of Pen & Sword
Aviation, Pen & Sword Maritime, Pen & Sword Military, Wharncliffe
Local History, Pen & Sword Select, Pen & Sword Military Classics,
Leo Cooper, Remember When, Seaforth Publishing and
Frontline Publishing.

For a c   contact

47 Church   AS, England

Contents

Preface

The invasion of neutral Belgium by German forces on their way to take France brought Britain into the conflict that became the First World War on 4 August 1914. German expansion threatened not only British overseas responsibilities but the very sovereignty of Britain itself, and huge numbers of young men from all over the Empire volunteered to fight off this threat.

The Germans established an extraordinarily long line of strategic points, often with very well-constructed posts and trench systems. The Allied forces likewise set up a parallel network. Frequently there would be artillery bombardment by day and then, by night, patrolling, repairing the line, supplying and the moving of troops. Men would spend spells of seven to ten days in front-line trenches, then in close-support trenches and in front-line trenches again before moving back to reserve areas.

From time to time, concerted efforts were made to break through the opposing front line. In February 1916, at Verdun, German forces advanced for six days but were brought to a standstill by enormous losses and the unsustainable stretching of their supply lines.

After months of stalemate, it fell to the British to attempt a decisive breakthrough. Early in July 1916, a week-long artillery onslaught started on the Somme. In addition to the five colossal mines that were detonated, this was designed to destroy the barbed-wire entanglements, the trenches and strongpoints, and to decimate any enemy who survived the bombardment.

In fact, many of the Germans were sheltering safely in their dugouts, 40 feet underground. When the shelling ceased for the advance, German machine-gunners emerged into what was left of their trenches and mowed down the approaching British and Dominion troops with devastating results. Twenty thousand were killed and twice as many wounded on that day, and only a quarter of the front line was breached.

There followed some five months during which positions were attacked and counter-attacks resisted but gradually the Germans were pushed back, field by field, until in November the objectives set in July were finally reached.

The 8th Battalion King's Own Royal Lancaster (KORL) Regiment gained honours in many actions throughout this campaign – the Bluff, St Eloi, Delville Wood, Guillemont, Serre, and in 1917, Arras, the Scarpe, and Zonnebeke. 'The Fighting Eighth' received much praise from the commanders of 76 Brigade and 3rd Division

By November 1917, many of the squadrons of the Royal Flying Corps, to which Leonard was then appointed Chaplain, were flying from airfields in the same general area.

For four months from March 1918, the Germans launched a massive offensive but they were held by the British and Allies who, in August, broke through an 11-mile section of the front line. Although the tide had been turned there was still fierce fighting until the bitter end – at the eleventh hour of the eleventh day of the eleventh month of 1918.

Acknowledgements

Family and friends who saw Pat Leonard's letters in their original handwritten form encouraged their safeguarding and publication. We thank them for their support and enthusiasm. There are others too, and they deserve our specific gratitude.

The curators of the following museums all gave information and advice which allowed us to fill a lot of the censored gaps in the original letters: Army Chaplaincy (David Blake), the King's Own Royal Regiment, Lancaster (Peter Donnelly), and RAF Records & Research (Stuart Haddaway).

Steve Smith, John Burgess and Dries Chaerle of Toc H provided some pictures, and strong support for the project.

Norman Gilham gave advice and the loan of useful records about the RFC.

Ray Mentzer of 'Photos of the Great War' allowed the use of several images from his valuable web-based archive, and John May ARPS helped with the acquisition and enhancement of other photographs.

Finally we thank our wives – Mary and Natalie – for enduring many months when our principal interest revolved more around 'The Fighting Padre' than them.

Glossary

Soldiers' Slang

'Signalese':
Ack, Beer, Don, Emma, Gee, Aitch, Eye, O, Pip, Q, Esses, Toc, Vic: thence Emma Gee for Machine Gun, O Pip for Observation Post, Ack Emma for Air Mechanic, Toc H for Talbot House ...

Shells:
Archibald – from anti-aircraft gun
Black Maria, Coal Box, Jack Johnson – heavy shell with black smoke
How – Howitzer 15in with 4ft 6in shell (or German 4.7 Howitzer)
Krump – heavy shell
Whistling Rufus – from naval 9in gun
Whizzbang – from 18 pounder field gun
Also HE, Woolly Bear, 15in, 5.9 etc

Expressions:
napoo (il n'y a plus) – is no more
Olive oil – au revoir – see you
Blighty One – injury serious enough for repatriation

The setting on the Western Front

Chapter 1

Introduction

Born in 1889 and brought up in a clergy family in Cumbria, Martin Patrick Grainge (Pat) Leonard went from being Head of School at Rossall to Oriel College, Oxford on a mathematics scholarship. After graduating and obtaining a Territorial Army Commission in the King's Own Royal Lancaster (KORL) Regiment, he served as a curate in a Manchester parish before being accepted as Chaplain to the 8th Battalion, KORL, from September 1915 on the battlefields of the Somme. He transferred to the Royal Flying Corps (RFC) late in 1917.

What follows are verbatim extracts from letters written by him, week by week throughout the First World War to his parents, a few to other members of the family, and to friends at home. These were, of course, in addition to the many hundreds of letters he wrote to the relatives of those killed or wounded in action.

Much personal material has been omitted, together with everything from the period following the Armistice. Very much a 'front-line' priest, his descriptions provide an unusually objective view of army life and the job of the multi-tasked chaplain who was expected to undertake the roles of counsellor, comforter, caterer, censor, entertainments officer and sports supremo ... They describe how the Chaplain found himself leading this 'ripping Brigade Church Parade' or that baptism in a shell crater by candlelight. He also emerges retrieving the wounded under heavy shellfire, smoking with Tommy in the trenches, and even, just once, beating the General at chess. They truly reflect those years, with all its joys and sorrows, triumphs and disasters, and flashes of irrepressible humour.

During his time with the RFC, Pat Leonard made frequent flights with 'those wonderful men in their flying machines'. This gave him a

1

bird's eye view from the observer's seat liberating his spirit from the mud of Flanders, whilst seeing how vital and how acutely dangerous was the role of the Corps.

Referred to in the British press as a 'veritable fighting parson' (from his prowess in the boxing ring), he played rugby for the RAF, was mentioned in despatches and was awarded the DSO for bravery.

Ninety years have passed before this opportunity arose to share his account of a time on the Somme, often regarded as unmitigated disaster, which, nevertheless, called forth human qualities of which we should all be proud.

John Leonard   Philip Leonard-Johnson

Chapter 1

The Mad Major ... and the Guardroom

From the trenches in Sanctuary Wood and Ploegsteert to billets in Eecke

12 October 1915. Here I am at last in *la belle France*. At present I am billeted in a little village [Outtersteene, SW of Bailleul] occupied this time last year by Huns, but time has wiped out all the scars which the passage of war must have left – an occasional cross in the corner of a field is all there is to show now that the war has passed this way.

I am with the 7th Field Ambulance. They have opened up a rest hospital here for slight cases so I make this my headquarters and go up to the trenches held by my Battalion for a day or two at a time. I could have wished that we weren't so far back – about eight miles – but luckily a motor ambulance goes so far each day and I can get on from there on some borrowed horse.

We are holding now one of the finest pieces of line on our whole front [Ploegsteert Wood]. The trenches are well made and sand-bagged – with planking at the bottom and well drained, so even in the wettest weather we should be free from excessive mud. I don't believe the Germans could ever take them, so strong are they. Moreover they are the only ones in which it is possible to get in and out by daylight.

I am becoming quite an expert horseman. On Sunday I borrowed a blood mare from one of the officers here, and went for a long tour of inspection, and incidentally tried my luck over a few jumps, luckily

3

without disaster but with a marked absence of finesse or elegance. However, I am becoming quite good by degrees.

I enjoyed my first night in the trenches very much tho' the rats ate half my tobacco while I slumbered – after that I got up and spent the rest of the night talking to the look-out men, and watching our shells burst, and the Germans sending up Very lights to see that we weren't meditating a violent onslaught. We stood by at dawn for an hour – the weirdest hour I've ever spent. Out of the mist your imagination could picture hordes of Huns silently advancing in serried mass!

One little excitement I had was when I went out into our listening post between the lines, and our own men started popping at us thinking we were Germans. I was out with two other fellows – of course it was pitch dark. They went each way to see that our wire was all right, and left me to listen. It suddenly struck me what an ass I should feel if a German on listening bent suddenly turned up, for of course I don't carry any weapon of defence or offence, and knowing nix of German would be hard put to explain that my presence there was entirely amicable and unprofessional.

I hear we are to give up our trenches tomorrow to a Brigade which got rough handled further down the line, and we are to go north a bit – probably a much warmer quarter.

There's a great fellow in these parts – known as 'The Mad Major'. He owns his own monoplane and goes over the German lines everyday to practise dodging shrapnel. When the Huns get his range he does a loop or a perpendicular *vol plan* and side steps a few hundred yards, and as soon as they alter their sights back he goes to the old place among the shrapnel smoke. He's a great fellow, even the Canadians admit that he is *some* flier [Captain 'Steve' Cochran-Patrick]. My opinion of the Canadians has gone up – they don't care a dump for the Huns and read novels up on the parapet! Every night fifty or sixty of them are out between the wire looking for Huns – their CO has offered £50 & ten days' free pass to England for the capture of every prisoner! And my word they work hard for it, but the Germans lie doggo.

We came over from Southampton to Le Havre by a small Isle of Man boat, packed like herrings, each man wearing a cork life belt which luckily weren't necessary tho' they successfully prevented us from sleeping. We cleared Southampton as the harbour lights were beginning to twinkle and dusk beginning to fall. It was rather a fine sight, our last view of old England for some time at any rate.

Outside, we picked up our escort, a fast, ugly looking destroyer, which followed us like a shadow, and successfully frightened away submarines, if any were about.

At Havre, while waiting to disembark, we saw a long trainload of wounded; slight cases, straight from the trenches, caked with mud and looking, poor fellows, most awful skeletons. And they shouted to us the good news of our advance, and we landed with high hopes that the beginning of the end had begun.

Amid the rain we disembarked, and then marched to a very muddy rest camp, where we spent the night in tents, and next day got on board a train to bring us up to the front. We hadn't Pullman cars! The men were in cattle trucks, with straw to lie on, and there in that train we remained for twenty-four hours, dawdling along and stopping every now and then. About 10 pm we stopped to stretch our legs and had some hot coffee and cognac served out by French soldiers. Then on again all through the night. 2 pm next day we arrived at a bleak, windswept, rainy little siding [Doullens]. There we got out our wagons and horses and ambulances, and started to march to our billets. Oh what a march! Frightful roads – all *pavé* and holey – incessant rain, weary and hungry, backs breaking under the load of our packs. However, at last, when all hope of getting anywhere was gone, we arrived at a little French village and learned that we were to find billets there for the night. By this time it was quite dark, so our task was not easy. However finally we all got settled down and had our first bite of food since breakfast thirteen hours before! Never before had I realised the recuperative effects of a steaming bowl of good French coffee – how we enjoyed it, and next day we rose fit for anything.

Already I feel I have enough experiences to write a book. They must keep until after the war.[1]

13 October 1915. It is so hard to keep track of the days. Each one is so like the last, and even Sunday sometimes has nothing to mark it as distinct from Tuesday or Friday. At last we have orders to move, my Brigade has been in the trenches a week now, but they come out tomorrow, and are then to be transferred further up the line towards ——[Hooge]. As the Ambulance is staying where it is, I am leaving them and rejoining my own Battalion.

[1] After only 3 weeks!

All the country around here is very flat and open, no hedges or very few, but the French are very clever at breaking the monotony by planting long avenues along the main roads. A main road that I have been using a lot lately is one long avenue of poplars stretching for a good seven miles – the road itself is *pavé* and very bad for biking, but it looks very picturesque, especially with its long line of motor lorries drawn in on one side, waiting for dusk to begin their slow and tortuous journey up to the trenches and batteries with stores and fodder for man and gun.

Our chief form of recreation is watching aeroplanes shelled. But as we can rarely see whether they are our machines or Taubes, we hardly know whether to rejoice or weep at the fruitless expenditure of shrapnel. It really is rather amusing to see the shrapnel burst like little spots of black ink in the blue sky, and wonder where the next will be. After a moment or two the black spot becomes unravelled as it shakes itself out into a ball of fluffy cotton wool which hangs suspended in the sky for several minutes. Sometimes altho' you cannot see the aeroplane you can trace its course by the line of bursting shrapnel.

17 October 1915. Since my last letter I have left the Ambulance [at Bailleul] and rejoined my own Battalion and marched with them to a new sector of our lines, about eight miles north of where I was. At present we are waiting to relieve the other half of our Brigade which is already in the new trenches. We are under canvas, surrounded on all sides by other camps. The country is extraordinarily flat and uninteresting, with a marked absence of distinctive features. The weather moreover is misty and cold, so we are not as comfy as we were, but still not so bad. I luckily have managed to procure a canvas and wood hut which I share with the Transport Officer. It is quite comfy, about twenty feet by ten. I wish you could see me as I write sitting on my bed – i.e. on the floor.

I've just got back from a Parade Service – out of doors of course and rather cold. I had two Celebrations this morning, the first at 7 am for the men. I rigged up a little altar with cross and lights in a bell-tent, and the men crowded round – very primitive but very nice. At 8 am I had another, this time in a hut for the officers of the Brigade. No small work packing up everything and transporting it elsewhere for each Celebration. Twelve officers came including some of the Staff Officers. We had such a ripping Service, again very primitive but less so than the one in the bell-tent. No altar rails or pews of course, but a folded blanket formed altar rails and kneelers combined.

We have to put up with a lot of uncertainty and disappointments. It often happens that after I have made all arrangements, fresh orders come out and we have to march away without any Service. But still it's all part of the game. I miss very much my regular little evening prayers with the men of the Field Ambulance in their billets. But still, I shall find many opportunities, I expect, for work here and in the trenches.

18 October 1915. After lunch yesterday (Sunday) I found that transport was going up to the trenches with water, so I elected to go with them. The Transport Officer found me a very nice horse to ride, steady and game and with the manners of a gentleman. So at 2.30 pm off we started on our ten-mile trek. As our water carts were full we had to walk all the way. It was an interesting ride through shelled-out villages and past old trenches and shell holes, but nothing to be compared with what was to come. At 5 pm we found a nice sheltered field where we out-spanned and off-saddled for tea.

Incidentally in getting into this field, the leaders of one of the carts got excited and the rear wheel got badly jammed in a deep ditch, and the whole thing tilted over at about 45°. Finally, we managed to get it out by hitching on six mules and digging the side of the ditch away. But it was no small job, I can tell you, with the mules straining and rearing all over the place, and the riders whipping and slashing about and the other men heaving on a drag rope.

After this little interlude, we soon made tea and had an alfresco meal *á la picnic* at Stenkrith. At ten minutes to six, we hitched up and rode off to meet our guides. They failed to meet us, or else we tried to meet them in the wrong place for we saw no sign of them. However as we knew men were short of water we pushed on in the gloom trying to find our way by the map or from scraps of information gleaned from stray stragglers.

The last part of the journey up was highly exciting, through a City of the Dead [Ypres] – once a beautiful city of noted beauty, now a heap of ruins – not a whole house standing; nothing but a few gaunt tottering walls and masses of debris. We were lucky enough to find a guide there, who took us through the narrow streets, past burned-out factories and the remains of small shops – what had once been, I suppose, the busy commercial end of the city. At the far end the guide left us, and then began the last stage of our journey up to the communication trenches, past all sorts of dangerous corners and bits of open country where we could hear the bullets whistling overhead, and the roaring shriek of our own shells as they hurtled high above us towards the German trenches.

At last we reached our dumping spot, and what a sight! To the onlooker it was a meaningless confusion of men and stores. Mud-grimed ration parties for many different regiments clustering round their transport carts, water parties with empty petrol cans to carry the precious fluid up to the firing line, wounded waiting for someone to get them away to a place of rest and safety, new regiments burdened with a miscellany of a hundred different things waiting to relieve men who had done their six days or more, old regiments staggering away for a few days rest, horses grazing quietly waiting for their wagons to be emptied. Everybody busy working quietly and methodically, though how they ever found what they wanted or re-found their trenches again seemed miraculous. And all the time the tremendous and ceaseless roar of the guns, the hum of the bullets, and the evil vicious tapping of the machine guns played their part in the devil's concert.

I hardly realised that I was under fire and that any minute a shell might find us. I wish I could paint the scene for you. Imagine a moonlight night with a heavy ground mist, and all round a ring of bursting shells, and flares and lights of all descriptions, and nothing else but this muddle of waiting and working mud-stained soldiers. Here a heap of stores, here a water cart with its attendant waiting queue of men, here a heap of barbed wire on drums, here a faintly recognizable mass of resting soldiers, here the horse-drawn wagons disgorging bales of sandbags or ammunition or bully beef, and above the ring of mist, faintly pencilled, the tops of fir trees. Oh no, and I can't tell you what a wonderful sight it was, or make you realise the patient pathos of it all. You would have to see it all, and the little garden of crosses near at hand, to understand it.

Well, at last, our carts were empty and the return journey commenced. It was now 10 pm and the mist was clearing, so we could see more, and incidentally be easier seen, so speed was the order of the day. We were soon out of that ring of flash and bang and roar entering once more the City of the Dead. From time to time heavily over-coated sentries stopped us, not with the conventional 'Halt, who goes there?', but the quiet question, 'Who are you?' And our reply, 'King's Own. Goodnight sentry'.

This time as no shells were falling in the city we didn't bother with the side streets, but went boldly through by the main road, through the great square with its skeletons of famous buildings looking magnificent in the bright light of the moon. All the hideousness was hidden, only the glory of the ruin was there.

As we trotted smartly through this great wide square, it seemed a sort of sacrilege. I felt we ought to walk through this cemetery of famous buildings and beautiful churches. Once through, we heaved a sigh of relief and the rest of the long trek home seemed tame and monotonous. I almost slept in the saddle, and would have done more than once, but for the stumble of my horse as he stepped on the edge of the shell hole or a deep cart groove in the hard *pavé*.

But all things come to an end, and at midnight we turned into camp, cold and stiff after ten hours and nearly the whole of it spent in the saddle.

22 October 1915. I wasn't able to post No. 5 until yesterday as we have been continually on the move since I wrote it. Meanwhile, the most excellent cake has arrived and a pc from Father but I have had no letters for ten days. I suppose they are following me round and will in time catch me up.

Last Tuesday I had a long ride. Over twenty-four miles on a very fat short-stepping cob – it wasn't much of a joyride as I went by myself to Outtersteene where my original billets were, to see if I could trace my letters and buy a few things in Bailleul where the other day I saw Wilfrid [brother-in-law].

On Wednesday, we had orders to move so I proceeded to pack up. Despite its uncouthness I had settled down quite happily in our camp and was sorry to leave it, especially as I had just manufactured for myself a bed out of four pieces of timber nailed together to form the framework, and had made a spring mattress by crisscrossing backwards and forwards some cable wire, which I procured from a neighbouring Field Telegraph Company.

When all was ready for our departure I got a note asking me to bury one of our poor fellows killed in action, so while the Battalion marched off in one direction, I rode off in the other. The Battalion has got six days rest in the rear of the line, and I had to go up to the line to get the body and bury it. It was 7 pm and quite dark when I started and after jogging along for nearly two hours, I met the body being brought down on a limber, and together we made for the little cemetery where many of our poor fellows rest in peace.

It was a strange and weird experience. The little corner of a field railed off with its crop of plain wooden crosses, and the new-dug grave with a dimly discernible group of gravediggers and stretcher bearers standing round, hardly illuminated by the faint moonlight.

After tethering my horse outside and putting on a stole over my uniform I went to the graveside and by the light of a pocket torch read the Burial Service over the poor fellow, who by the way came from Ulverston.

Of course we could have none of the pomp or ceremony of a military funeral, but the big guns boomed the death knell, and machine guns in the distance fired the volleys over his grave. It was my first military funeral out here and moved me very much. It was all so weird and solemn.

Then back once more on my long ride to bed. When I arrived at our new halting place I found the town [Poperinghe] in darkness and everyone asleep. Imagine me riding up and down the lonely streets, my horse continually slipping on the cobbles, trying to find someone to tell me where my billet was. At last at 2 am I found a house to which, after I had rung the bell until I broke it, I gained admittance and just as I was (for my baggage was I knew not where) lay down on the hard floor and slept the sleep of the weary. Altogether Wednesday night will not easily fade from my memory.

Yesterday (Thursday) we rested all day in this same town, and I managed to have my first hot bath since landing in France. How I enjoyed it, a big washing tub full of boiling water and a wee drappie of disinfectant and me. *Ma foi* it was a treat.

Then at 6 pm we started to march again. Apparently they are afraid to move troops by day for fear of being spotted by aeroplanes, so all night we tramped along through the rain until, when we could hardly go another inch, we came to a large French village [Eecke], not far from Wilfrid's headquarters, and there in barns and farm-houses we found rest. I believe we are to be here six days. I don't fancy the idea much as we were really better off in camp, for here we are packed like sardines. However, it is all part of the game, and despite everything I am enjoying myself immensely.

23 October 1915. I am sitting in the parlour of the farmhouse at a round oilcloth-covered table, writing this: four others are all employed writing home. There are in our little Mess: the Doctor who has been out since the beginning and snaffled a Military Cross at Festubert; the Transport Officer, a mad Irishman with a brogue; the Quartermaster, an old regular and one of the best; and lastly our Interpreter, a Frenchman, who *inter alia* is marrying an English girl. We are quite a happy little family and make our billet as comfy as possible. The farmhouse is old and solid, with splendid oak-beamed ceilings and stone-flagged floors, but very cold and draughty. Across the way in the barns are about 100 men billeted; and between them and us an open cesspool! I wish you could see our bedroom – an empty flagged room the whole floor space occupied by the stretchers on which we sleep, and our kits.

It is a strange life we live these days, or rather 'these nights', for most of our work is done at night. In years to come whenever I see a moonlit night, I shall think of jogging along these long *pavé*-avenued French and Belgian roads.

The other night I was up near the front. In point of fact, I was just in front of our heavy batteries, waiting to meet one of my Battalions coming out of the trenches. As I was blowing on my hands and thinking of the insignificance of mortal man, and the fatuousness of firing hundreds of heavy shells at an unseen trench miles away, I came across another Chaplain who invited me into his little shack. He is living in the only house in a shelled-out village, a little four-roomed cottage in the middle of a battered row. In the front room he and his servant eat and sleep and dispense tea and coffee to tired soldiers passing back from the trenches – a real good Samaritan. In the back room downstairs lives his horse, its manger nothing less than the old sink. Upstairs in front a shell has battered in the wall and made a mess generally. So, nothing happens there, but in the back room he has rigged up a little altar, and there every day he has a Celebration with his servant, and perhaps a strange soldier or officer, who having lost his way over night, has found hospitality and a blanket, as congregation.[2]

When I arrived they were just having their evening meal, bully beef and bread and tea in their enamel mugs; their illumination a candle stuck in an empty bottle, and a little wood fire in the hearth.

---

[2] This was Mellish – see later regarding his VC.

I was in the middle of a cup of tea with them when the Battalion came along, so I went off with them. When we got on to the main road we found a long fleet of motor buses ready to carry us to our billets – old London motor buses painted green, with all the windows removed and boarded up, and absolutely unlighted. It's rather a fine sight to see a long line of these top-heavy buses loaded up with war-worn soldiers, moving along these long straight *pavé* roads with their beautiful avenues of lofty poplars each side. As they pass in the darkness, you can see nothing but the sea of faces, looking pale in the moonlight, looking down upon you.

Since we have been out, we have been extraordinarily fortunate in the amount of fine bright nights we have had. It will be a very different thing when the rainy season begins.

My last two or three letters have really been written in Belgium, tho' through force of habit I have headed them 'In France'. Now however, we are in France, once more, far from the klonk of guns or rifle fire in a large straggling village called Eecke not far from Hazebrouck.

I've been very much tickled by some of the dog-teams I've seen in the barrows out here. One turnout I saw had three big mongrels harnessed abreast dragging a big barrow loaded up to the nth including the driver who sat on top of everything and rattled along at a good eight miles an hour. The extraordinary thing is that these strange breeds seem to like pulling carts behind them, for they strain away and look quite hurt when they are asked to stop.

Our original trenches were in Ploegsteert Wood, and very nice too they were, only one casualty in the whole week we spent up there. In fact until the last day when they strafed us a bit, we were really in serious doubt as to whether there was anyone in the opposing trenches. Nobody seemed to mind when we spread the cloth on the parados for afternoon tea or sat on the parapet for a better grip of the foot when paring one's toenails.

After that delightful experience we trekked further still away from you to a horrid bulge in our line [Hooge], and there in forty-eight hours we lost six men killed and several more wounded. The whole place is one huge cemetery, and the trenches mere furrows in the ground. Luckily the Division to which we are now attached has come back after five months continual trench life, for a few days rest, and we have come with them – rumour says we do not return to that particular sector, for which the Saints be praised, but go south once more, or else cross the sea to Serbia. But rumour as you know is at best a lying jade, and we wait in some suspense to see what will befall us.

25 October 1915. Saturday was a nice sunny day, so in the intervals of arranging and preparing for Services I washed my shirt and socks, also my pyjamas and other articles of intimate apparel. It was a great achievement, and despite the fact that my things accumulated a certain amount of dirt in the drying process, they certainly look cleaner than they did. This morning I completed my domestic labours by doing an hour's ironing; war certainly is a wonderfully liberal education.

Sunday afternoon I rode over to the farms where the Welsh are billeted and looked up some of my flock and had a Confirmation instruction. On my arrival home I found our transport in a high state of ferment – all the horses and mules were saddled ready for a great cross-country race. Much as I mistrusted my ability to ride a line across country, I had no option but to compete, so in a dithering funk I got my horse into line. It really was a joke, the mules lashing out in all directions and showing a marked penchant for a bolt in the wrong direction, the horses on the other hand seemed to have a strong opinion on the colour question, and continually edged away from the mules. It may have been out of fear of flying heels, but I rather imagine that theirs was an attitude of supercilious aloofness. However when the flag fell my horse started so abruptly that I at once lost an iron and for the rest of the race, including the one and only jump, I hung on as best I could, my feet vainly seeking to lock themselves beneath my horse's girth and my hands clutching mane and reins and saddle in one comprehensive and abject frenzy of self-preservation.

My progress wasn't dignified but my horse could go so I didn't finish last. Where exactly I did finish, I don't know. I was too much occupied keeping on and I didn't recover my *sang froid* until my horse had quietly trotted back to its place in the transport lines!

What a land of paradoxes this is. Here we are living like bushmen and Neolithic barbarians in holes in the ground, with sheepskin clothes and eating our food with our fingers, and next door we have started a Divisional Cinematograph for the troops! Moving pictures on the battlefield. Isn't it grotesque?

26 October 1915. All the funerals have to take place at night for fear of shells or machine guns. It is a weird experience, the little band of mud-stained soldiers standing round the open grave, the body wrapped in his greatcoat or blanket, the Burial Service read by the light of a flash lamp or, if near the German lines, no light is possible and then I have to repeat the Service by heart. The whole scene has a wonderfully moving effect upon me, it is so much more real than the conventional funerals at home.

28 October 1915. All this week, we have had vile weather, though I have been out a bit most days. On Tuesday, I borrowed a horse and rode off to the place where I first met Wilfrid [Bailleul] – nine miles away – to look up my friends in the Field Ambulance, and to draw some money from the Field Cashier and make a few necessary purchases. The horse I was riding was a bit fresh, and had a nasty habit of always wanting to go the wrong way and standing on his hind legs when I remonstrated. Altogether he was rather a handful, and once made me very annoyed by turning sharply into an open field at the side of the road and banging my knee in passing against a tree. However, when I got him out again I took it out of him by making him canter until I was sore!

Yesterday I arranged to meet an ambulance at another town [Hazebrouck], but as it never turned up and I had wasted half an hour waiting for it, I decided to go off with one of our officers who happened to pass in a car. While we were there, we noticed that something was afoot. The Square or Grande Place was cleared of traffic, and little knots of people and English officers were standing about expectant. Just then an aeroplane came fussing about over-head; the assiduous looking at watches was somewhat noticeable, so we guessed that the King must be going through shortly.

It was in fact as we expected, and soon a car full of Staff Officers went buzzing through, followed at intervals by a small fleet of motor-bikes carrying Scouts. Then after a pause came a closed car of vast dimensions, flying the Royal Standard. I was standing by the edge of the pavement and had an excellent view of His Majesty who I thought seemed gratified at the way I saluted him, though inconsiderately he looked the other way at the critical moment! Following him came Sir John French and about three cars full of red hats and big bugs of various sorts and variously coloured noses. It was quite nice to see them all, and I liked the way the natives shouted '*Vive le Roi*' and waved their hands and hats with great zest. The British soldier out here appreciates the gracious visits of the King.

I've got hold of a rather nice trophy in the shape of an unexploded German hand grenade. I would like to send it home, but a new decree has come out forbidding the PO to accept such things on pain of confiscation, so I must bring it home when I come on leave.

1 November 1915. We are still here [in Eeecke], being gradually bored to extinction, for we have absolutely nothing to do all day except watch the rain transform the farm yard into a troubled sea of mud. As you can imagine, the cesspool in the middle is now perfectly pestilential and the home of all the unclean beasts of the brute creation – fat and odoriferous sows wallow on the marge thereof, and dead carcasses float aimlessly about the discoloured and slimy liquid – all we want now is a flock of carrion crows to complete the picture of desolation and decay.

While we have been resting here we have run a footer competition for the Divisional GOC's Cup. We have got a fairly good team out of the Battalion and began well by successively defeating the 4th Gordons, 1st Gordons, 10th R Welsh Fusiliers. This afternoon in the semi-final against the Divisional RFA we met our Waterloo and were beaten by the only goal scored. It was a poor exhibition of football, the ground was a quagmire and the ball wet, heavy and slippery, so the match degenerated into a scramble in which we were beaten by the better and heavier team.

2 November 1915. It is still raining, and I suppose it will continue to do so until the crack of doom. Luckily we are well equipped to withstand the elements. In a pair of gumboots and a voluminous mackintosh cape one can splash about without fear of getting wet. Today I am going out to try to get up a concert for the Battalion tomorrow night. Poor boys, they have nothing to do here except sit in their barns and gamble. Of course they do a certain amount of drill and a route march occasionally, which hardly suffices to break the monotony of resting.

Last Sunday I was lucky enough to get my Parade Services in between the downpours. At 7.30 am I rode over to the Welsh to give them a Celebration. It was bitterly cold, and I had to get off once or twice to quicken my congealed blood.

15

The place arranged for the Service was the Quartermaster's stores – an old cow byre – at one end I arranged my altar of packing cases, all round the sides were other packing cases and bales of bully beef and biscuit and gas helmets and articles of clothing and boots and legs of ham and all the hundred and one things which live in a QM's stores. The mixture of odours – leather, ham and stale cow – was calculated to intrude on our devotions, but as a matter of fact, it didn't. Twenty of the Royal Welsh came, headed by the Colonel, Adjutant Major and about twelve other officers. The floor was covered with straw and folded blankets, and they knelt down just as they came in. It really is extraordinary how near God seems to be at these little Services out here, and the more discomfort and uncomfortable the surroundings, the more real is the spirit of worship. Certainly experiences like these bring out the nobility and grandeur of our own simple Liturgy.

Guy Fawkes Day, 1915. My week so far has been chiefly made up of routine work with very few thrills worth recording. On Tuesday I rode into Hazebrouck where I saw the King t'other day and did some shopping for the Mess. It was quite uneventful except for the pouring rain. On Wednesday, we were startled and shocked by the news that one of our Brigade – a Welshman – had drunk himself silly and then loaded his rifle and run amok. Before he could be disarmed he had fired nearly twenty rounds killing one and wounding another, and had his Sergeant on the ground preparing to out him with his bayonet.

The poor fellow who was killed was buried yesterday, and the murderer is awaiting trial. I don't know what will happen to him. The doctors seem to think that he is mentally deficient. In any case it's the most awful thing to happen and has cast quite a gloom over us all.

6 November 1915. Today has been proclaimed a general whole holiday and the sun is shining brilliantly. Nearly everybody has gone off to see the final of the GOC's cup. I, poor wretch, am the only one who can't make holiday for it is the day of preparation, and when I have finished this I will have to visit innumerable Orderly Rooms and make arrangements for tomorrow. I have a Celebration and four Church Parades tomorrow, each one separated from the other by distances varying between one and three miles. It is like fitting in a

Chinese puzzle, and I anticipate dashing madly à la John Gilpin on a foam-flecked steed from Service to Service, stung to frenzy by the fear of being late.

We are managing now to get a fairly regular supply of newspapers, though they are always a day old when we receive them. However, that is better than nothing and helps us to get fairly *au courant* with events.

9 November 1915. I missed rather a treat on Saturday by not going to see the football match, for afterwards there was a very swagger distribution of medals by a French General. The Guard of Honour consisted of Zouaves and Gordon Highlanders, and Brass Bands played appropriate music and the French General saluted the recipients in the proper way on both cheeks, and altogether it must have been a great show.

After lunch our Quartermaster's son – a Sergeant in the 18th Hussars – such a nice fellow – arrived on a bicycle. He had come twenty-two miles over the most atrocious roads to see his father, and had to get back again the same night. You can imagine how heavy the going must have been when I tell you it took him four and a half hours to make the journey. He has been out from the beginning, and this was the first time they had met.

We have lost a member of our little Mess – our Doc has gone off to hospital with a temperature and a wicked cold. We are wondering how his relief will fit in. Let's hope he's a nice fellow. We live so much in each other's pockets, that it makes all the difference to our happy home, and our mutual peace of mind and comfort.

We are having a Confirmation towards the end of this month. I spoke as strongly as I could at all my Services on Confirmation, but so far I have only got a few names in. Today I rode around my Battalions to fix up some classes, and afterwards rode over to rather a famous monastery standing on the top of the only hill in the neighbourhood – Mont des Cats by name. It is a Trappist House now used as a rest camp for slightly wounded cases. The monks – or at least some of them – still remain and funny looking coves they are too. When I blew in on my steed I sighted some of them and mistook them for cooks. They wear a dirty white costume, half pyjama and half nightshirt.

The buildings themselves are not much to write home about, but the place has a certain interest from the fact that it was the scene of an affair early in the war when Prince Max of Hesse was killed. I met the Chaplain attached to the Ambulance there, and he took me round and showed me all the spots of interest. He tells me they deal with a 100 cases each day, that is a hundred dirty, trench-worn, tired, nervy, wounded soldiers arrive each day, and a hundred rosy-faced, clean, smart, healthy men go off each day after their week's rest; every man in a new clean outfit. The baths are quite a feature. As soon as they arrive they have a hot tub – perhaps the first for months, their clothes are taken away and stored and repaired. Fresh underclothing and uniform is served out to them – and so the merry game goes on.

On Monday, most of our fellows saw one of our own aeroplanes come down. I'm thankful I wasn't there. The plane caught fire and crashed to the ground and both airmen killed. Our only satisfaction is that it wasn't due to the Germans, but to engine defect.

12 November 1915. Well we are still here, still resting, more than ever bored, and less than ever to do, though somehow or other the days pass quickly enough and I never seem to find time hanging on my hands. Pottering about among the men and messing around generally, fill the days up, but afford no food for letters home. Today after breakfast I donned my numerous devices for keeping the rain out, and wandered down to the Welsh billets, called on the Mess, saw some men, then ambled about until I came to the Guard Room, where the murderer is still confined. The Guard Room is a sort of tumbledown stable, and the prisoner was lying huddled in a corner under some blankets, his handcuffed hands hidden beneath them. I sat down beside him and tried to talk to him, but it was far from easy. In the first place, the presence of the guard had a fettering effect upon my tongue, and the man himself wouldn't say a word. Finally I asked him, after one or two awkward pauses, if he would rather I didn't come to see him. He shook his head so nothing was left but to clear out. After that, I went to see some of our fellows in a barn, then to our own Guard Room to see a poor lad who is waiting for his sentence.

He was sent out on a listening post after thirty-six hours con-tinuous work, and fell asleep. He's only a boy and tired nature was too strong for him. Such a nice kid, I hope they won't insist on the extreme penalty. Probably they will give him another chance, but in

18

any case the suspense – he's been waiting fifteen days now – is worse than the punishment itself. And so the day passes.

I am thinking of writing a book in letter form of my experiences out here. It would be so much simpler to send a copy to my friends than to write the same sort of thing to each one of them separately. What do you think of the idea? At present I haven't got as far even as the title. Have you any suggestions for a snappy and attractive little title? – something that would make the book sell well.[3]

16 November 1915. Yesterday afternoon, as there was to be a cross-country gallop I thought it might cheer me up a bit if I joined in. So I borrowed a horse and had a ripping ride across an easy bit of country – no big jumps except one which I scrambled through – the other jumps were only ditches and small hedges. I was on a little shaggy tub of a horse – the only one I could borrow – very short of leg, and almost as short of wind. So I followed the field at a steadily increasing distance. A nasty fall and the consequent bogging of Williams' horse gave me a chance to catch up, as the whole company had to get off and pull the poor beast out.

When we started again, I got away well and was close up to the leaders when another horse who had lost its rider at the last jump came after me. Having caught its eye I saw it had no evil intent against me. It followed me through love, I suppose, and not through anger or annoyance. Reassured on this point, I caught it and led it back to its muddy and slightly heated owner. I had the satisfaction of feeling a little hero, but lost the remaining chance I had of finishing with the leaders. However it was a thoroughly enjoyable ride and a perfect day – bright, frosty weather and the ground with that snap in it which horses love.

In the evening there was a big boxing competition billed as the finals of the 3rd Division. As room was very limited, only five officers were invited from each Battalion. However, being a Brigade Chaplain I got in on the 'nod'. It was a strange show, a medley of boxing, wrestling, a funny man, and a glee party.

The boxing was short and sweet, each event ending in the first or second round with a knockout. In one event – I think lightweight – we were robbed of what promised to be a very pretty bout by a very nice piece of sportsmanship. Early in the first round, one lad hit

[3] And now, more than ninety years later . . .!

the other as he was falling. Quite an unintentional foul. The fight
was stopped for a moment, the judges conferred and the lads told to
fight on. The offender, however, took the first opportunity of being
counted out. Personally I think it was unnecessary and quixotic, but
it was proof of the right spirit of sportsmanship.

The boxing on the whole was disappointing, but the referee
afforded much amusement by the way he hopped about like a
dancing-master, doing the hundred yards in even time. Between
each bout we had a dose of the funny man who sang and pattered in
broad Scots so that I understood never a word. Much more enjoyable were The Glees. The party were the subalterns of the Gordons
and very good they were. The titbit of the evening, however, was
the wrestling match – an exhibition bout between two ex-world
champions of the catch-as-catch-can species. They are both men in
our Battalion, but it was the first time I had seen them at work.

To a layman, it was incomprehensible – they squirmed about,
turned somersaults with the utmost goodwill and enthusiasm, and
grunted & gasped like good 'uns, and incidentally lost much skin off
their naked bodies on the hard boards and a still greater quantity of
liquid fat. It was extraordinary and highly diverting – but as a sport
seems somewhat tame.

17 November 1915. Last Sunday and Monday I had a terrible
experience – a Welsh man in our Brigade about ten days ago went
mad with French beer and ran amok and killed a comrade. The
FGCM found him guilty and condemned him to death. It was my
duty to break the news to him and prepare him for his end. It was
a terrible ordeal. He was to be shot at dawn on Monday. Most of
Sunday night I spent with him, he was quite penitent and made his
confession and his peace with God. Monday morning I was with
him for about an hour before the end. He was quite composed and
extraordinarily brave and faced the firing-party without the slightest
sign of fear. A real white man – out of drink – and a model soldier
who would as likely as not have snaffled a VC.

I had to be present the whole time, and afterwards buried him.
Poor fellow, the manner of his death made some atonement for the
failure of his life. The whole business made me feel perfectly ill. May
I never have a similar experience.

Chapter 2

Vaseline, Glycerine, and the Suffolks

From 'Happy Christmas, Tommy' to the German attack on Verdun. Holding trenches at Verbranden Molen; rest at Reninghelst

21 November 1915. At *last* we have ceased 'to rest' in the military sense of the word. We marched out of our barns and stables yesterday and moved about ten miles nearer the front into what are probably our winter quarters. That is to say we come back here after each turn in the trenches, a week in and a week out.

We are in camp on the outskirts of a French village [Reninghelst], the camp is a quagmire pure and simple, mud everywhere inches deep. You can hardly realise what mud is at home, even when I tell you that every step you take you go in well above the ankle and in places up to the middle of the calf. The men are in tents & huts which cluster round a big windmill which stands, as all well conducted windmills do, on the top of a hill.

My home is rather apart from the rest; I have managed to procure a hut to myself in a field which still possesses some grass. In the same field, which is only small, are the tents and huts of our genial QM, our Transport Officer and our Interpreter; with us also are our servants, our horses, and our grooms – a happy self-contained little family.

My hut is quite a palace as huts go, some twenty feet long and half as broad. It is divided into two by a couple of Army blankets. In one half I sleep and live, in the other half which by the way is unlighted, live my servant and groom.

My half contains a table, a bed, a chair & a stove! All hand-made by the last occupant – a regular Quartermaster Sergeant of the Rifle Brigade.

The furniture really shows more signs of expert manufacture than does the hut itself which is made of boards & galvanised iron. It is a sort of patchwork only very open-work & the winds whistle through its myriad cracks – but even so it is many times better than a tent.

This I expect will be my headquarters during the winter & will be the centre from which I will sally forth like St Paul of old on my Missionary journeys, up to the trenches for a night or two, over to the Field Ambulance occasionally, back to the reserve billets from time to time. But after each journey coming back home here.

Thursday was quite a red letter day for it saw the arrival of my horse. I have had to wait a long time for it, while Brigades and Divisions and ADVS's and Remounts and other people have signed and countersigned my original indent but it was worth it, for I have got a real beauty – a mare who behaves like a lady, and yet has spirit and pace and jumps like a flea. She belonged originally to a General Hoskins or some such name, and was cast for a skin disease. She is all right now & shows no sign of ever having had it.

Friday was so full that I must chronicle it hour by hour. In the morning I tried my mare by riding her round to my various Confirmation classes & in looking up men to play in a hockey match.

I had arranged this match between the officers of the Suffolks and our Mess. The Suffolks were very keen but our fellows kept crying off, so that an hour before the match was timed to begin I had only eight men! It was here that my mare came in, and we started punctually at 2.30 pm with twelve men!! The mistake was only discovered at half-time. However as the Suffolks were all in shorts and had played together before, & we were all in our ordinary breeches and puttees and had never played as a team before, they allowed us to play the extra man. Despite this, sad to relate, they beat us 4–3. It was a fast hard game & I am still horribly stiff from my unwonted exertions. After the match I went in for tea with them, and then rode over to a neighbouring town to see another Chaplain on matters connected with the forthcoming Confirmation. Then back to my billet for a bath & a change.

What a vision of comfort if not luxury the word 'bath' calls up; visions of glistening white walls and porcelain bath of gigantic proportions, and unlimited boiling water and warm towels and bath-mats and scented soap and all the rest. My bath was in a canvas bucket, my water cold, my soap carbolic (necessary out here), my bath mat a piece of sacking. One of the supremest joys of leave must be baths, hot & cold running morning, noon and night.

In the evening I went to dinner with the Suffolks. They were having a farewell oyster supper & very kindly asked me to share in the fifty dozen deep sea beauties which they had procured.

I managed a humble two dozen and a seven-course dinner to follow, and felt pleasurably tired, well fed and warm with a nice cigar to enjoy, when the wilder spirits dragged me off to dance in the kitchen to sweet gramophone-made music.

Ladies being less easily procured out here than oysters we had perforce to dance with each other. It was great fun. The stone-flagged floor, unseen in the dim religious light cast by a single candle, beaten and caressed by the feet of a dozen young men tunic-less & heated, hugging each other & performing the latest steps from London. Foxtrots & Turtle Run etc etc. We kept it up until mid-night when I tore myself away & went home for a few hours in bed before having to pack up for our move. We started early yesterday (Saturday), the Interpreter & I rode over *à cheval* & arranged about our billets and water supply and other similar details.

The day of arrival in a new place is always a day of fasting because the cookers and the cooks or the food invariably lose each other. So we made our own arrangements. Being a native he discovered a cosy little back parlour where we ate pork cutlets & drank bad red wine at one franc fifty the bottle. Madame is a dear old motherly soul who told me her whole history between the courses, and has invited me to have other meals there.

25 November 1915. Nothing very much has happened since my last. The time has been spent in making my hut more comfortable and less open to all the winds that blow. Among other improvements I have had the floor up and re-laid it, so I hope now not to lose quite so many things between the cracks!!

I haven't been up in our new trenches yet [Verbranden Molen]. Half the Brigade went up on Sunday, and the other half, the King's Own and Suffolks, relieve them on Saturday. I shall probably go up on Monday for a night, unless I am sent for before. But I don't think that is very likely as we have fairly good and safe trenches. A Lance

Corporal Carter came for a Confirmation instruction, which lasted nearly an hour; then a Private Fletcher who is in trouble because his father is dying and he cannot get leave. He wants me to argue with the powers-that-be and plead for him. I will do what I can, but I'm afraid it won't be any good.

Next the Post-Corporal, who wants me to order a supply of envelopes for the men, and to get a censor stamp to save delay, so that I can stamp the letters instead of sending them all the way up to the Orderly Room. I don't for one moment expect this will be possible, but I shall have to try, and so the day goes on.

30 November 1915. You must have been having as much frost as we have had lately. My word it has been cold, the ground like iron and a cutting wind withal, which has found no difficulty in getting through the walls of my little shack. In my spare moments I have been busy stuffing up the most persistent cracks, and have covered the walls inside with empty sandbags and sacking. It has certainly made me much more cosy though it still leaves something to be desired.

The last two days I have been feeling very cheap and seedy, a mild attack of flu, pains in my back and head and a lazy feeling which has made my work seem less of a pleasure than it usually is. Today I stayed in bed for breakfast and feel much better, in consequence. This evening I'm going up to the trenches to have a look around, bury one of two poor fellows, and make arrangements for my Confirmation candidates to get leave from the trenches for the Service on Thursday. It is going to be a great 'do', a regular fête day, two Bishops, 100 candidates, and tea for all in the YMCA tent. I have been busy the last week putting the final polish on those whom I hope to present. They are a mixed crowd, I mean their occupations are mixed, and their homes various – one is a cook, one is in the trenches, two are in rest billets, and five are in the Field Ambulance, so of course I can never get them all together at once.

The five in the RAMC came and had tea with me in my hut last Thursday. We all packed in somehow & had a very jolly meal tho' primitive; we all had to share the same knife and spoon, and we dispensed entirely with plates. The mugs I borrowed from the YMCA, but the food was good and plentiful. You should have seen our smiling faces – it was quite a success. Three of them sat on the bed, two on orange boxes (which serve me as cupboard and washstand), and I as host sat on the one and only chair.

3 December 1915. If I don't get a letter written tonight, I can't see any chance of doing so until Monday, and I have a lot to tell you about. In my last I said I was going up to the trenches [at Verbranden Molen] in the evening, and go I did, and had the time of a lifetime. Every afternoon transport starts off from the Quartermaster's stores here with rations for our men in the trenches. They take it out about seven miles to our 'dump' where ration parties come down from the trenches to collect their food & letters and either carry the stuff up in sandbags, or push it up in little trucks on a light narrow-gauge railway. I intended to go up with the transport this particular day in order that they might show me the way. However I was delayed by interviews and had to follow after them. All went well and I caught them up alright, but at the expense of overheating my mare, so I got off and walked for some time. When I essayed to remount, my saddle slipped round on me, and the last of the transport saw of me was trying to put it on again. Now for a little word painting! A narrow road, a constant stream of transport, a pitch-black night, and mud everywhere, and to crown it all a horse restive and nervous by reason of the gun flashes and reports. By the time I had got the saddle and saddle-blanket properly arranged once more, the transport was some way ahead. However nothing daunted I pushed past wagons and guns and men and ambulances and all the rest until I caught up with what I took for the tail of our transport column. This I followed for sometime until we were held up by a block in the road. Before I knew where I was I was surrounded by a heaving, struggling, pushing mob of strange men with strange wagons and stranger oaths. It was then I discovered my mistake – as it afterwards turned out, my little crowd had branched off down a side road. However, I didn't know it at the time and spent hours wandering about this unknown land in the completest darkness, made darker still by the occasional flash of a bursting shell in the distance – asking everybody I met if they knew where the King's Own dump was. Of course nobody did for it takes a man all his time to find his own.

I forgot to tell you that all this time my feet were being tortured by a new pair of boots I was wearing. Finally tired and sick I was all for giving up and going back to camp, but the bit of the old bulldog strain within me urged one more try, and by the supremest good fortune I chanced upon the transport of the 2nd Suffolks, who hold the adjoining trenches. From them I borrowed a guide and started up on foot to the front line. If my journey *à cheval* was bad, this was a thousand times worse – along a path across fields ploughed by shells far worse or more thoroughly than any farm plough; I call it path by courtesy, it was really a ditch of mud, beaten into a soft yielding consistency by the countless feet of ceaseless ration parties. Up this path I plunged in my new tight boots, falling down, sitting down, nearly taking involuntary headers into shell holes full of dirty water, slipping sideways or backwards every step, and nearly dislocating my hips every time I pulled my leg out of the holding mud. Had my boots been less tight I might have had to add 'lost footwear' to my list of misfortunes.

However at length I arrived and did my business, saw my pals and repeated once more the strenuous journey to the dump and my horse. The return to camp was uneventful except for periodic clutches at my mare's neck to save myself falling off in my sleep.

Yesterday (Thursday) we had the Confirmation Service. As expected we had two Bishops – Taylor Smith and Khartoum, and ninety-eight candidates, many of them straight back from the trenches with mud caked upon them and their equipment, neither of which had they had time to remove. It was an impressive sight, impressive because of its simplicity and childlike reality. A large wooden hut used by the YMCA as a recreation room, with a platform at one end on which we erected a little altar. On the floor below, an ordinary cane-bottomed bedroom chair for the Bishop and a folded army blanket for the candidates to kneel on. Six chaplains formed a surpliced choir, another played the piano for the hymns, the candidates in rows on forms, the Bishop in his robes, and the Holy Spirit. After the Service and two inordinately long addresses by the CG we all had tea and buns together, and then back to work again, the trenches for some, hut-building for others, stretcher bearing for others, and for others road-making or cooking or camp fatigues.

While we were invoking the power of the Holy Spirit to help us live, poor Major Williams, our CO since the Colonel went sick, was solving the problem of death. He was hit by a fragment of a trench mortar in the morning and breathed his last at a few minutes to five. He is our first officer to be killed, and we shall miss him frightfully. He was always so cheerful and bright, and good-natured – one of the most hospitable men I have ever known. Poor old man we buried him here behind the line this afternoon in a little military cemetery. Young Bardsley too we have lost for a time; he was hit in three places on Tuesday, but not seriously, and is doing well, I believe. He is the son, you know, of the Vicar of Lancaster.

It is now quarter to one so I think I will turn in, but I will leave it open in case I have time tomorrow to add a word or two.

Saturday. I have been out all the morning in the pouring rain and wind trying to arrange Services tomorrow and have just got in. The leaden sky and cheerless mud and hopeless outlook was all forgotten or transformed into rosy sunshine by the sight of your letter dated the 30th November.

6 December 1915. The order has just come that we are to clear out of our snug little field; it is wanted for the Brigade to build standings for the horses, so we shall have to move, but the difficulty is where we can go. Nearly every square inch of land is already occupied by camps and hutments and transport.

If and when we find a site, I shall dismantle my hut and carry it with me and rebuild, for I don't hanker after the discomfort of a tent. It is always the way in life, get a nice place and everybody wants to turn you out, get a rotten one and you can stay there as long as you like – or live. Well, it's all part of the game I suppose, and something may yet turn up.

It's 9:45 pm and we are just back from a most enjoyable trip. Les our Interpreter – a real white man and one of the best – and I rode over to [Poperinghe] and did some shopping, cigarettes and razor blades, and envelopes and so on. And then met Rowe our QM, and Clare our Signalling Officer and arranged to have tea together and go to the Fancies. The Fancies are a musical party of the Follies stamp, run by the 6th Division. The party consists of five officers, one private and two Flemish girls called Vaseline and Glycerine who sing English songs in broken English. They are the quaintest couple you ever saw. Very wooden and lifeless, and it is quite evident they don't understand a word they are singing. They made me howl with laughter. The men are all excellent and everything they do is good. Quite one of the best and most enjoyable shows I've ever seen, despite the difficulties at every point. The hall is a big showroom,

I think, lighted by acetylene motor lamps – for gas and electric light is all cut off so near the front. The stage effect is splendid – all home made so to speak. The first half of the programme is a pierrot entertainment, the stage & hangings all jet-black, the pierrots in white and black, and the stools on which they sit black and white check – very striking and novel, and the singing and fooling absolutely first-rate.

The second half of the show is a sort of review, screamingly funny and very topical. What was so refreshing was to see one man appear in faultless evening dress. I think that pleased and thrilled me as much as anything. Of course the place was packed out; it's the same every night I believe, and the audience most appreciative. It is quite the best two francs' worth I've ever had.

12 December 1915. The weather all last week has been atrocious, we are still up to our necks in Flanders mud, but as we all wear fishermen's waders or 'gumboots, thigh' as the official name has it, we don't mind how much mud we are asked to wade through.

Last Wednesday I had a Celebration at the Field Ambulance in order that my Confirmandi might make their first Communion; and the evening before I arranged a little Service of preparation. The only place available was a vaulted cellar. It reminded me of the catacombs. As each man came down the stone steps out of the gloom into the little circle of light thrown by a couple of candles, I felt that we had been transplanted back to the dawn of Christianity and were meeting in secret – 'The door being shut for fear of the Jews'. The roof was too low for us to stand up, so we sang a hymn sitting and had the rest of the Service kneeling. Quite a number of fellows came, and to the Celebration next morning, which we had in the operating tent.

The Ambulance and I are lucky in possessing two priests in the ranks and a fine Quartermaster Sergeant, who is an excellent church-man and helps me in every way.

The same evening, the Suffolks invited me to form one of a party for a theatre and dinner. The idea was irresistible so once more I went to the Fancies arriving just at the end of the first half and found that they had kept me a seat in the front row. Afterwards we adjourned to a humble looking estaminet for dinner. It was a lesson in the folly of judging by exteriors, for they keep a prodigy of a cook there. Our menu was oysters, soup, lobster mayonnaise, asparagus and eggs, chicken, quails on toast, Camembert, coffee and liqueur brandy. And this is war! Not a bad little dinner for within sight and sound of the guns! On our way back it was raining hard and no moon or light of any kind, so dark in fact that we dared not trot along the muddy, broken, shell-torn road and so got soaked to the skin, but it was well worth the wetting.

The next day was notable for a wonderful hot bath – my third I think since I've been out here. An old brewery has been converted into baths for the troops. The officers' bathroom is down in a sort of basement. Two pipes run overhead with a rose screwed in at intervals, and underneath each a washing tub. But the water is plentiful – as well it might be! – and boiling.

Imagine six healthy-looking young men sitting in six washing tubs, in a dimly lighted basement, full of steam and the smell of soap, and a shower of hot water splashing on the head and shoulders of each one, and you will almost hear the grunts and exclamations of joy which proceed from their six mouths as they see the white flesh appearing through the grimed-in mud of Flanders.

On Thursday I had a Celebration at the YMCA hut, chiefly for the Chaplains of the Division; followed after breakfast by a Chaplains' Meeting in my hut – I being Senior Chaplain in the absence of Campbell our real SCF who went sick with a fever, but has since returned to duty. After the meeting I helped to censor the films of the Divisional Cinema. We've had the same programme for about a month until every frequenter knew every inch of every film by heart, and clamoured for a change. So at great expense and trouble we managed to get some French films – hence the need of the censor.

The next day (Friday) I went up to the trenches for twenty-four hours. My mare was a bit lame so I borrowed the Interpreter's. What a dance it led me! It started by trying to have me off, but failing, set off as if possessed by seven devils. I couldn't hold him in, although I nearly sawed his head off. All the brute did was to wag its head from side to side, but didn't slacken speed. Finally I got it to trot, and what a trot! Its back legs felt as if they were a foot too long, and bumped me nearly out of the saddle, so in desperation I got off him, sent him home in disgrace by my groom and continued my journey on a limber. A ration limber is a springless affair, pulled by mules, and filled with bags of bully-beef tins and coke, and other hard and knobbly articles. Moreover, these roads are not noted for their surface, the middle portion is *pavé* & generally full of holes, the sides consist of deep mud, usually a good foot lower than the middle. Whenever two vehicles meet both have to get one wheel off the *pavé* in order to make room to pass. My journey therefore was not a bed of roses, as you may imagine, as we met several wagons and limbers en route. On arriving at the dump I called on the Brigade Headquarters, and they very kindly gave me tea. They live in a large old farmhouse which is the target of every German gun within miles, but which so far has escaped damage.

Then the weary grind through the mud up to the trenches. Before starting one is advised to write one's will and fix on a lifebelt. But unfortunately I found the mud a trifle too thick for swimming, and as it is too deep for walking the only thing was to plunge and wallow through it as well as possible. That night I slept in my Burberry in a dugout, no blankets being allowed. Luckily it wasn't a very cold night, or I don't think I should have slept at all.

Next morning I made a complete tour of all the trenches [at Verbranden Molen] and found everybody very cheery and bright. They all seemed very pleased to see me, which was gratifying. Tommy is a wonderful fellow. How he manages to live and thrive and keep cheerful under such conditions is nothing short of wonderful. In the trenches he has to stand up to his knees in water, and under constant strain, always wet, generally cold, frequently hungry and often sleepy and yet, except for an occasional grouse which means nothing, he smiles, and whistles and jokes, as if he hadn't a care or trouble in the world.

I was much amused at some sailors whom Jellicoe or the Admiralty have sent over here to see at first hand the conditions and work of the Sister Service. There were three of them in our trenches, three big burly Petty-Officers. When they arrived the Hun very kindly gave them a firework display, and before they left they were able to distinguish between trench mortars and rifle grenades; aerial torpedoes, and Jack Johnsons; Black Marias and Coal Boxes; Whizz Bangs and HE (high explosive); shrapnel and Archibalds and all the other devices for taking the life of poor Tommy.

They experienced too the joy of standing in muddy water well above the knee; and of sleeping in a muddy leaking dugout. They tasted trench-tea and found it wanting, and altogether got a thorough insight into the joys and sorrows of trench life. As they were leaving, they were asked how they had enjoyed the experience. One and all protested that he preferred the North Sea. You should have seen their eyes bulge when they saw the mud for the first time. They said they didn't know mud grew like that anywhere!

As I was coming down yesterday evening (Saturday) I was trying to find the grave of two of our fellows who had been buried by a Sergeant in my absence, so that I might say a prayer over them and have their resting place registered. As I was peering about with my flash lamp I was mistaken for a spy. A Sergeant of the RAMC watched me for some time, and came up and asked me what I was doing. Quite evidently he didn't believe my story, so put some leading questions, such as what trenches were we holding, what was my Brigade, and the name of my Divisional General and so on. I of course answered quite correctly for the most part, hugely enjoying myself, but I couldn't for the life of me remember the number of our trenches. That was quite enough to him. Quite politely, he suggested that I had better see his Captain. I demurred and said I was in a hurry. Quite untrue but I wanted to egg him on and see his next move. He again suggested that his Captain might be able to help me; I said I didn't think he could and that I wouldn't worry him for the world. Poor fellow, by this time he was certain he'd caught a spy red-handed and sternly and firmly insisted that his Captain wished to see me and that I must see him. So reluctantly I went along deepening still more his conviction that I was a wolf in sheep's clothing. I wish you could have seen his face fall when I was ushered in before the Captain, with all exits carefully barred, and I found the Captain was an old friend of mine who greeted me effusively!

17 December 1915. Last Monday I kept as Sunday for one of my Battalions as they only came out of the trenches early Sunday morning. Poor fellows, they were wet, tired and dirty, so I couldn't pull them out for Church Parade before they had had a night's sleep, and after all, every day is the same out here and Monday seemed quite Sundayish with a Celebration and a Parade Service out of doors [at Ouderdom]. Luckily it was bright and sunny but nippy withal.

However I spoilt the illusion by going to the Divisional Cinema in the evening. The cinema is run in a large thatched barn which holds nearly 500 fellows, and is packed every night. I am now on the Executive Committee and so am very keen that it should go well. When the Customs and Post Office officials are kind, we try to have a change of programme twice a week but don't always succeed.

31

The profits go towards providing hot drinks in the trenches. Rather a sound idea, don't you think?

On Wednesday I went up to the trenches again, this time to stay with the Suffolks and had quite an amusing time. The Suffolks are extraordinarily nice to me. While we were having dinner in the dugout, which by the way is quite palatial and possesses a sofa and a fireplace, to say nothing of a window and door, they had a bed knocked up for me and I spent a most comfortable if somewhat chilly night.

Nothing very exciting happened, except I got nearly strafed once by a shell which came over my head and burst 15 yards behind me. When I got back I had a hot bath. This time in a canvas bath borrowed from Rowe our Quartermaster, in my little hut in front of a nice red charcoal fire. It was priceless. As I bathed I had the gramophone playing all the latest waltz and gaiety music. Quite a sybarite.

Today (Friday) has been filled with small fry of various sorts. Celebration in the YMCA at 7.15 am [at Reninghelst], breakfast at 8.15 am, writing and sending in Returns, and various official work until 11 am. Then walked up to Headquarters and saw the Adjutant about various things and arranged a gramophone concert for this evening. Back to lunch at one o'clock. Then down to the cemetery with the Pioneers to put up a cross over Major Williams' grave, then in to see the Senior Chaplain and help him with the censoring of the day's mailbag. Then after ten, once more up to the King's Own camp to arrange the hut for the concert, then the concert itself, which by the way was very cheery. Then a little sick visiting until dinner time, and now I'm back once more in my hut thinking it is nearly time for bed as my candle is flickering out and Mr Dream Man is throwing dust into my eyes.

20 December 1915. I have opened all the parcels and am perfectly charmed and delighted with their contents. How good you are to me. You have given me everything that I wanted and nothing that I didn't.

Since I last wrote we have been treated to a real-life gas attack and a big artillery engagement. Luckily we were back resting, so played the onlooker, thank goodness. The gas attack was early Sunday morning, and even back here, eight miles behind the line, we could smell and taste and feel traces of it. The artillery display was deafening. One continuous roar like heavy thunder. The guns were firing so fast that you could not distinguish the separate reports. It sounded appalling; thank goodness I wasn't the target at which they were all aiming.

Sunday was a beautiful frosty bright day. Coming out of our hut after breakfast we heard the sound of a machine gun hammering away above us somewhere. At first we could see nothing, but as our eyes became accustomed we saw the most thrilling fight among the clouds. It was hard to see quite what was happening, but we could see the aeroplanes circling round each other, and the whole time bursts of the murderous machine guns. We learnt afterwards that it was a fight between eight English Scouts, and two German armoured fighting machines. It sounds most unequal, but I believe the Germans managed to get away. We couldn't see the result as they flew out of sight, still fighting hard, but we thought one of the German planes was on fire for it seemed to leave a line of smoke in its wake. If only you could have seen the blue sky and the white fleecy clouds, and the aeroplanes dancing and swooping and hovering round each other! It was a perfect picture: except for the tap tap tap of the Maxim it didn't seem like war.

Since the death of poor Major Williams we have got a new CO – a Major Smith from the Gordons. He seems a fine fellow with a nice kind face, but firm withal.

On Saturday I had a row with Barnes, our Adjutant, over Church Parade. He had ordered a route march on Sunday morning, and said we couldn't have a Church Service. However, I soon got the General on his track and he had to climb down, and we had the Services on the strength of it – a Parade Service followed by a late Celebration to which twenty-five stopped.

The order of eviction is still hanging over our head, but apparently somebody has issued a stay of execution for we are still here, though probably the next week will see us in new quarters. I shall be sorry to leave my little orange box and scrap-iron hut, for I have become quite attached to it, but if we must we must. There is a big gun firing as I write. It sounds as if it was in the next field for every time it belches forth a shell my shanty quivers and rattles like a palsied tinker.

I am thinking of giving a lecture one day on the psychology of Tommy's headdress. It is as numerous and as various as the leaves in Val Ambrosia. First you have the official stiff round cap denoting smartness and NCO's stripes as a rule. The same cap with the wire taken out looks like the bed cap of *la jeune fille* and is worn by those who prefer comfort to smartness and by the lately out who ape the veteran of fourteen months. Both these varieties are further disguised by covers, some with a flap behind, some without. The former transforms the wearer into an old sun-bonneted countrywoman, the latter is useful and is worn by the careful Beau Brummel.

Then come a gamut of Scotch caps, Glengarries, tam-o'-shanters large and small, close-fitting and wide of brim, some with bobs on top, some without. Some exposed to all the winds that blow, some swathed in mackintosh covers – and every man seems to wear that which is right in his own eyes. Then we have the steel helmet that looks like Patsy's last year's summer hat, what I believe is called a plain shape. This worn by bombers and snipers at a rakish angle is rather prepossessing and gives an Old World appearance to the trenches, which is further enhanced by the latest devices for taking life, modelled on the crossbow and catapult.

There may be other varieties of headgear sanctioned by the War Office which I have forgotten, but I must leave them to mention the unofficial coverings of Tommy's brainbox – worn by the lazy, the unlucky, and the absent-minded. First the woollen stocking-cap in various shades of khaki & brown, then the knitted tam-o'-shanter, equally variegated, and lastly the Balaclava helmet. This also is worn in a rainbow collection of colours including scarlet – for this particular specimen is worn by my servant when off duty, as a constant reminder to me of the dangers of the scarlet lady. I may perhaps add that this atrocity is the work of Mother's loving hands. At least I have always understood that she made it for Father to wear at the Nice Carnival; or was it for his trip to Spain – I forget which and my servant doesn't care for it keeps his ears warm.

27 December 1915. You can judge how rushed I've been when I tell you that I never had a chance of opening my Christmas mail until this morning.

Christmas Eve I rode to all my billets to arrange time and place of Services. It is a long tour round and I had all my meals out. Christmas morning I was up betimes at 5.30. My first Celebration was at seven o'clock at the Field Ambulance in a small operating tent. It was packed out with officers and men. It was a ripping Service and had quite the Christmas spirit, and we had two Christmas hymns. Then back to my hut for a cup of coffee and off once more on my horse three or four miles to a Field Company of the RE. I gave them a Celebration in the Recreation Hut – and they very kindly gave me breakfast. Then back once more to my hut for fresh supplies of wine and wafers, and off at once four miles to the Royal Welsh Fusiliers. They too had a Celebration, though as they had just come in from the trenches only about twenty came to the Service.

Then back once more to my hut for Christmas dinner. This consisted of mutton cutlets and plum pudding. The former were a bit tough, but the latter was most succulent, and we concocted a rum sauce which gave the finishing touch. Dessert was chocolate and almond raisins, which you sent some time ago. Afterwards a Benedictine supplied by some friend of the Interpreter. After dinner I only had time for one of Father's cigarettes before I again mounted my horse and rode the nine weary miles up to the trenches, arriving at the Brigade Headquarters in time for tea.

Christmas night I spent in the trenches; everything was very quiet, though there was no fraternising with the Hun this year. In fact a great bitter strafe had been arranged for the Birthday of the Prince of Peace, but better feeling prevailed and the day passed quietly.

Next morning after three hour's sleep, I ploughed my way down the two muddy miles to Brigade HQ [at Woodcote House] and gave them a chance of making their Christmas Communion. Meanwhile an artillery engagement was beginning, so we worshipped the Babe of God, not to the accompanying voices of the Angel Host proclaiming their Hosannas of Peace, but to the loud raucous voice of the Heavies.

I had arranged to go back to the trenches for lunch, but the General advised me not to do so, for if I once got into them I might not be able to get out again if the bombardment developed into a regular strafe, so I set off instead on my way back here. I had arranged for my horse to meet me at 4 pm, but as there was no way of letting my groom know my changed plans, there was nothing to do but hoof the nine miles back to camp on my own flat feet. It is a tedious road, and the journey was not improved by the waders I was wearing. I got very hot and tired, and nothing passed me, so I couldn't get a lift.

However I didn't grumble as I was lucky not to be hit coming out. The Huns were shelling the road I was on, but funnily enough every shell fell about thirty yards behind me. They seemed to be following me at that distance, all down the road. Luckily for me it was oblique fire, and the splinters carried over the hedge instead of coming straight on down the road and catching me in the small of the back or the seat of my pants.

When I got back I had a sort of tea-lunch and then made off for my last Service – evensong at the Field Hospital in a big ward. Here, I found a Presbyterian Padre [Thomson] had also arranged for a Service half an hour after mine was timed to commence, so postponed mine and we had a joint Service. I took the prayers and lesson, and he gave an excellent address on the Wonder of Christ – 'His name shall be called wonderful.'

I crawled back to my hut looking forward to a few restful hours in front of my fire with my Christmas mail but found instead an invitation to dinner from the Colonel of the 1st Gordons. It amounted to a command, so of course I had to go. It meant a tramp of a couple of miles each way, but they gave me a very nice little dinner and were very charming to me. At 11 pm I tore myself away and got back absolutely dog-tired and tumbled into bed more than half asleep, with my letters still unread.

This morning I made up for lost time and didn't get up until 9.30 am. I sat in bed and smoked a cigarette and had a gorgeous time with my letters and parcels – so many I hardly know the exact number, but getting on into the twenties. Today has been pretty slack, and, except for a trip up to camp to make some arrangements for a 'do' we are giving the Battalion when they come out of the trenches, has been spent by me writing and smoking.

17 January 1916. Well here I am back again wallowing once more in the turgid mud of Flanders [Camp B, Rosinghill], surrounded by all the familiar landmarks and the same old muddy khaki. Those few blissful hours of leave seem now only a dream of surpassing wonder and beauty – a delightful fantasy, but grotesquely unreal. In fact I can hardly persuade myself that the long expected leave has come and gone. However, the memory of it is very sweet, and it was simply heavenly seeing you all again.

I have been busy starting a Coffee Bar for the men, buying in stores and stoves, and teaching the Bartender his business.

In addition, I have been building a new hut for myself up in the camp. I find it is really more convenient than my old one, and am more on the spot altogether. I have occupied my new hut since last Friday, but for the first two nights my only roof was a tarpaulin thrown over the top – a bit cool as you can imagine. Now, however, I am getting everything into shipshape and making quite a snug little home for myself.

On Monday I got up a concert for the Battalion. It was a strange event. All the pianos in Flanders are in the dugouts, I think, for I couldn't borrow one for love nor money. However, the performers didn't seem to mind the absence of an accompaniment but warbled away sweetly and keeping the time extraordinarily successfully. Tommy loves his emotions to be tickled. There are only two kinds of songs Tommy likes, the sentimental type which tells of the white-haired mother and her darling child, sitting by the fire or starving in the attic, and the vulgar comic. Nothing else goes down at all, but whether it's sentimentality or vulgarity it's got to be laid on thick, and the thicker it is, the more Tommy enjoys himself.

Luckily, for these two types of songs a piano is not indispensable; in fact it is apt to rob the performance of its full flavour and therefore to be a bit of a drawback.

On Monday, when I couldn't stand any more caterwauling about the dear old home, I turned on the gramophone which was a welcome change. At half-time we dished out hot tea flavoured with rum, which was immensely popular and loosened their tongues in the choruses to such an extent that a Hun aeroplane was erroneously reported to be overhead.

The last few days we have had quite a lot of sunshine, and all the world seems young and gay; the camp is less muddy than it's been for months and we have just heard a rumour that the Engineers are going to fit us all up with electric light! Another of the paradoxes of civilised warfare!

I'm just off now to hold a choir practice for the Suffolks. We're going to try to sing the Responses and the Chants at the Church Parade next Sunday – rather ambitious at an open-air Service [at Ouderdom], but the Royal Welsh Fusiliers sing the whole Service regularly, and beautifully they do it too.

3rd Sunday after Epiphany 1916. The camp now is really looking quite well. My hut is right at the back of it, as I write I can see all the huts in front of me, partly hidden by the trees. Our camp is built in a thin sort of wood, chiefly to avoid the eagle eye of the Taube I believe. The ground of course is very soft and mushy, but now we have an elaborate network of 'duck boards' leading from every-where to everywhere else.

A 'duck board' is a kind of ladder laid on the ground with the rungs fairly near together. They are in great demand out here and are now quite ubiquitous. They are an excellent invention but at night in damp weather the source of much bad language. In gum-boots a walk along a duck board resembles a walk along a greasy pole, only there is no duck or leg of ham at the end!

During the last week or so we have managed to get the Coffee Bar in working order, and it is proving a great success and boon to the men who nightly fill the hut and munch slabs of cake washed down with tea, the while they read the week-old 'dailies' or month-old Tatlers and Bystanders. The organisation of even a simple thing like a Coffee Bar and Reading Room out here entails quite a lot of work, for it is making bricks without straw from the word 'go', and supplies of cake and chocolate and milk and everything else have to be horse-drawn from the town six good miles away. Even the water for the tea is brought from a distant main, first in water-carts and then by a water fatigue in old petrol tins.

The trip up to the trenches was quite uneventful. The Hun was amazingly quiet. I really thought that he was withdrawing to a second line some miles further back, but no sooner had I got back to camp than I got word through to say that the Germans had exploded a mine under our front line and blown several of the Suffolks up. It's a rotten way of going out, but most of them were asleep at the time and would never have known what hit them.

Apart from the sorrow of losing so many good men and true, my hands will be full for some days writing to the bereaved parents and wives. It is a sad and difficult job but I think it is worth the trouble, and I hope brings a little comfort to their aching hearts.

Today – it is now 11:15 pm – has been a busy Sunday for me; three Celebrations with a total of seventy-four Communicants, two Church Parades and a voluntary evensong and sermon this evening. The Services are not so tiring in themselves, but it is the packing and unpacking of my Communion bag & robes, the long rides between each Service, and above all the constant strain of trying to keep up to time and avoiding or counteracting the unexpected, which is always a very present menace on active service.

We had rather an interesting air-duel this morning. A perfect cloudless sky and a bright sun. The Taubes were high up and hardly visible without glasses, but they caught the sunlight and looked like two brilliant diamonds. Our machines are painted a darker shade and don't reflect the light so well. Even with glasses it was impossible to tell how the fight was going and they drifted out of sight until nothing could be seen, but still we heard faint tap tap tapping of their machine guns.

25 January 1916. Your letter dated the 22nd has just arrived much to my joy. I have received a letter from Hal [his brother] written in hospital on January 2nd. He says how weak he feels, and his temperature was still in the region of the 100's, so I don't suppose he was back with his Regiment when he sent the pc of January 6th. On a field postcard 'I am quite well' has to cover a multitude of meanings, generally it means nothing more than 'I still exist'.

As I sit here trying to write, the famous Pipe Band of the 1st Gordon Highlanders is practising within twenty yards of my hut. I love them as a band, especially when I can see the swirl of the kilt and the swagger of the Pipe Major. But sitting here unable to see them, I fairly hate them. Each Piper is playing his own favourite lament regardless of the others, and the drums are practising rag-time, I think, so you must take that into consideration if my letter is more disconnected or futile than usual.

My new hut is now quite comfy and snug, I am sending you a grand plan of it. As huts go it is above the average, being commodious and airy – a little too much so sometimes! The great drawback is that it has only got one real window, rather low in the wall and rather minute at that. The other window is covered with canvas in default of glass, and doesn't therefore add much to the gaiety of nations. However I shall be shortly nestling on Luxury's Lap for the electric light is no mere rumour. Already the wires have been laid, and the green shade is hanging majestically from the centre beam, though as yet no globe has appeared and no current has been turned on.

The Coffee Bar is now a *fait accompli* and is doing well – much appreciated by Tommy and Jock – Jock has an insatiable appetite for cake which I am now buying by the case – fifty-six lbs to the case. In the busy time one case lasts about half an hour! In fact, one man does nothing else but cut up cake into penny and twopenny slices!

Our aeroplanes are very busy these days, and the Huns are not backward either. The air seems thick with them, and the sky is perpetually mottled with the smoke balls of bursting shrapnel.

There is rather a good aeroplane story going the rounds now, which I'm told 'on the very best authority' is quite true. One of our pilots went up at night to drop bombs on a German headquarters. Whether he succeeded or not is not known, nor does it affect the story, but as he was coming back his engine began to misfire or misbehave in some other way, and he was forced to come down. As soon as he landed he whipped out his revolver and emptied it into his petrol tank, smashed his wings and set the whole thing on fire in order to prevent it falling into the Germans' hands. While he was thus engaged two other RFC men appeared on the scene and asked him in Expeditionary English (which I need hardly tell you is peculiarly lurid), what he thought he was doing. The poor fellow nearly died of fright. Feeling a little hero he had destroyed his machine within 100 yards of his own hangar under the impression that he had landed on German soil.

I had this from an RFC man who is at present attached to us for a rest. Rather a quaint conceit on the part of the authorities to send a nerve-shaken pilot into the trenches to recuperate!

The last flight he did before he joined us was to take a French Corporal, disguised as a German peasant, and drop him with a basket of carrier pigeons thirty miles in rear of the German lines. What a wealth of feeling the unfortunate Frenchman must have put into his '*au revoir*' as he saw the aeroplane rise into the air and make off for home & safety, leaving him alone in a hostile land, dependent for his living and his life on his own wits.

My toothache I am glad to say is better but the ache has now descended and nestles beneath my belt. I must have eaten too heartily of the curried bully beef we had for lunch.

31 January 1916. The electric light has, contrary to all expectation, made its appearance. It is the last thing in modern warfare, absolutely *le dernier cri*, so now doubtless we shall be moved away within the next day or two. The camp has been brought to a high state of comfort and completeness, it might very properly be used as a model encampment. But nothing of the sort will happen. The proper army procedure is to turn the unfortunate Battalion out and allow the camp to grow moss and mildew while a new camp is sited in the middle of the thickest mud patch in the vicinity!! The idea, I believe, is to prevent us from becoming too attached to the fleshpots of Egypt!

I forget if I told you that I am the proud possessor of a dog. One of the men in the Field Ambulance brought out a terrier pup as a mascot, but now that the pup has increased in size and appetite he finds himself greatly embarrassed, and so has asked me to take it off his hands, which I have done. 'Spot' is the plebeian name to which the hound answers, but he is nevertheless an affectionate little beast, and will I hope protect me from mice and rats when in the trenches.

The irresistible connection between the cold and coal reminds me of a story against some of the King's Own. Out in no man's land there is a battered house, about halfway between us and the Germans. Nothing of the house remains except a heap of debris, and the cellar which a bold patrol discovered the other day. The cellar, like all well-trained cellars, was well stocked with coal which the patrol rightly coveted for their trench brazier. So next night out they crawled again, over the parapet, through the wire, to the treasure trove with sand-bags in every pocket in which to bring back the coal. Then later in the evening they reappeared, covered with coal dust, and burdened to the ground. But it was a happy and warm little party which stood round the brazier for the rest of the night to the envy of all the poor cold fellows in the neighbouring bays.

Next night one of the most envious ones crawled out with his sandbags and repaired to the cellar where he proceeded to fill his bags to bursting point. On his return he proudly exhibited his bursting sandbags to his friends, but when the brazier was brought out and the bags were opened and everybody was cheering up with the idea of thawing his toes and fingers, instead of coal appeared very much battered and discoloured brick ends!

6 February 1916. In addition to my Coffee Bar and its accounts, I am now acting as PRI (President Regimental Institutes), which includes everything from the Beer Canteen to the Hairdressers Saloon. Every morning a queue of men come to my hut with vast sums of money which I have to book down and treasure, while others come for orders to buy stout or candles or chocolate at the neighbouring town. So far from being a spiritual pastor, it seems that I am being initiated into the mysteries of commerce. When the war is over, what I won't know about feeding and lubricating a Battalion won't be worth knowing. In my spare time I act as Caterer of the Officers' Mess and have succeeded in improving the menu at the cost of increasing the mess bills. But after all it is a false economy to eat tinned butter when you can get fresh. Up to the present we seem to have lived out of tins, our whole existence has a tinny flavour. Everything in the BEF comes out of a tin – milk, butter, jam, cigarettes, fish, fruit, vegetables, meat, matches, coffee, biscuits, even our water for it is brought up in old petrol cans. Our very lives seem to be contained in tin, and death too for that matter, for it generally comes over from the Hun lines in the form of a jam pot filled with high explosive.

I remember in a recent letter I said that now that the electric light had really come and everything was going well, we should also have to go. And so it is, orders have come to move out – in fact half the Brigade have gone and we follow on Tuesday. We have been relieved by a new Division and we are going back to a spot near St Omer for a month's rest. It sounds very nice, but rest is a misnomer in army circles and means just the reverse. There isn't a single man who wouldn't rather remain where he is than go back for a month's constant fatigues and parades. It's like exchanging the freedom of Oxford for the restraint and discipline of school.

The Gordons – our camp mates – marched off this morning just as I was going to my first Celebration. It is quite a relief not to have their pipers practising at my door. I had never realised before what a strange race Scottish pipers are – a peculiarly self-contained, introspective breed, placid volcanoes. They strut about detached from their surroundings, playing the mournful lament so dear to their hearts.

Each evening they tear themselves away from the dream world in which they habitually live, and assemble in a wide circle to play Tattoo. Even then, although they play in harmony with the others they still wear the vacant detached look of hermits. As a matter of fact the Band is really first class, and the drums particularly are excellent. Such a swing and dash and precision about them. They are quite a treat to watch but it is the pipers who hold me spellbound. Each one beats time with his right foot, but not with the toe as ordinary mortals do, but with the heel!

Yesterday we were invaded by a Labour Battalion. They came down upon us like locusts from the east, and have sent bar takings at the Beer Canteen to a dizzy height. Apart from that they don't appear to be good for much, unless it be natting or chair-warming.

The imagination fairly blinks at the picture they provide. All of them are hairy grandfathers, with swivel eyes, or drooping eyelids or club feet – a most weird collection. However, they find their sphere of usefulness on the roads and railways – both of which sadly require all the loving care these gentlemanly old ruffians can devote to them.

Chapter 3

'We have won our Spurs'

The Battle of Loos: The Bluff – March 1916; St Eloi Craters – April 1916

11 February 1916. On Monday last we were relieved by a new Division and handed over to them our trenches and our camp, and on Tuesday morning early we began our long journey back here. The first part we marched, about eight miles, to a railway siding where we entrained. The distance was not great but the time the train took to cover it was beyond belief, and it was teatime before we crawled stiffly from our cattle trucks. Tea was a primitive meal, partaken hurriedly and with our loins girded, in a goods shed nearby, and then began the last stage of our journey. By the time we were clear of the town the shadow of night had fallen and we plodded along the high road hoping every minute to come within sight of billets. We had been told that they were only five miles away, but after we had marched eight we began to think that our informant had been unduly optimistic: it was then that we discovered that we had missed our turning and it wasn't until 11:30 pm that we finally arrived tired and hungry and somewhat short of temper.

It was then quite dark and drizzling, what little moon the calendar led us to expect was hidden behind clouds, so we had to get the men and horses into their widely scattered billets as well as we could in the dark.

Headquarters, with whom I live, found that the billets prepared for us were in an imposing chateau [Hellebrouck], but we cared little for that as the grate was cold and the cupboard was bare, so we went to bed to forget troubles in dreamland.

44

Next day the sun was shining brightly, and we looked out on a scene of rustic beauty which after the dreariness of battered Flanders was quite refreshing. A wide expanse of lawn cut by a winding stream, and dotted with shrubs and trees through which white wooden bridges over the rivulet could be seen. After enjoying the beauty of the grounds we turned to examine the chateau – I had plenty of opportunity for this as I was unable to leave the purlieus of the house for a necessary and intimate reason!

The Chateau is a pretentious building; viewed from the front or the back it might easily pass as the country seat of a Belted Earl with its big frontage and many windows and pillared doorway, but as soon as the side is seen the deception is apparent; it is only one room thick – a sort of vertical flat. We learn now that the builder was an American which accounts for everything!

The drawback to this style of architecture is that privacy is impossible, for one has to go through every room to get from one end of the house to the other. This doesn't matter so much downstairs, but it's rather trying for the occupants of the middle bedrooms. Luckily we are a bachelor community, but the imagination refuses to picture what happens when the house is occupied by a cock & hen house-party in the piping days of peace.

Yesterday we were startled by the Guard turning out, and the Bugler playing the General Salute. I was in bed at the time but I looked out of my window like any Peeping Tom and saw a dazzling cavalcade prancing & curvetting up the drive. It was Sir Douglas Haig and his Staff come to shoot his card on the Battalion. He looked very fine & soldierly and was followed by a Trooper carrying a Union Jack on his lance, and five or six Generals resplendent in their red hats and brass fixings, with a small army of Staff Officers in attendance while bringing up the rear were three very smart Lancers, with their lances at the carry, and their steel points catching and reflecting the rays of the sun. It was quite an imposing sight, and was the first proof I had seen that the pomp and splendour of the Army is not yet departed.

Yesterday, as I have hinted, I stayed in bed until tea time. I have had a slight touch of dysentery, I think, which made me feel very cheap and seedy. Nearly everybody has been troubled in the same way, we are inclined to think that the water is the cause, but it may be the effect of all the tinned food that we are condemned to eat up near the front lines. However, I am much better today and I feel quite merry and bright again.

6 March 1916. The Brigade has been in action and has not disgraced itself [the Bluff, the Bean]. The trenches which the 17th Division lost have been recaptured and a small portion of the Hun line as well, and we are back once more in our huts trying to efface the memory of the past few days and repair our clothing and equipment.

In the last three weeks we have lived an intolerable life of suspense, with our assault and its cost hanging like a black cloud over our heads. Our tongues have been tied and our senses fettered by the tragedy which lay ahead of us; but now all is over, and pride in our victory is mingled with relief that all is over and our sorrow for the good men and true whom we have left behind.

The Army Commander, General Plumer, inspected the remnant of the Battalion today; and while congratulating us on our achievement, reminded us that our engagement was but a small unimportant local action. It came as a shock for, in our small world, it did and does loom very large.

However, I must tell you about it from the beginning. Ever since we were recalled from rest we knew that we had been chosen for the inevitable assault, and our time has been spent in rehearsing the part that we were to play.

Facsimile trenches had been dug some distance back, drawn accurately to scale, giving both our line and the Hun's in complete detail. Over that ground, day after day, we practised the attack, until each man knew by heart his position and his part. The assault had been arranged originally for Tuesday evening an hour before dusk, but the hard frosty weather made it necessary to postpone it until later. Finally, when all preparations had been made, we marched away from camp on Wednesday evening, ready to 'go over the top' at 4.30 Thursday morning.

It was a great and impressive sight when the Battalion paraded in its fighting kit. Fighting kit consists of nothing superfluous. Each man carried in addition to his rifle and bayonet, 180 rounds of ammunition, his entrenching tool, two hand grenades, three sandbags tucked in his belt, rations for twenty-four hours consisting of a tin of bully beef and biscuits, and a steel helmet. No packs or greatcoats, but instead, a look of dogged determination. Every third man carried strapped to his back a spade with which to consolidate the trenches when they had been won. And of course every pocket bulged with gas helmets and field dressings, identity discs and wire cutters.

Every man who was to take part had, sewn to the middle of his back just below the collar of his tunic, a large yellow patch with various black marks. The idea of this was to distinguish at a glance friend from foe, and anybody seen in the trenches without his patch was to be shot at sight, for we meant to have no Hun tricks played on us.

The King's Own were given the post of honour in the centre of the line, with the 1st Gordons on our left, and the 2nd Suffolks on our right. We alone were to go on and capture German trenches, the other two Battalions were to stop when they had regained our own lost trenches.

As the hour of the assault drew near the excitement was intense, until at 4.30 am the whole line got out of its assembly trenches and marched forward in three big waves. The Germans were taken completely by surprise. We were into the first line before they knew what had happened. Until that moment, there had been no sound, but then almost at once began the most awful noise imaginable, the incessant rattle of rifle fire, machine guns and bursting shells.

In less time than it takes to write it, the whole countryside was alight with Very lights and the blinding flash of high explosive: words fail me to describe the tornado or the terrifying crack and roar of the guns, each one firing as fast as the crews could feed it, until it seemed impossible that human beings could live in such a hail of flying lead and steel. But still the line pushed on until they had reached their objective and occupied the German third line.

All this time I was with the Doctor at the Regimental Aid Post, so let me try to describe it to you. Just behind the trenches from which we assaulted was a sandbagged dugout, low and dark and small. In this was crowded the Doctor and his staff of Dressers and Bearers and all the paraphernalia of his art, and to this the wounded were brought to be roughly dressed before being carried down to the Dressing Station some two miles in rear.

Soon after the beginning of the attack, cases began to arrive, mostly walking cases, for stretcher cases could not be brought down then. Some of the wounds were ghastly, but the Doctor patched them up as best he could and waited for dawn and the stretcher bearers from the Field Ambulance, and while we waited our hearts were cheered by the sudden appearance of a large crowd of Hun prisoners, seventy-five or more, who had been captured in the first line. For the most part they looked dirty and tired, hungry and very frightened. They had surrendered tamely at the first sight of cold steel.

I said that the attack was launched in three waves. The reason for this was that we meant to capture three lines of Hun trenches. The first wave went straight over everything until they reached their objective – the third Hun line; the second wave did the same, so that the Germans in the front line when they opened their bleary eyes saw two lines of men jumping over them and carrying on straight ahead. You can imagine their plight, cut off from the rear and attacked by the third wave in front. They lost no time in throwing off their equipment and holding up their hands, the while they shouted 'Kamerad' at the top of their panic-stricken voices.

Just outside the Aid Post these prisoners were marshalled into fours and marched away through the bursting shells to the Brigade Headquarters some distance in rear. It was almost pathetic to see the eager way in which they tried to pacify their guards by handing over their watches and their trinkets. One even pulled out a photo of himself and thrust it upon his warder!

But I am getting away from the main story. By this time it had dawned, and the stretcher cases began to arrive, and still no bearers from the Field Ambulance to take those who had had their wounds dressed out of the inferno to a place of safety. All this time the Huns were shelling fiercely to prevent reserves from coming up. They sight their guns so that their shells form a curtain of fire between the trenches and the reserves. It was just on the edge of this curtain or barrage that the Aid Post was situated, so that it was of vital importance to get the wounded away as soon as possible, but it was this same barrage which prevented the Field Ambulance bearers from coming up to us.

At last things became impossible for the dugout was filled to overflowing, and the great bulk of the cases were lying out all round in the open. In fact many were killed there as they lay on the ground after the Doctor had dressed their original wounds.

About this time, the first of our badly wounded officers arrived. Poor boy, he was simply riddled and his arm blown off. Delay meant certain death, for the cold was intense and nobody had a greatcoat of course. The only thing that could save his life was to get him down to the Hospital at once, so off we set with him, successfully avoided all krumps & after much labour got him down to Bedford House – the Hospital. However, our labour was in vain for he died of his wounds soon afterwards. Poor boy, for he was only a boy, was the perfect hero and never murmured once tho' we jolted & shook him terribly as we carried him on a broken stretcher over the broken ground.

When I got down there I got the Field Ambulance to send up their bearers for, after all, the barrage was more terrifying than dangerous.

Meanwhile, things had gone well for us all along the line, and we held and consolidated the trenches that we set out to win. But for the artillery, our losses would have been inconsiderable, for the German infantry man is really quite a poor fighter and showed no relish for a stand-up fight. However the Hun artillery never paused a moment from hammering away at our trenches and above all our communication trenches up and down which ammunition, bombs, sandbags, messages and wounded had to pass. At the end of the forty-eight hours that we were up there, the trenches were practically nothing but a series of krump holes filled with dead and wounded and discarded or broken equipment and rifles – an absolute shambles. I can't tell you of the awful experience it was, or the sights which would have made a heart of stone bleed. Men lying as they fell and trampled underfoot, crushed down into the all-pervading mud by the living who simply couldn't avoid them.

The second night I spent in the front line, for it was much safer than further back where the barrage was incessant and murderous. I managed to find a dugout which hadn't been blown in, and there with eleven or twelve men, Gordons and King's Own, I spent the night, dozing off from time to time despite the noise & the cold. In the dugout was a Gordon wounded in the stomach in the first assault. Poor lad, he had been there then nearly twenty hours, and it was to be nearly another twenty-four before he was got away to Hospital, and yet he never complained or uttered a word of pain. Truly the courage and spirit shown by all ranks was magnificent. Everyone there deserved a decoration, and the official communiqué says 'the trenches which we lost on February 14th have been retaken with small loss and 250 prisoners'. *C'est tout!*

Finally, after more than forty-eight hours, wet through the whole time, with practically no food and insufficient covering and unceasing strain, we handed over the captured trenches intact to the relieving

Brigade and staggered back to our camp leaving nearly 50 per cent of our original number behind.

We started from here at 7.30 pm Wednesday evening and arrived back at 7.30 Saturday morning, so there is small wonder that many of the men were lightheaded when they found themselves in safety once more. It was a really sad sight this morning when the Battalion paraded to receive the congratulations of the Army Commander. I wonder if you remember a picture which appeared sometime ago entitled 'The Roll Call' – a Scottish regiment drawn up after an engagement, tattered and torn and almost decimated. I thought of that as I saw the remnant of our Battalion drawn up – a mere shadow of its former strength and glory.

The winning of our spurs has cost us dear, though the exact figures are as yet uncertain. Three officers killed and nine wounded, fifty-five men killed, sixty-five missing, which I'm afraid means blown to pieces, for the Huns were too overwhelmed to make prisoners, and about 250 wounded. It is a heavy price, but we rejoice that it is the price of victory and not defeat.

We are hoping now to be allowed to go back and finish our interrupted rest, but at present there is no sign of moving. As I write the snow is falling and the sky is grey and leaden, quite in keeping with our frame of mind.

Many of the men found time to pick up wonderful and interesting souvenirs from the German trenches. I'm afraid I never thought of anything but getting through alive – the only souvenir I got was a very plebeian cold in the head, but I daresay when we move again many of the men will gladly exchange their souvenirs for the price of a drink or two, so I may be able to bring you back a relic of the fray. No German helmet though for they all wore those pork pie caps.

I'm afraid I haven't done justice either to the splendour of the assault or the terrifying and awful experiences. Nor have I given you the faintest picture of the magnificent way every man behaved or the courage and endurance they displayed, but I cannot write more now for my hands are full of letters of sympathy to the families of those who answered the call.

11 March 1916. We were recalled, as you know, from a month's rest at the end of six days to clear up the mess made by the relieving Division, on the distinct understanding that when the work was done we would return and complete our rest cure. After three weeks of constant strain, we 'went over the top', did all that we were asked to do, and I think I may say without boasting, did it jolly well. On our return from the trenches, battered, weary and sadly reduced, we are kept hanging about for a week in this most uncomfortable camp, daily expecting the order to move back and therefore unable to settle down to anything, but instead we receive an order to go up to the trenches again, or at least what remains of them, in order to consolidate what we captured, re-dig what the Hun artillery destroyed, and generally act as bottle washer and scullion combined. Of course we know it is active service, and so forth, but why make us promises which are never redeemed? We wanted no bribe to make us do our best, we would have fought not a whit less hard, had we not been buoyed up with the prospect of rest. Nothing is gained by making these false and valueless promises, while our faith in the ability, nay rather the intelligence of the authorities is undermined.

I was really sorry for the Battalion when it marched away last night. Companies which went up to the assault 160 strong, went up yesterday sixty or seventy all told, led by a Lieutenant or Company Sergeant Major.

The bitterness of my grouse is not for myself, for I personally am very cosily ensconced with my old friends the Quartermaster and Interpreter in a roomy and draught-proof hut divided into a sitting room, where I am now, and the sleeping apartment where I hope to be shortly.

I didn't go out with the boys this time, for three reasons.

1. There is little room for interested onlookers in the trenches, as they are now.
2. I have got a pestilential cold in my head, which refuses to abate.
3. Tomorrow being Sunday, I have to prepare and arrange the Services back here.

So here I am toasting my toes at a nice warm stove, and yarning all sorts of hot air to fill an envelope home.

14 March 1916. We are back once more in our old camp [Rosinghill], with the electric light in full swing and my own hut much improved by the last occupants. The walls and roof are completely lined with canvas, which gives it a clean and pleasing appearance, and keeps out all undesirable draughts and winds.

51

Much has happened in the month that has passed since we marched away for our month's rest [at Vlamertinghe] near St Omer. We have been through the furnace of affliction, we have seen sights which we would fain forget, we have lost many good men and true, whom we ill could spare, we mourn for many a pal who has answered the last great call, we have tasted the joys of victory, we have won our spurs, we have lived as it were in a new and strange world of blood and fire, and now we come back here, as it were to home, to recover from a mental and spiritual bruising and pick up again the old threads of peaceful trench life and weekly concerts and Coffee Bars and all the other adjuncts of normal existence out here.

Rowe, Leo and I decided to take advantage of the weather and view the ruins of Ypres. I had been through on my way up to and down from the trenches many times, but I had never stopped to wander amid the debris and the side roads. Luckily, the Hun was as peaceful as the day, and we strolled amid the ruins of the Cloth Hall and the Cathedral unmolested, picking up bits of stained glass and so on as souvenirs of our visit.

Ypres now is wonderful in its ruin, not a whole house is standing, nothing but a few gaunt walls and piles of brick and plaster and debris of every description. Of the Cloth Hall hardly anything remains, even the outer shell is slowly disappearing under the continued strafing of the Hun guns. The Cathedral is even worse in many ways. I entered through the East Window and down over the mound of rubbish which buries what remains of the High Altar. It is a novel way of entering a cathedral, but in this case the easiest. All the original doorways are blocked by huge pieces of masonry and beams and rubbish. Inside it is almost impossible to reconstruct the very plan of the building; all is confusion – great piles of stonework and bricks and broken wood and lead melted into the most grotesque shapes, while above all, two or three great pillars lying as they fell, broken into their original circular slabs and looking for all the world like a row of Dutch cheeses.

It made a wonderful picture: above, the blue sky, dappled with smoke balls of the bursting archies, and stabbed with the glittering wings of the aeroplanes, droning backwards and forwards but at such a height that they seem to be motionless. Below, the feeling of utter desolation and decay, silent as the grave and yet alive with khaki figures strolling about in knots of two or three, visible through the broken walls, intent for the most part on picking up souvenirs, though many are stationed there to guide the transports through at night, and to prevent the would-be looter from looting what little furniture or household stuff still remains intact.

When the war is over some enterprising American will run up a skyscraping hotel in the Grande Place, and Mr Cook will offer all sorts of unrivalled opportunities for the becheckered sightseer to view poor shattered Ypres and the belt of desolation that runs from the sea to the Swiss frontier.

20 March 1916. The last week, I have 'merely existed', and more than once wished that I didn't, but it wasn't until Saturday night that I really began to feel that life was not worth living and so went to bed. I'm not too sure that my distemper hasn't been brought on by the sheaf of doleful letters which I have been busy writing since we returned from our show at the Bluff. If the first requisite for a *corpus sanum* is a *mens sana*, then it seems only logical that a mind unnaturally depressed by the incessant eulogising of the dear departed and the repeated sympathising with the bereaved is calculated to have a very deleterious effect upon the health.

On Friday I got up a concert for the Battalion to cheer them up before going up to the trenches the following day. I think I have told you of the Mudlarks – our Divisional pierrot party – though I don't think I told you that their marquee was blown down by a Euroclydon some three weeks ago. Since then they have been more or less out of work, so the brilliant idea struck me of getting them to give us a concert in our own Recreation Hut.

It took a good deal of blarney to persuade them to leave their comfortable billets for the rough accommodation of our hut, and I had to tell them the tale of how when the prophet was unable to go to the mountain, the mountain was patriotic enough to come to the prophet. History does not relate as far as I know why the prophet was unable to make the journey, but I suggest it might be due to a bad attack of trench feet, which was the only thing which prevented the King's Own from going to seek amusement and recreation outside the purlieus of our camp, and – well, to cut it short, they came bringing with them their costumes and piano. Never had our hut seen such a merry evening – every seat and inch of standing room was crowded with perspiring but enthralled spectators. All the members of the Mudlarks are professional entertainers and we had a perfect feast of wit and pathos, sentiment and humour, all neatly set to music, to say nothing of sleight of hand, for among the artists was a first-rate card manipulator who performed prodigies of magic with hard-boiled eggs and silk handkerchiefs and tissue paper.

At the end of the show, which was really first-rate, we doled out the usual tea and rum. This helped materially to swell the volume of sound when I proposed three cheers to the Mudlarks, and sent all home with an inward glow of satisfaction and contentment, which I am sure was worth untold reinforcements in the trenches next day.

On Saturday I was initiated into the cult of Charlie Chaplin. Our Divisional Cinema advertised an entire programme of Chaplin films, so tho' I have as you know a decided antipathy for moving pictures, I went off with the Quartermaster and the Interpreter to enjoy the show. And enjoy it I did, though my eyes and nose were streaming with cold, and every time I laughed I had a paroxysm of coughing, but despite all that I am now a decided and eager votary of the cinema idol. He is the quaintest and cleverest little man I've ever seen, and for once in a way *vox populi* if not *vox Dei* is at any rate *vox mea.*

21 March 1916. The last week has been perfect summer weather, warm and sunny, all the mud has dried up hard and firm, but not so dry as to choke us with dust; it really has been beautiful, which emphasised my foolishness in getting another cold and spending two days in bed. However, now I really am better and have at last got rid, I think and sincerely hope, of the cold which has been hanging about me since the beginning of the month.

I think there is no doubt now that we shall be moving shortly into a quieter part of the line; which will be very agreeable to us all, though unfortunately it entails leaving our old camp and my very cosy and luxurious hut.

You will be sorry to hear that my pup 'Spot' is doing dot-and-carry-one just now. He persisted in running immediately in front of my pony until at last the inevitable happened and he got his back paw trod on. Then the noise started; such a hullabaloo that all the villagers and soldiers came out to see what or who was dying. If you could have seen poor old Spot standing in the middle-of-the-road holding his paw up, with his nose pointing at the heavens, and the look of outraged innocence on his face, yelping like one possessed. I felt an awful worm, and the gathering crowd glared at me as if I were some low wife-beater or body-snatcher. Finally as I was in a hurry and in some fear of my life, I left Spot in a neighbouring house and rode on, sending the mess cart later in the day to fetch my lord home. Now, by dint of much licking, the damaged paw is almost completely restored to health, but Mr Spot is cute, and still makes all he can out of it, winning sympathy and one unending meal from tender-hearted Tommy.

26 March 1916. We are providing nightly fatigues, many hundred men strong, who pass the hours of darkness in carrying bombs and sandbags, wire and spades, planks and trench mortars from one place to another, from the dump to the trenches or vice versa; and arrive back in camp tired, wet and blasphemous some few hours after dawn. It's useful work and so on and so forth but the most boring imaginable to carry up bombs for other people to throw, or to carry up planks and nails for other people to hit their thumbs over, and to lose your beauty sleep into the bargain must be the limit of refined torture and indignity. I hardly wonder that they would all prefer to stay in the trenches. The usual six or seven days in, followed by the same number back in camp, is not at all a bad sort of life, but what we have been doing for the last three weeks is anything but conducive to gaiety.

The rewards for our little 'stunt' have been issued and the ribbons presented. Our share of the spoils are four Military Crosses and six DCMs, though we hope there are still one or two DSOs for our Colonel and Majors. In any case, we have done as well as any Battalion in the Brigade and are quite satisfied, though naturally we feel that it is only a very limited number who have received the recognition that practically every man deserved.

Today has been rather a strange Sunday as I had two of my Church Parades in the afternoon. The King's Own as I told you were doing a carrying fatigue last night and didn't get back until 5.30 this morning, so they broke their fast at 1 pm and went to church at 2 pm. Having just eaten heartily of steak and onions, I didn't have that pale spiritual feeling which is born of early rising and an empty stomach. But out here one's own feelings and prejudices have to go by the board, and our spiritual coat, as our physical or material one, has to be cut according to our cloth.

Spot's foot, crushed by my pony between his hoof and the hard *pavé* road is fast recovering, and is now nearly serviceable once more, despite the fact that a heavy footed Scot in his uncouth and clumsy way stepped on it again in trying to avoid it, when they met on a narrow 'duck board'.

28 March 1916. Our expected move hasn't come off yet, we are still in the same camp 'standing by' at present. There has been fresh activity in our sector. 'The Fighting Third' – our Division – has been in action again and has captured some more German trenches yesterday and today. The fruits of the victory have been visible – batches of very dejected and dirty German prisoners have been continually passing down the road past our camp, under an escort of mounted Military Police. They are marched as far as Poperinghe where they entrain for the Base and Merrie England. So far our Brigade hasn't taken part in this engagement, but we are going up to reserve dugouts this evening, and may be called upon to help repel a counter-attack or consolidate the trenches captured. Nothing at present is certain, but whatever it may be, I expect as soon as it is over we will get away to a nice quiet part of the line.

Tomorrow evening I am going for a twenty-four-hour 'Retreat' in the ecclesiastical sense of the word only – arranged by Neville Talbot for chaplains out here. But more of this in my next.

31 March 1916. Behold me sitting here with a lovely black eye, very un-clerical and most unprepossessing! Luckily the Battalion knows how I came by it, or I am sure they would think that I had been brawling in the local estaminet, or at best indulging in an unsuccessful display of muscular Christianity. It was on Wednesday night and the Battalion was going up to form a local reserve just behind the trenches, for an attempt by one of the other Brigades of our Division to bite off another small German salient at St Eloi. You will probably have seen in the papers that the attempt was successful, and as it happens we were not actively engaged.

However on this particular occasion, a thoughtful Staff provided us with buses to take us from our camp to our destination. It was my first ride on a London bus out here, so, full of life I climbed upstairs determined to wring the last ounce of pleasure from a new sensation.

I was in the fourth bus of a long line of twenty-five which stretched into the dim distance. It was a long ride of about ten miles, and at the slow crawl to which the badness of the road reduces even the fiercest motorcar, it was night long before we got to the end. Pitch black and very cold, my thirst for new sensations seemed doomed to be frozen and blinded unquenched when suddenly something gave me a terrific belt in the eye which jerked my head back, and then with a feeling of being scalped my cap was skinned from my head and shot into space!!

A whole gamut of sensations, as painful as they were unexpected and unappreciated, crowded into the space of a molecule of time, and it was a minute or two before I could realise that I had run into a low-hanging telegraph wire stretched across the road. As soon as I was articulate, I shouted for the bus to stop, for being frugal-minded I could bear the pain of a fast-closing eye better than the pain of losing my cap.

Some hero gallantly volunteered to go and retrieve my bonnet now some distance in rear, and on we went again. The mystery really is how I, sitting on the back seat, was caught by the wire which missed the full house sitting in front of me.

However, to continue, when we got as far as the buses could go, we disembarked and proceeded to march to our final destination. With one eye closed, and the other weeping with sympathy, I had to be led by the hand, as St Paul of old, until we arrived at the place where we were to spend the night. Luckily my billet was in a house. Most of the Battalion were in huts and dugouts in a wood, but the Company I attached myself to had the barns and houses which still remain more or less intact in a much shelled village near the front.

There in the stone-flagged kitchen I laid me down with four other officers, and with straw beneath and a British Warm above, I managed to keep tolerably warm and therefore to sleep. Next morning my eye was fast closed and swollen, and I was still capless for the hero who got off to get my cap rejoined us later in great form and thrust into my hand what he was pleased to think was my cap, but which refused to do more than perch on my head. On a closer examination it proved to belong to some Tommy of our Battalion who apparently had been caught on one of the other buses by the same wire that outed me. They say that when the whole twenty-five had passed, the road just there was carpeted with khaki caps, and that now all the little boys and girls of the neighbourhood are sporting them!

That evening, I was due at Poperinghe for a much-needed twenty-four hour Retreat. I am sure that when I arrived the assembled chaplains thought it was a penitentiary rather than a Retreat that I was in need of.

The Quiet Day had been arranged for the Chaplains of our Division, and we had managed to get Neville Talbot to take it for us. Life out here is necessarily dominated so largely by the material side of war, and everything is so physical, that the spiritual is crowded out. We have so much serving of tables to do, that it is hard to keep the other side of our work uppermost. Physical force, physical health, physical comfort or discomfort are the ever-present fundamental basis of all thought and care, and they combine to smother the faint voice of the spirit. I know that I find it increasingly difficult to keep my lamp burning brightly, for the individual soul is very much dependent for its vitality and growth upon the capacity of the souls around it. Living among worldly people, and shut in by the cult and worship of physical force, it is not really surprising that we so quickly become unspiritual.

A Quiet Day for meditation was what we all needed, and I more than most, for I was becoming dead and cold. The place chosen for our little Retreat was Talbot House in Poperinghe.

Talbot, who is out here as Chaplain to another Division, has rented a large house and has fitted it up as a haven of rest for officers and men alike. Downstairs is devoted to recreation, and the gratification of the stomach; the first floor consists of a certain number of bed-rooms for officers going or returning from leave, and writing and reading rooms for the men. Above them on the next floor are quiet rooms and more bedrooms, while at the top of the house in a large and lofty attic he has fitted up a most delightful and beautiful little chapel. The attic is lofty as I have said, with a pointed roof and oak beams across, with a loft at one end in which stands the harmonium. The other end wall is hung with heavy curtains and banners taken from Ypres Cathedral and other ruined churches in the neighbour-hood. In the centre stands the altar raised on two steps. Behind is a sacred picture as reredos, and hanging from a beam above is the red glimmer of the sanctuary lamp.

All down the middle runs a beautiful Turkish carpet with two carved oak standard candlesticks halfway down. The lighting is all done by candles, a gilt candelabra hangs from the middle beams, while each form placed obliquely down each side of the room has a tall wooden candlestick fixed at each end. The combination of the rich colour of the hangings and carpets, and the soft light of dozens of candles makes the little chapel an ideal haven of rest, and a perfect little house of God.

Here we lived for the twenty-four hours except for one meal which we had in a downstairs room, while Talbot read extracts of Pilgrim's Progress to us. As the house is always full, and all the bedrooms are used nightly by officers on leave, we slept on stretchers in the chapel itself. It seemed a little strange & out of place, but really it was rather a nice idea when once we got over the shock of the unusual. Altogether it was a very delightful and helpful experience, and my only regret is that the time we had wasn't much longer.

Now I am back in the world of war once more, just off on my pony to arrange Services for Sunday. It is a beautiful sunny day, warm and balmy, a blue sky and the pleasant droning of the aeroplanes taking the place of the buzz of the busy bee. We are still in the same sector and the date of moving is continually postponed, but next week really ought to see us clear of the Salient and either back in rest or in a quieter part of the line.

6 April 1916. Oh the joy of being between sheets again, and seeing a tablecloth! We are back in rest at last [at Eecke], enjoying to the full our few days respite from the clash and roar of the guns. After the blood and fire and mud of the trenches, the peace and restfulness of this little French village is perfect bliss, and the joy of a napkin is unspeakable.

Strangely enough we are back near where we spent our first rest, though not in the same billets; but under what very different circumstances. Then we were new and raw, fretting at the enforced rest, and eagerly awaiting the chance to get back to the trenches and the Huns. Now we are veterans who have had more than enough of war, and only anxious to be allowed to have our rest unmolested.

Since my last letter, we have been in action again – twice within the month, and have again lost heavily. But I must tell you all about it from the beginning.

On Sunday night after all my Services I rode up to see my Battalion, who as I told you were in reserve during the last attack at St. Eloi. I was intending to pass the time of day with them and then get back to camp and my little hut for the night, but when I arrived I found to my infinite surprise that the Battalion was paraded in fighting kit, just preparing to march off and go over the top at two next morning to take a crater and some trenches which still remained in the enemy's hands, despite repeated efforts to wrest them from them. I got the shock of my life for I no more expected it than the Battalion did itself.

However, having made a name for ourselves at the Bluff, we had to justify it and so off we set. It was a dark misty night, the lie of the land and the trenches were practically unknown to us, and none of us were very full of the fighting spirit. Everything seemed to point one way, and that was that we should lose ourselves and fail to do whatever was demanded of us. I am sure no one was very sanguine of success. However, away we went. I took up my position with the Doctor at the Regimental Aid Post, and went through a living nightmare while the Battalion advanced to the attack. Soon a few wounded came in, slight cases only, who brought news that all was going well, though the Huns still remained in the largest mine crater. As there was little to do at the Aid Post, the Doctor and I went forward to find out what was happening. It was still very dark, Stygian hardly does it justice, and how the Battalion managed to find its way is still a mystery and a miracle. To understand the difficulty of the situation I must go back a few days and explain what had happened previously.

Our Miners had placed five gigantic mines under the Hun front line, which were exploded on the morning of the original attack. When the mines went up, the Fusiliers dashed forward and occupied the German second line, but in the subsequent fighting the Germans had managed to win back some of their trenches, and the largest crater as well. It was to win back the lost ground that we were employed, but nobody really knew quite where the Germans were, for apart from the gaping craters, the ground was pulverised and pockmarked by the combined artillery of both sides and the whole character and aspect of the country was altered. Really it beggars description, even the imagination of an Edgar Allen Poe could not picture such a scene of absolute chaos and desolation. The large crater for example is 100 yards across and more than 50 feet deep. It seems impossible to imagine that man could make such a hole in the ground; in fact, it looks more like a valley in which some evil spirit brooded, a valley of death in which even vegetation couldn't live.

It was under the lip of this huge crater that 200 Huns working frantically had managed to burrow like rabbits, with machine guns sited to sweep the surrounding country. In these burrows they were safe from artillery, and it was only by bombs & the bayonet that they could be dislodged. You can imagine the task then of our Battalion, but I'm proud to say they managed it, and by daylight we held the crater and a line of trenches beyond, capturing eighty-five prisoners to boot, all that was left of the original 200 when our Bombers had finished with them.

However, our victory cost us dear, for during the attack or soon afterwards our Adjutant and two other officers were killed, while many men also made the supreme sacrifice. But for the darkness and the mist, which really made it impossible to see more than two yards ahead, I think our casualties would have been very much heavier. All the day the Hun was remarkably quiet, and we were able to consolidate the trenches somewhat. I call them trenches, but that is a courtesy title for there was practically nothing left of them but ditches of mud full of dead Germans. Literally the mud was up to the middle of our thighs, and moving about was almost impossible, for the labour of forcing your legs through this thick creamy mud was great.

After I had managed to get all round and had seen what was left of the Battalion, I laboriously made my way back to the Aid Post to organise a stretcher party, which I took up as soon as it was dark, to bring back our badly wounded, and if possible the bodies of our dead officers.

Under the shadow of night we went over the top, being infinitely easier than keeping to the trenches. We had with us eight stretchers and forty bearers, and managed to make use of them all, though unfortunately we were unable to find the bodies of our dead among the krump holes and mud and darkness.

One German wounded amused me very much. He was lying in a trench with a dislocated shoulder, a bullet wound in each knee, and a crushed foot – he had been buried by a shell and dug out by our fellows when they captured the trench. As he lay there he kept on repeating something in German – the only word of which I could gather was the word 'mark'. I asked an officer with me who knows a little of the language what he was saying, and what do you think it was? The poor fellow was offering two marks to us to get him away! And what is the mark worth these days – is it 5d or 6½d? We got him down alright, but if we had been out for money I don't think there would have been any offers at that price, for it is no small job to carry a stretcher case two miles over that broken country in the dark. We started away from the Aid Post at six o'clock in the evening and got back again at three o'clock next morning! Which will give you some idea of the difficulty of the ground, for the distance there and back is at the most four miles the way we went, and probably not more than 800 yards as the crow flies.

I have never in my life been so tired. Luckily we were relieved that night, and coming out along a very long and winding communication trench I couldn't keep my eyes open, with the result that at each turn I went bang into the side of the trench and woke up with a start and a jolt.

All the next day we slept as we were, the mud caked on our clothes and hands – even faces were hideously dirty, for I forgot to say that before the attack the Battalion was issued with Vaseline and soot and every man had to black his face, partly to prevent the whiteness of his skin giving him away as he advanced, and partly as a sort of unspoken shibboleth – a white face in the trenches that night meant Hun and therefore death.

The following night – Tuesday – we slept in bed – in billets at Poperinghe, and the next day we entrained for this delightful little village. Ordinarily I should call it 'one-eyed', but by way of contrast it is beautiful.

My own billet is in a spotlessly clean little cottage at the bottom of a slope, nestling under the shadow of the village church. I have a diminutive room of which a four-poster bed with appropriate hangings occupies exactly one half, while a table and wash stand jostle each other in the other half for a place in the sun.

It is now after midnight, so when I have finished this I will turn round and be in bed. My billet-keeper is a charming spinster of uncertain age, but full of the milk of human kindness. She is always offering me coffee of nectarish goodness, and doing all she can to make my life here one long dream of content.

Friday. The Senior Chaplain has just been in to see me, and tells me the glorious news that I can get away on Monday for eight blissful days in Blighty. I can hardly believe that it is true, and expect he will be back in a minute to tell me he is only pulling my leg. Eight days in England, *ma foi!* How perfectly and supremely gorgeous.

19 April 1916. A gigantic pile of letters was waiting for me when I got back early this morning, rather appalling for they were all from anxious or broken-hearted relatives, but they have helped me to settle down after a hard morning's work among them. I can hardly believe that I have broken the threads even for eight short days. Luckily we are still in the same rest billets, so I enjoyed the sheets for the few hours I spent in bed this morning, though the bed is not as comfortable as the one I have just left.

24 April 1916. I have had quite a busy time since I got back preparing for and arranging my Good Friday and Easter Services. Good Friday was an unkind day, wet and depressing, but Easter Day dawned very fair and warm. Nature seemed to be eager to keep the Festival and to share both in the sufferings and triumph of our risen Lord. For myself, I had a very happy day yesterday. Five times I celebrated the Holy Mysteries, three times I preached and twice I said shortened evensong – seven Services in all. Three of them were in a cinema so-called. It is really a sort of village hall, but used now as the bed sitting room for about fifty men of the Royal Flying Corps, who at 7 and 8 am, while the Services were being held, were occupied with their toilet and their breakfast. I had one end for my little altar, and they had the other end. The nicest Service of the day, I think, was Sung Eucharist in a barn for the Field Hospital. The priest who was in the ranks of this Ambulance with the help of the Quartermaster Sergeant arranged things excellently. The barn is covered deep in straw, but otherwise empty. The end wall was hung with a full-size Red Cross flag, the cross being directly above the altar which as usual was composed of packing cases and draped with a Union Jack. They too supplied the altar lights which saved me from unpacking and assembling mine.

A great number came and we sang the one Easter hymn contained in our little book as the introit – 'Jesus Christ is risen today'. I forgot to say that many of the men had to sit up in the loft above, from which they looked down as from an organ loft upon the altar below. When I turned round to give them the Easter message I was inspired by this banked-up sea of faces. It really was a very inspiring Service and the spirit of devotion could be almost felt, so present was it.

As soon as the Service was over I had to pack up and gallop off to my next, some miles away, this time held in a sort of archway through some farm buildings, the ends closed with army blankets. The only drawback in this case was that I had to kneel in a puddle of half-congealed mud!

The evening Services for the ASC and RAMC were both in barns lighted with candles. I must confess to a great liking for these primitive mission Services. The straw and the dim religious light, and the men sitting or kneeling round is really very inspiring and helpful. It is also elemental, childlike and simple, and therefore so convincing.

Today I have been present at a most gallant and thrilling ceremony. Mellish, one of the Chaplains of our Division, has been awarded the Victoria Cross for an unequalled act of gallantry at St. Eloi. Seventeen times he went out into the crater and brought in wounded men under a constant hail of shells and bullets. You can judge of its severity for three men were killed as he was bandaging their wounds out there. Today he was presented with his ribbon by General Haldane, and no man deserved the honour more, for he is a perfectly charming man, a real white man and a saint. There is no Chaplain & very few men whom I would rather see decorated. The whole Division was represented by detachments from each unit, drawn up in a hollow square to do honour, as the General said, to a very brave man & a very gallant gentleman. By the way, do you remember I told you once about a chaplain who lived in a cottage in the shelled-out village, and kept open house for wearied Tommies coming back from the trenches – well, this is the man who has earned the Victoria Cross.

Luckily nature was kind this morning and a brilliant sun looked down upon the scene and caught and reflected the glittering bayonets of the assembled troops.

The fourth side of the square was occupied by a line of some twenty officers and men who were to receive the DSO, MC, DCM or MM ribbons, while in front in solitary grandeur and visible discomfort stood Mellish. In front again stood a group of Generals and Staff Officers resplendent in their red and brass fixings.

Before each man in turn the General took his stand, read out the deed which had earned the decoration, pinned on the ribbon, and perfunctorily shook hands. Then repeated the process with the officers until all had received their ribbons except Mellish. He, poor man, stood stiffly to attention as one hearing his death sentence, while the General made a speech and eulogised his courage and his deed, and then while all the world stood silent and expectant pinned on the red ribbon and called for three cheers, which were given *con amore*. Then came the General Salute followed by the Royal Salute for The King, and as a grand finale three cheers for His Majesty.

As you may have gathered we are still in rest billets, for which we sing continually Te Deums of thanks, but I expect we will move up into the line towards the end of the week.

My one-armed hostess simply smothers me with her kindness. Just now she has brought me a bowl of steaming soup with which I have burnt my tongue, after a fruitless refusal on the grounds that I am just off for my lunch. She never takes 'no' as an answer, but insists at all times on me consuming glasses of coffee or plates of chips! She's a kind soul and I shall miss her mothering when I have to leave this delectable little billet.

28 April 1916. We are moving tomorrow so I must send you a line today, for letter writing has to go by the board when we pull our roots up and replant them in a new place.

Ever since Easter Day we have had the most delightful weather, brilliantly sunny days and starry nights, with the result that we all feel years younger and many degrees better & brighter than we did when we arrived.

On the strength of it we are having an open air concert tonight. I have found a field which forms a natural amphitheatre – a nice semicircular grassy slope on which the Battalion will recline at ease, while the piano and performers will be mounted on a wagon drawn up in the middle. If it is cold, we are thinking of having a big camp fire which will also serve as footlights for the horse-drawn stage. I think it will be a great success for I have got an all-star cast, and the weather promises to be kind and balmy.

This week has really been a week of singing, for on Tuesday we had a great Brigade entertainment in the cinema hall – the RFC were turned out of their bedroom for the time being, and an eighteen-foot ring erected at the stage end. It was a very mixed grill for we had the Divisional Band blaring out selections, and an excellent concert party, and some very spirited boxing jumbled together to entertain the assembled generals and privates.

All the big bugs were there in their scarlet and gold, and as many men as could be packed into the rather limited space.

It was a first rate show, and everything went with a swing and a dash, especially the boxing which was extraordinarily spirited and commendably clean. The only fly in the ointment was the atmosphere, which was superheated and heavily loaded. I had an excellent if somewhat contracted seat near the ropes, and enjoyed myself immensely.

On Tuesday we played the Final of the Brigade Football Cup & we were decisively beaten by the Gordons. As we lay on the ground fanning off the flies & fierce rays of the sun, we grew quite hot at the sight of the panting players strenuously charging up and down the field. Later in the afternoon I had to hike to a neighbouring town to bury a Gunner who had died of heart failure after running in a race on a strenuous training of French beer. When I arrived I found no grave had been dug so had to rout out the Warden of the Cemetery and in my best French borrow his spades and tackle & supervise the digging of the grave – a strange life.

1 May 1916. The concert on Friday was a great success & I think much appreciated. It was a warm balmy evening and the camp fire was unnecessary either for warmth or light. I wish I could have photographed the scene.

Our piano perched up on a rickety old farm cart in the middle of a semicircle of reclining and smoking Tommies and Officers, drinking in the cool & scented evening air and the sweet harmonies & foolish quips & jests of the performers – a very peaceful and pastoral scene I can assure you.

The following morning we were up betimes, had broken our fast by 5.30 and soon afterwards commenced our long trek up to the front. We started early to avoid the midday heat but even so it was a long & dusty march and we arrived in our new billets [at Locre] shrouded grey in dust with an unquenchable thirst and a desire to bathe in some cool and limpid stream. However there was no bathing and very little drinking, for we had to find billets for the men and ourselves, and get something prepared for a much-needed meal.

My job was to get the Officers' Mess in working order, no small job in a place where such shops as still exist sell nothing but onions & tallow candles, or French beer and post cards. However we managed eventually to get a stew going, and some tinned fruit. In the intervals of catering I dashed round looking for suitable places for my Church Services, and arranging details with the different units concerned. I had managed to get a nice billet in the *Curé*'s house but at the critical moment the Brigadier arrived with his Staff looking for a billet, so I had to offer him my room with as much grace as I could muster & turn out.

Unfortunately by this time all the best billets had been snapped up & I wandered from house to house in vain. Finally, when I was thinking of woolly worms, I found an attic above a small shop in which, in addition to much household lumber and a miniature old clo'shop & jumble sale combined, hung strings of odoriferous onions & heaps of dried beans & other stocks of the commodities on sale below. In this savoury collection a bed was discovered, so for the time being I sleep there, but spend as little of the hours of daylight as possible.

The first night we all turned in early intent on getting a good night's rest after the fatigue of the march; I was quite prepared to have my rest disturbed by unwelcome pilgrims of the night, for the blankets provided looked anything but newly laundered, but I was not prepared for what did happen. At 1 am all the guns in the neighbourhood gunned with colossal speed & noise, and hard on the heels of the first salvo began a great clanging of gongs – the dread signal that the Germans were making a gas attack. Soon the whole place was astir with officers and men hurrying to their alarm posts. As I had previously lost my gas helmet I hastily threw my British Warm over my pyjamas and hurried to the Quartermaster's store for another one. However we smelt no gas, so having stood by for some time listening to the incessant firing and watching the sky lighted up with the German and British flares, we went back to bed & slept untroubled until 6.30 am when I had to get up for my first Celebration. However the alarms of the night kept away all but the very faithful few.

After breakfast I got word that some cases were coming down to the Field Ambulance from the trenches where the attack had been made, so I hurried down to see if I could do anything. It was the first time that I had seen the effects of gas poisoning. Nothing that I have ever read prepared me for the agonising sight that I saw. There were some twelve or thirteen men lying on their stretchers in tents, writhing in their gasping efforts to get their breath and tearing at their throats, coughing and moaning and wrestling with the poison. I never shall forget their damp greenish faces, contorted with pain and flecked with the froth which continually forms at their mouths.

It's hellish, perfectly hellish, and the men who use such a weapon deserve no mercy & no consideration. Our Brigade will never take another prisoner, of that I am sure. The heartrending thing about gas is that one can do practically nothing to relieve the pain or help the poor tormented sufferers. They were having oxygen while I was there, but it seemed to give little or no relief. The great majority will in time recover but some I am afraid will simply fight and struggle until the poison fiend overcomes them – a slow lingering and absolutely agonising death. But enough!

In the evening I had a joint Service with the Presbyterian Padre. I took the Service and he gave the address & a very good one too. I'm not sure how far I like or approve of joint combined Services but perhaps they help to make us know each other better, and so tighten the bands of unity, tho' not of uniformity, from which Good Lord deliver us.

Last night we were again roused in the night by the clanging of the gas alarm, but apparently the attack was not pressed; and apart from causing a few casualties & much devilish suffering, the Germans have gained nothing but the undying contempt and hatred of a few more thousand Englishmen.

The weather is still extraordinarily beautiful, fine and warm and brilliantly sunny – war seems so utterly out of place.

I must dash. Two of the poor fellows I saw have passed away this morning and are to be buried this afternoon, so I must make arrangements – the Corporal has just been in to tell me.

6 May 1916. The last week has been chock-a-block with sunshine and dissipations of all sorts – a very happy little interlude between the rigours of war. We have been billeted in a rather gawky Belgian village [Eecke] some three and a half miles – as the crow flies – behind the front-line trenches, protected from view, tho' not altogether from shellfire, by a very famous and beautiful sugarloaf hill which rises about halfway between us and the Huns, and from which we dominate his positions. I must not tell you the name, but perhaps if I whispered 'aniseed' and offer you a drink you may guess it [Kemmel].

We are only a few miles further south than where we were all the winter, but one can hardly realise that it is the same country. This wooded hill seems to be the gateway to a piece of rural England. Even war can't prevent nature from coming out in her new spring suitings of tender green and apple blossom – and very chic and well-dressed she looks. However I will tell you more about it when I have seen more of it, at present I have only made one or two tentative attempts to explore the trenches, but the Battalion goes up today and I follow on Monday, after my Sunday activities.

The chief event of the week I suppose was a great Mess dinner which we had on Wednesday, to which we invited our General and his Staff. All day, in my capacity as Caterer, I spent in and about the kitchen, advising, supervising, and generally getting in the way and very hot. At length, as is usual, the great moment arrived, but instead of the General came a note from him saying he would be three-quarters of an hour late, so to pass the tedium of waiting we adjourned to the back of the house for a boxing display between the Padre and a Sub. In a moment of foolishness I offered to box three rounds with anybody my own weight. Judge then my consternation when the assembled Mess pushed forward a newly joined Subaltern who on his own showing was an ex-champion of some sort. Fortunately however for me, he had been bottling up a good deal, though I didn't know this until later. Old Rowe acted as my second, and fanned me with his *mouchoir* while I sat on his capacious and well-padded knee.

On the call of time I advanced trembling, determined however to get one clip in before they carried me away. As soon as the formality of joining hands and walking round each other had been performed, I led with my left and landed full on his mouth, which seemed to let loose all the powers which work windmills. For before I knew what had happened I was in the middle of a perfect hail of swinging arms. After mixing it for a bit I made a series of strategic movements to the rear, followed closely by this dancing dervish.

However, despite my fears, I found I could land pretty easily and it was then I realised that my opponent was not altogether, what the medicos call '*compos mentis*'.

The friendly timekeeper fearing that I would get eaten up, called time about half way through, for which I was thankful as my reverse gear was getting tired.

The second round was more or less a repetition of the first, and the third was the same until I got in a lucky clip on his jaw and dropped him. It wasn't a knockout but it terminated the proceedings and we dashed off for a wash before the General arrived.

The dinner was not bad in view of the difficulty in getting supplies, but the after-dinner entertainment was great. The General [Plumer] in his kindly genial way went down to sit among the Subs to drink his port, and by chance sat next to my late opponent with whom he tried to chat, but his answers were a trifle distrait; conversation was beginning to flag when it was abruptly closed by the disappearance backwards of the Sub. Whether it was the dizziness of a slightly concussed brain, or the whirling fumes of Bacchus, or a sudden rush of blood to the head due to the close proximity of a live General, or a combination of all three, I cannot say; but the sudden disappearance of the General's *tête à tête* and the crash of dancing glass as his toes caught the underneath of the table was a moment fraught with some surprise and consternation.

Yesterday the Army Commander summoned to his side all the Senior Chaplains of the Divisions with their seconds in command. We went in style in a staff car to the Army Headquarters [at Cassel], had a conference among ourselves, in which as usual the brethren with anything to say sat silent, while those who had nothing to say, said it at great length. After nearly three hours of this in a hot room, there was a universal sigh of relief when the chairman announced that the hour for tea was at hand. General Plumer very kindly gave us tea in his own house, so we sat cheek by jowl with Generals and Staff Officers and consumed tea out of dainty cups and daintily nibbled still daintier confectionery. Afterwards we listened to an excellent address by the General himself – most illuminating as we got a few kindly hints from the layman's point of view.

Chapter 4

Fighting Padre in the Fighting Third

The Somme – the Battle of Delville Wood, July 1916; the start of the Big Push

12 May 1916. It's been rather a breathless week in more senses than one, hot breathless days full of breathless activity, and yet there is little to write a letter about. It has been our first week in the new trenches, and has been spent in exploring the network of trenches which in the Year of Grace 1916 are considered necessary for safety and comfort.

Our front line is pretty good on the whole though it contains one short bit very much knocked about, and of ill-repute. Known as the 'Glory Hole' it owes its name I understand to the fact that three VC's were won there. It is a nasty spot, and so far all our casualties – which are not many I am glad to say – have occurred there.

My permanent headquarters are in the gawky village [Eecke] of which I spoke in my last letter where I live with our Quartermaster – the famous fat boy of Peckham – whose heart is in proportion to his hulk. We share a bed, smoking, sitting, study, drawing room, with an excellent view of the country between us and the trenches. At night we can see quite plainly the constant stream of flares and Very lights, shooting into the air, bursting out into their brilliance and falling in a graceful parabola to the earth and extinction again. It was a wonderful sight to see these flares all along the front from Ypres to Armentières.

Right in front of us rises the wooded hill [Mount Kemmel] of which I spoke in parables. Over the shoulder of it, up and down the most delightful lane, canopied by the spreading branches of the trees each side, we ride until we reach on the far side a sweetly picturesque little village nestling among the trees. In the middle near the church stands a rustic bandstand, now feeling tired from the effects of German shells, a few of the small cottages at the near end still inhabited by old men and women, who potter in their gardens, all oblivious to the booming of the guns within a stone's throw of their homes. The far side of the village is shelled out, but still retains something of its charm – it must have been a delightfully quiet little village – the haunt I should think of honeymoon couples and artists.

Passing through the now deserted village, past sentries in sand-bagged shelters and along the road towards the front trenches, you suddenly come upon a most splendid chateau standing down among the trees, and girdled with a moat – absolutely untouched. How it has escaped is a miracle, but there it is for all the world to see, and occupied now by a company in reserve.

Before the war it must have been a most desirable place. The grounds of course have gone to seed, the hard tennis court is hidden by rank weeds among which pheasants take their ease and success-fully avoid the avid tendencies of Mess Presidents and hungry ex-poachers.

In the grounds too is our little Cemetery where already three of our Battalion have been laid to rest, two yesterday and one this morning.

Battalion Headquarters at present are in the Doctor's house, also hidden from view by trees, and protected by sandbags on the Hun side. There we sit at table, and sleep in beds, and control the fate of nations. It is very comfortable but too far from the front line, so we move soon into dugouts which are now being dug in a more convenient situation.

From the Doctor's house to the trenches runs a long winding communication trench, rejoicing in the name of Via Gellia, and not belying its associations either.

Two Battalions of the Brigade are in the trenches, one is back in this gawky Belgian village as reserve, while the fourth one is in huts and dugouts built just on this side of the hill, and protected by the contours from the attention of German shells. Week by week we change and change about, one week in the trenches, one week in the Shelters, another week in the trenches, and then a week back here, so that one week in every month we come back here for rest and refreshment – a very sound and workable plan.

At the Shelters there is a YMCA hut in which I have Services. I had one there last night, and am having a Celebration there tomorrow morning for the Battalion which will be moving up to the trenches to relieve us.

17 May 1916. Sunday was a red letter day – a day replete with rare and unexpected happenings. It began in the orthodox manner with a very nice little Celebration in the Recreation Hut [at Locre convent] for the Field Ambulance at 6.45 am. Then a hard gallop to the Headquarters of the Divisional General [at Westoutre] and a Celebration for him and his staff at 8 o'clock. He very kindly asked me in for breakfast, and I very foolishly refused, and got back to my own billet to find my faithful servant Leah, scarlet in the face and with a watery eye withal – no, it wasn't that at all! The poor boy is a teetotal abstainer, but he had managed to catch the most unpatriotic complaint of German measles.

Having safely removed him to the Field Ambulance I rode up to the Shelters to see if I could arrange a Service for the King's Own who came out of the trenches late the night before. While there, a car drove up & two red hats got out and came into our Mess. One was an old friend of the Colonel's and the other – his Staff Captain – was none other than Bairnsfather – THE Bruce Bairnsfather of Bystander fame. He is a charming fellow, quite young and very keen, and not at all averse to talk about his art, so before he went I got him to do me three little sketches – types of Tommy Atkins – the 1914 type in a Balaclava helmet & heavy black moustache and determined mien, the 1915 type in a soft hat and better temper, and 1916 in a steel helmet and broad grin. I will bring them home when I come – meanwhile they are on show in the Mess.

Last night we had a visit from a Hun aeroplane. I heard nothing, but this morning after a Celebration at the Hospital I was shown the result of one bomb which he dropped. It fell plunk on the top of a bell tent and blotted it completely out. By a miracle it was the only one of the cluster there which was unoccupied. All the neighbouring tents were pepper castered, but luckily no one was hit – and men still deny the existence of GOD!

22 May 1916. The heat is terrific, and we stagger about with tongues aloll and a perpetual thirst. Adequate bathing arrangements exist only as a mirage in a tortured imagination and everything is sticky, but the country is at its very best. The hedges are white with May blossom, and the trees and fields brilliant in their coats of many hues. It's the weather for a punt on the Cherwell with a vision of white muslin and frills, a life free from care, a pampered life of downy cushions and lobster salads. War is grotesquely out of place, it's much too hot to work up anything like a satisfactory hate of Brother Hun, and the concentrated and shimmering heat of the trenches dries up the very sap in our bones, and makes torpid somnambulists of us all.

Last Wednesday the Chaplains of the Army gathered at Poperinghe to meet His Grace of Canterbury. It was an historic occasion, and we were a very motley crew, Chaplains in the wideawakes of sunny Australia, and the khaki twill of the tropics, Chaplains in steel helmets who have never seen the front line, Chaplains garbed in kilt and sporran, Chaplains with beards and Chaplains without, all met to pay homage to the great man.

He, noble man, was gracious to us all, though he must have thought that his suit of sober black was peculiarly out of place at such a fancy dress ball!

The proceedings commenced with the inevitable Conference, held luckily out of doors so that the flagging interest of the weaker brethren found food for thought in the glory of nature and the skill of our airmen.

When all were exhausted, even the most persevering of the hot-air brigade, the Senior Chaplains of each Division were presented to his Grace the Archprelate. Our Senior was on leave so I deputised for him. It was a tense moment fraught with potential greatness when hand grasped hand, and eye met eye. Words were superfluous. I must say I liked the old man and was much impressed. He seemed less of the diplomat and more of the Father in God than I had expected.

When I got back I found that a new draft of five officers had just come up from the Base to join the Battalion. They don't seem to be a very great acquisition, and have already 'got their wind up' (*anglicé* for a state of panic). The usual evening and desultory artillery duel they characterised as 'pooping off like blazes' and 'a dickens of a strafe' and anxiously enquired if the roof was bombproof!

Unless they buck up considerably, I am afraid their stay with the 8th won't be very protracted, for now that we have made a name for ourselves, our CO refuses to have any sort of wallah dumped on him.

Tuesday. Today I have spent in the trenches. It's been another glorious day and the Hun has been fairly subdued. I am writing this in a moated Chateau which still stands, more or less intact, about 1500 yards behind the front line, and which is occupied by the Company in reserve. Just across the way is the house of the village doctor – who departed, I suppose, on the first call to arms to minister to the needs of wounded Poilu. It is now the Battalion Headquarters, and is the house in which du Maurier was killed earlier in the war.

About 300 yards behind our front line, we have two strongpoints, bristling with machine guns etc. These are known as SP 10 and SP 11 respectively. While going from one to the other this afternoon, I had a little practice in dodging whizzbangs. Luckily the Hun is a man of method and a creature of regularity; which makes it possible to know to a second when the next shell will arrive, and if one is nippy it's quite easy to get across the open bits undamaged but doubling is warm work this weather. However, we are having some sports in a week's time and I was glad of the chance to practise for the sprint.

Up in the front trench is a dugout occupied by two of our officers, in which a swallow has built her nest. Not as you might suppose in the darkest corner, but on a beam right in the middle of the dugout and in full view of the doorway. In fact, you have to duck your head to come in, and even so are on a level with the nest. There she sits solemnly blinking at you, and quite unconcerned. I didn't see the nest abuilding worse luck, but the first time I was up the little home was completed, and the happy mother was sitting on her four eggs, while the proud father fluttered busily about or watched his clever little wife at work hatching.

Since then there has been a rift in the happy family, either father is a blaggard or a bigamist, for a fifth egg has appeared and with it another hen, who seems anxious to bring up the entire family and to oust his first love. If wifey goes out for a breather or to stretch her legs, in whisks number two who takes possession of the nest. When wifey returns, the racket begins, each appeal in turn to a father who seems unwilling to give a definite ruling and rather enjoys the shindig. Wifey is plaintively tearful and tearfully indignant in turn, but number two is a hussy and tries to brazen it out. I'm afraid father is very weak, and if he doesn't make up his mind soon I can foresee a very pathetic little tragedy.

26 May 1916. I'm sitting at the open window of our billet in the gawky Belgian village which straggles some three miles behind our trenches. From my seat I can almost see our line, hidden by day behind a thin belt of trees, which however is not thick enough to screen the ceaseless rise and fall of the Very lights which begin all along the line as soon as the shades of evening fall.

I had a very happy and amusing time up in the trenches this last time. I got back yesterday after spending three days with the Battalion.

In my last letter I told you about the Chateau in which the company in reserve dwell. But I didn't tell you all. It's a place of perpetual thrills, and better than any picnic. In the morning we jump out of bed, mine by the way was an old spring mattress balanced precariously on four empty petrol tins, and jump into the far from limpid waters of the moat. The morning dip is generally short and sharp, the real business of bathing begins later when the sun is up and the water is pleasurably warmed. The Company there this week under young Bardsley have constructed a raft out of doors and planks of wood, which supplemented by an ordinary washing tub provides endless scope for aquatic acrobats and much amusement. I enjoyed scrambling on the raft and falling off again and still more Bardsley's vain attempts to get into the tub, and most of all his look of consternation when a large piece of wood fell with a resounding whack near him; he thought it was a piece of HE shell I think, and was preparing for a hurried retreat when he caught sight of our CO peeping from behind a bush from which he had thrown the small log. Altogether it was a most delightful bathe, until in an unwary moment I touched bottom and stirred up the mud. Then – but I draw a veil – och the smell of it! Dead Frenchman I think, and dead rats I know, for shortly afterwards I saw a bloated and distended brute floating within twenty yards of our pool.

31 May 1916. We are back in rest billets again, greatly intrigued as to the meaning of this unexpected move, and faint and half-stifled in an atmosphere thick with rumours. The general idea is that we have been taken out of the line to form the nucleus of the new 'army of pursuit', which we hear is being formed to harass the tired Hun back to Berlin. Another rumour mentions Mesopotamia, and still another Verdun, so meanwhile we wait in patience to see what the future has in store for us.

On Saturday I went up again to the trenches, so I was free to join a party of officers for whom a special little treat had been arranged. The Artillery had invited a select number to be initiated into the mysteries of their art. Now in one important respect the Artillery is like a golfer, and the same axiom holds good for both – 'keep your eye on the ball' – in other words the Gunner must see where his shells are falling in order to correct his aim and adjust his fuse. In most parts of the line there is a FOO, that is Forward Observation Officer, always in the front trenches and where the ground is favourable. The best place for observing is from a hill a short distance behind the line. Where hills don't exist they sometimes rig up a sort of 'machan' in a tree, or observe from a convenient factory chimney if they can find one which has escaped the attention of Brother Hun.

Where we were however, the famous hill of which I spoke [Kemmel] is ideal for artillery observation, and is almost unique in this respect. Lucky indeed is the battery who can observe from the safety of this hill, instead of risking the lives of its officers by sending them up to FOO in the front-line trenches.

The top of the hill is honeycombed with tunnels running through from the back to the front facing the trenches and ending in a narrow slit shielded from view by the growing grass, so that the Observation Officer can sit there with his telescope to his eye and see all that happens within miles of him, without a chance of himself being seen or detected.

These observation posts or 'O pips' as they are known in military circles are wonders of engineering skill, and are guarded with the utmost care, so that we were extremely lucky to have a chance of seeing the most famous one of all. The day was an ideal one for observing, bright and cloudless and an entire absence of haze.

At the bottom of the hill we were met by a guide with passports for us, who led the way through the trees ever upwards along a path which twisted and turned in order to use every bit of cover and prevent it from being seen by prying aeroplanes.

As we neared the top we were challenged by a sentry who allowed us to pass on the testimony of our guide. Then suddenly at a turn in the path we came to a black hole in the side of the hill into which we went for some dozen yards until we were stopped by a closed door. The other side of the door we found a square dugout with tables and chairs, the former in front of a long horizontal slit, and covered with telescopes and telephones. With his eye glued to the telescope sat the

Observation Officer who bade us welcome. At the moment he was observing the fire of his battery and after each shot telephoned the result to the battery commander in a language incomprehensible to the layman, consisting mainly of numbers and uncouth mono-syllabic words.

When the battery had finished firing we each in turn glued our eye to the large telescope and saw Germany for the first time. Nine miles behind the line we could see a road alive with German wagons and horsemen, moving along slowly and quite unconscious of course that their every movement was observed by the foe.

It is the most novel experience to sit and watch shells bursting in the enemy's trench without dread of the effects of their retaliation.

On Sunday I had time for a Celebration [at Locre] before we started our long trek back again to the same village we left a bare month ago [Eecke]. It was a boiling & scorching day, so we took our time and halted twice and unspanned our transport teams for dinner and tea, both eaten *á la picnic* in fields by the side of the road.

For some reason, we are a popular Battalion, and the entire village turned out to welcome us back again. They had just come out of church after *Salut* or *Bénédiction* when we arrived, and were consequently dressed in their Sunday bibs and tuckers which added to the gaiety and magnificence of our reception.

I'm back to my old billet being mothered more than ever by my one-armed hostess, who seems to have more to tell me about than there is time for the telling, for she talks twenty-four to the dozen now, and keeps it up all day long.

Leah [his batman] has come back again after his short holiday with the measles. I hope they gave him a good carbolic bath and disinfected his clothes, for I have no wish to be a victim now that the fine weather has come. Visits to the Hospital are a luxury in the winter months, but quite unnecessary now.

4 June 1916. On Thursday we had a great open-air boxing carnival, to which we bade many visitors from the various units of our Brigade. The ring was pitched in the grassy field in which once before we had a concert. On the sloping bank all round sat the spectators who overflowed even to the edge of the ring itself. It was a motley crowd of footsloggers – English, Welsh, and Scottish, Engineers, Artillery, Army Service Corps, and the RAMC.

The programme was a good one and all the bouts were keen, and what was lacking in skill was invariably made up in vigour and hearty goodwill.

In addition to the competitors in the various weights we had a special six-round contest between our heavyweight champion, and a brawny Gordon Highlander, who until he fell with a clip to the jaw towards the end of the first round, bore the proud title of champion of the 76th Brigade.

We also had a wrestling match between a King's Own man – ex-lightweight champion of the world – and a Gordon piper who though beaten was not disgraced.

As far as I was concerned the *pièce de résistance* was the Officers' Catch Weight Competition in which I entered trembling. In the first round I drew our MO – Dr Pearson and a sportsman. I lost a little in weight, but gained a good deal in reach. The rounds were arranged to suit our want of condition and training at one-and-a-half minute rounds with the same length of time between each. It was a tough fight ending in the third round with a punch to the jaw which knocked me down and silly, but I managed to get up and was luckily saved from the coming *coup de grâce* by the call of time. We had both gone at it hard and were neither very pleased to hear that the judge had disagreed and ordered a fourth round. However we got to work again, and by supreme good luck I managed to pull it off on points. The Doctor was good enough to say he had never enjoyed a fight more, and I cordially agreed for, though it was hard and vigorous, we both entered for the sport of the thing and fought as good friends fight.

In the Final I met our Transport Officer, who has little science but a hard punch and rather whirlwind tactics. I managed however to keep him out and score the necessary points at the same time, and got the verdict at the end of the third round. The only damage done was a sore jaw from the Doctor's clip, and a strained left arm which I did when I fell, but both are all right again now, and I feel fitter than I have for weeks.

On Friday we had a Confirmation at Bailleul to which I took my two candidates, borrowing for the purpose a motor ambulance from my friends at the Field Ambulance, for the distance to Bailleul is rather further than I care to walk or ride.

Yesterday, being the King's Birthday, was observed as a fete and gala day. A red-letter day in every way. In the morning the Brigade paraded in review order in a large level field. The Suffolks by immemorial custom wear roses in their caps on 4 June, and very brave they looked. Their horses and their drums are decorated too with the red and yellow roses.

The whole Brigade was drawn up opposite a flagpole at the saluting base, at the head of which the Union Jack was broken at the moment of the Royal Salute. Afterwards followed a march past and three cheers to His Majesty, caps being held on the point of the bayonets and waved furiously while the cheers were given. Luckily we are some miles behind the line, or the noise we made would certainly have put the wind up the Hun, and brought an intensive bombardment upon our heads.

10 June 1916. The Hun has displayed a certain amount of liveliness lately on land as well as on sea, and as the papers will have told you, has taken a fair stretch of our front trenches near Hooge. Our sudden return from rest is not unconnected I think with this reverse, though at present I am glad to say there is no talk of us taking an active part in the recapture of the lost trenches. After leaving our restful French village last Monday we spent twenty-four hours in farms and barns in another village, and on Tuesday evening crossed the frontier and so back here, where we remain more or less in reserve doing little by day, but finding large working parties and digging fatigues each night.

When we arrived back here last Tuesday we found that all our old billets had been snaffled by the Battalion who relieved us, so had to pull up our socks and find new ones.

I am happily ensconced in an empty house in a small room on the first floor back. I wonder if I can make you see the room: first the window, which looks out towards our trenches has evidently been at some time the target of naughty Belgian boys, two panes are badly twisted, but apart from a little loss of light no harm is done for the gaping holes are covered with a newspaper tacked firmly all round. Then the walls, they are as devoid of paper or covering as the ceiling or the floor. Their only ornament is where the damp has stained them, or the plaster has crumbled away. Half the room is occupied with an iron bedstead and a spring mattress, on which I put my valise and blankets and sleep untroubled and serene.

The rest of the furniture consists entirely of packing cases, one raised on legs to form a table, another on its end is my washstand, on which a green canvas bucket does duty for the china bowl which is not. A third, on its side, is my bookcase and my whatnot. Thus do we live, and believe me I love it. It sounds rough and uncomfortable, but really it isn't a bit, and I know that within six months of the end of the war I shall sigh for this Liberty Hall sort of existence.

This afternoon we had a Pierrot entertainment given by the Divisional Troupe, who rejoice in the name (self inflicted) of 'Mudlarks'.

The concert was given in an empty and very dilapidated sort of hall, every window broken and dust and plaster and bits of wood everywhere. Nothing could be more incongruous: a troupe of pierrots in their clean white tops and frills, with their flawless apple blossom complexions, sitting and singing amid this wreckage and decay, under the cold hard scrutiny of a tactless daylight.

This evening we are having a very special little dinner in honour of our Colonel, who as I think I told you was in the Birthday Honours List for a DSO.

He is a simply top-hole CO, a real white man and a soldier, whom everyone would follow through fire and hail, and whom every officer and man in the Battalion is delighted to see honoured and decorated.

14 June 1916. Our brains will be soon giving away under the strain of conjecturing what the future holds for us. For the last three weeks we have done nothing but move, as it seems aimlessly about the country from the trenches to rest billets, back to the trenches, then away to other rest billets, and now to crown all we have moved right back miles behind the line and in the most excellent billets, quite close to the Chateau from which we were recalled for the Bluff show. We are beginning to think that either the Staff can't decide what to do with us, or else they are trying to hoodwink the Hun with our rapid changes. We are known throughout the Army as the Fighting Division, and it may be that we are to be thrown into the coming battle from some unexpected quarter, to the consternation and defeat I hope of the Hun.

On Monday we learnt that we were moving again, and at nine pm we marched away through the rain to catch our train at Bailleul at what the French are pleased to call '23.24' pm. We all got wet through, and to add to our discomfort we found that the train wasn't big enough for us, and so had to pack the men into the cattle trucks provided, like herrings in a tin.

It was still raining when we arrived at St. Omer and we simply hated the idea of marching the nine miles to our billets through the wet hours of the night. For once in a way the Staff had pity on us, and told us to find billets in the town and finish our march next morning. So at three o'clock in the morning we got the men into a large cavalry barracks near the station, and went off in search of a friendly hotel.

We found one near the square and after much shouting and knocking gained admittance and demanded food. We hardly hoped for beds, but found that the hotel was fairly empty and that eighteen were available. The Major took in hand the business of allotting the rooms, and I went off and had four hours untroubled slumber until I was called again at 8 am. When I got down I found the Major looking very dishevelled and everybody in fits of laughter. It appears the Major, after seeing everyone safely off to bed, went to the room he had reserved for himself only to find that it was occupied by a lady, who indignantly demanded what he wanted, and so terrified the little man that he dared not ask for another room, but spent the night on the floor of the smoking room instead.

After breakfast we formed up and marched away as bravely as we could through the rain, which was still falling. The men were in a bad plight, for they had been unable to get their clothes dried and were still wet and starved from the night before.

However, the rain ceased and the wind dried them before they arrived at this picturesque little village while I rode on to arrange billets.

Incidentally, I had a bad half hour and much mental torture before I managed to find our village [Westrove, near Eperlecques], for the name on the map doesn't correspond with the local name, and I wandered about the countryside looking for the mythical village and being met at every turn by a blank denial from the natives that such a place existed at all.

However, we are all comfortably settled now, and if the weather clears up we ought to have a happy time here, despite the stiff programme of training which the Staff has drawn up for us.

After we had had lunch, the Doctor and I went off to inspect the men's billets. As usual they are billeted in barns and farm buildings where, when the straw is clean and plentiful, they are very warm and comfortable. Of course billets vary immensely, and where possible we condemn those which don't come up to standard. One for example was completely open on one side to all the winds that blow – imagine men trying to sleep there this cold weather – and it has been cold lately – with nothing but their greatcoats and a quarter of a blanket to cover them, for the allowance now is one blanket between four men.

The greatest difficulty with the billets however is the problem of water. The French farmer has an unenviable habit of sinking his well as near as possible to his manure pit, which renders the water a bit fruity, and makes it still more a matter of wonderment why he guards it so carefully and gives it to the soldiers so grudgingly.

I have just received a pathetic little parcel, a cardboard starch box full of dead roses, sent from England by a bereaved mother with a note asking me to put them on her son's grave. I wish I could, but we are miles away now from where he lies at rest. If we ever go back there, which I trust we never shall, I will buy some for her boy's grave.

20 June 1916. Another move and we are once more in our [Hellebrouck] Chateau with the wonderful grounds, where once before we spent six happy days before we went up to do battle at the Bluff.

If it was beautiful then in its winter leanness, it is still more beautiful now. The trees are gorgeous and the flower beds vivid splashes of colour, and the meandering stream a joy forever. There is an old punt-like boat which we pole up and down, and try to imagine that we are back in Oxford, though the faint booming of the guns is never absent and never really allows us to forget the tragedy of war.

We have received a great number of drafts, both of men and officers lately, and are now at full strength once more, and are undergoing a very vigorous training, so I suppose we shall not be left alone very long in this delightfully sylvan retreat. Nothing is known, but we feel the shadow of war coming between us and the sunshine of careless happiness.

We have lately lost our Interpreter who has been promoted to a Brigade, so it now falls to my lot by virtue of a little knowledge of the vulgar tongue, to go round arranging billets, settling claims for damaged crops, and generally acting as the connecting link of the entente. It is certainly good for my French, and for that reason I'm rather glad of the chance, but I never cease to marvel at the control which the French peasant has over his emotions, for horror and amusement at my murderous use of his language must be struggling for expression, and I should think that it must literally hurt him to listen to my barbaric attempts to be grammatical.

Since the date of my last letter we have adopted summertime: the change has been accepted by everybody military in the most unconcerned manner, but the villagers still stick to the old time and refuse to have anything to do with the black art of correcting the sun.

26 June 1916. We are still living in the Chateau, that is to say seven of us are billeted here: the Colonel, our two Majors – little Major West and a Major Hutchinson who has but lately joined us – the Adjutant, Quartermaster, Doctor and myself – a very happy & select little party, our new Major is from the Connaught Rangers tho' he comes to us from Sandhurst with a record of war service second to none. He is a most amusing fellow, full of good stories & a real good soldier. We are the guests here of a Madame West – a most quaint body of uncertain origin & nationality. She is a most philosophical old thing, and laughs at the damage which the constant stream of troops have done to her property. Her great stunt is inviting all her daughters & granddaughters down to meet us, so nightly we have guest nights and the needful feminine influence and finish up with choruses in the billiard room.

I suppose all good patriots hope that when the Big Push comes off we will succeed in getting the Hun out of his drain and keep him on the run above the ground & in the open – at any rate it was with the idea of practising the attack in the open that we proceeded on Thursday to a limitless expanse of rolling downland, and extended in long lines to attack a ridge some miles in front. The Doctor and I rode or at least galloped about behind the advancing lines looking for casualties to succour, and generally enjoying ourselves. The most interesting part of the proceedings was the aeroplane which watched us from above, & acted as scout to our advance. It came down from time to time to report progress etc, and I took good care to be near it whenever I could. They are wonderful things, but your imagination must paint the details I would give you but for the prying eyes of the ubiquitous & inquisitive Censor.

A host of peasant women and buxom farm girls were also attracted by the novel scene, and we had much squealing & mad rushes from them when the aeroplane taxied along the ground in their direction, which was increased by the frenzied plunging of Niger – my pony –

84

who took a violent and almost hysterical dislike to its noise & playful frightfulness. Among other things our Brigadier went up for a joy ride, which delayed proceedings a good deal and it wasn't until 10 pm that we began our three hours march for home, arriving eventually tired and famished in the sma' wee hours.

Tommy never fails to fill me with wonder. We were out all day and most of the night, on the move the whole time with nothing to eat but a drink of tea made in the field, and yet as we swung home the whole country side was awakened by his full-throated craving to return to Dixieland or Michigan or some other uncouth place in Ragtime-land, or his vociferous protestation that he was or would be true to some lady unknown, but masquerading under a galaxy of *noms d'amour*.

On another occasion we had a thrilling lecture on the Balkan tangle from a man in civilian garb from Trinity College Cambridge. A Professor Atkins who is spending his Long Vac in this way & who is extremely good. His lecture lasted three quarters of an hour, but we would all gladly have listened to him for longer.

We are all very much exercised how to get our kit down to the prescribed weight. During the winter we have accumulated all sorts of spare kit & junk of various sorts. Now the order has come for us to reduce it to the allotted thirty-five lbs, so I am sending a large box of kit home. There will probably be more to pay in carriage than the contents are worth, but if you will foot the bill I will repay you when I come on leave.

3 July 1916. The long expected order to move came on Saturday, just as we were finishing breakfast. The morning we spent in paying bills and packing our kits, and in the afternoon we marched away to St. Omer to entrain for an unknown destination. It was a long hot and dusty march along a particularly switchback road and we arrived at our siding minus some of our old sweats who couldn't stand the pace. However as military trains always start to the minute, we had to entrain and leave our stragglers behind to follow how and when they could. All night we journeyed slowly, until about five o'clock Sunday morning when we detrained [at Doullens] and had a hasty and inadequate breakfast in a brickyard near the station, and started to march to our billets some six miles away. While detraining we saw a fleet of our battle planes going over to strafe the Huns. Later we heard that they did most excellent work and accounted for two Hun machines, this at a cost of two of our observers killed.

It must have been a strange homecoming for the two Pilots flying back with the bodies of their Observers strapped to their seats in front.

6 July 1916. We had another march last night leaving [Coisy] at nine o'clock and arriving here at one o'clock this morning, having covered twelve miles in that time. It was a beautiful night and the Battalion marched well. The whole Brigade are billeted in this village [Franvillers] so there is 'some' congestion. I wish I could paint you a picture of a Brigade coming into a village in the small hours of the morning, seeking billets – officers rushing about looking for their Battalions or the billets to which to lead them. Curious and sleepy-eyed peasant women watching the troops or holding a flickering candle for the Billeting Officer to make his notes. In the shadows at the side of the streets, bodies of troops, recognizable by the count-less points of red from their glowing pipes or cigarettes, standing patiently waiting for the word that will release them from the burden of their packs. While down the middle of the street lumber noisily the transport and the field kitchens, the latter belching forth smoke and sparks, for the fires are lit and the water is already boiling for the tea which will be issued as soon as the men are settled in their billets. Whilst wandering everywhere and in every conceivable direction, officers' servants, orderlies, stragglers, and the whole gamut of lost and bewildered souls trying to find whither the Battalion has suddenly vanished, or attempting to solve the insoluble mystery as to why it is that at a time like this you can find with the utmost ease everybody else's billet, but your own. However, all eventually find somewhere to lie down, and in an incredibly short time the streets are deserted, the seething mass of men, horses, wagons and all the paraphernalia of an army melt away, and peace broods over a quiet village once more.

It is a strange life we lead, since Friday last week we have slept each night in a different place and will continue to do so, I suppose, until we reach Berlin! All day we sleep, eat and prepare to march, all night long we march. Thus do we hope to keep the Hun in ignorance of our movements, and of the place of our concentration.

Last night we marched through a village [Lahoussoye], where two days before a German Colonel had been shot for treachery. The people there showed us the wall against which he was placed. After surrendering, he had pulled off his helmet in which a bomb was concealed, and hurled it into a group of officers standing nearby!!

I'm afraid war is making me bitter. I can't help feeling that a bullet was too good for such a blaggard, hanging without a drop would even be too merciful a death.

Chapter 5

Longueval to the Bazentins

The Somme – the Battle of Guillemont, August 1916

9 July 1916. July 6th found us in billets in a French village [Coisy], having marched most of the night. All day we rested and at nine pm we began to march again, getting steadily nearer the front.

Soon after starting we began to descend by a winding road into the valley of a famous river [the Somme] which we could trace for miles each way by the green ribbon of trees which wandered twistingly at the bottom of the most wonderful panorama. It was a sublime view, never to be forgotten, the sky a riot of tender reds, deepening into a distant purple, while spread out below us this wonderful valley dotted with its sleepy villages and cut up like some Highland tartan into the various browns and greens and golds of intensive cultivation, fringed as it were with the dark green belt of trees, and beyond, seen indistinctly through the deepening twilight, the hills rising away again on the other side.

Down into this peaceful fruitful valley our long column wound its way. To our right and left other similar khaki worms could be seen, converging towards the bridgehead across the river.

That night after a long and tiring trek we made our bivouac in a wood. But before we could get to the wood, we had to get the Brigade over some very rough country, no road, but simply a track over a huge ridge of stubble, up one side and down the other. This took a long time as the mules were unable to pull the limbers up for a long time, meanwhile the infantry was halted near the top and we watched the flashes and bursts away on the skyline.

After crossing the ridge our road ran along the side of a canal until we came to the wood [Les Célestins] in which we were to spend what remained of the hours of darkness. The wood was a strange sight seen under the first faint twilight of dawning day – the men lying huddled together wrapped in nothing but their greatcoats. Some more enterprising or less tired made little shelters for themselves by stretching their groundsheets between four saplings, while others made campfires and sat dozing round them. It was the sort of scene that an artist could spread himself on. Our Headquarters, consisting of the Colonel, two Majors, Adjutant, Quartermaster, Doctor, one of two Senior Captains and myself slept under cover in a sort of hut open at both ends. Here we put down our valises and slept as soundly as a conscientious objector ever sleeps in his featherbed.

7 July. It rained steadily – imagine our poor fellows out in the remorseless downpour with nowhere to go and nothing to do but get wet. That night we again slept in the now sodden undergrowth, and I blessed the leaking roof above my head, but the morning broke fine and by seven o'clock there were signs of a hot day.

8 July. We learnt that we were moving up to take part in the heavy fighting, so I arranged Services of preparation and commendation. It was in the corner of a cornfield [in Les Célestins Wood] looking down into the valley below. My altar was a low box, not more than two foot high, and the officers and men knelt in a semicircle, very much like the picture in the Academy except that the only sign of war was the fairly distant rumble of the guns.

At 3.30 pm we marched away, and are now in bivouacs immediately behind the line waiting for the word to go up and over. It is a unique sight, all round us and all day long we can see the shells bursting, and the din of our guns is deafening. Luckily, we are in dead ground, unseen and unmolested. Above, the sun is shining brilliantly, and the air is alive with busy aeroplanes, and torpid looking 'sausages' as the military man in the trench dubs the captive balloons from which we watch the wily Hun. From where I sit I can count no less than twenty-one of these 'sausages' strung out in both directions all along our front.

10 July 1916. The word has not yet come to send us forward, so we are still in bivouac in the same thistley field. But although we have

not seen any real fighting, we have not been unconscious of the war for the last twenty-four hours. Yesterday morning we were shocked beyond measure to hear that our Staff Captain had been killed by a stray 'Woolly Bear' while out reconnoitring the ground over which we attack. Strangely enough, the man by his side was untouched, so the old words prove true today, 'the one shall be taken and the other left'.

Last night I buried him in the military cemetery which lies just behind our original front line, in a little hollow, which is now bristling with our guns. It was like being in an inferno, the guns were firing as hard as they could be loaded, on all sides of us, so that no one could hear a single word of the Service. There was no need, even if such a thing had been possible, to fire three volleys over his grave. The guns and the 'hows' [howitzers] did it instead.

We buried him just before it got dark, but it would have been quite possible to read the Service by the light of the flashes.

Before going down I had dinner with the Brigadier and the other officers of his Staff. They live in dugouts in the middle of a wood nearby. Some of the dugouts are really twenty or thirty feet down in the bowels of the earth. They were originally made by the French, and are in very vivid contrast to the ones we had in the Ypres Salient, for there they are really nothing more than sandbagged shelters the same level as the trenches.

This afternoon we had a little diversion from the tedium of waiting. The Hun saw fit to throw a dozen or so shells into our field, but fortunately his aim was not quite accurate, and the majority whistled overhead like an express train and burst just beyond. One however landed on two 'cookers' and completely did them down. A 'cooker' is a kitchen range on wheels by means of which Tommy gets hot food every day, for the cooking goes on just the same whether we are stationary or on the move. Each battalion has four cookers, so the loss of two means that half the Battalion will get no tea or stew for the next few days.

While we were watching the shells bursting behind us, another tragedy was being enacted in the air, and we turned round just in time to see an aeroplane hit by an 'Archie' (a shell from an anti-aircraft gun). It was the first aeroplane that I had actually seen brought down, and it was like watching a wounded eagle struggling against its fate; it came toppling down, turning over and over, righting itself for an instant, only to fall over again until it was lost to view behind a clump of trees. We haven't heard whether the air-man was killed, and so still hope that his machine landed on one of its wings, and so broke his fall.

11 July 1916. We have moved our bivouac today, a few hundred yards to one side, and are now on the reverse slope of the hill and sheltered from view by a wood. Here we hope to remain safe from German shells until the word comes to go up and over against the Hun third line. This precautionary measure has been taken because slumber was somewhat disturbed at four-thirty this morning by a repetition of the shelling we had yesterday. Luckily the range was again a little too long, and we had the satisfaction of hearing the shells whistle overhead and burst behind us and no material damage was done, if you except a box of Spanish onions and a case of bully beef sent skywards.

This afternoon some of us wandered over to see a fifteen-inch Howitzer in action – a monstrous looking machine firing shells four-and-a-half feet long, and weighing I know not how many tons. You can judge of their weight however when one shell is as much as a GS Wagon and two horses can transport. Even a huge motor lorry is overloaded when it has four on board.

The shells are raised and put into the gun by a gang of men hauling on a rope connected by pulleys and so on to a portable crane. The gunners work in shirt sleeves like Trojans and shower endless care and much oil on 'Grandmother'. When the shell is fired the noise is appalling, and everybody rams his fingers in his ears to prevent his drums from being broken. The most interesting thing however is that you can actually see the shell leave the gun and can watch its flight in the air for two or three seconds. It looks for all the world like a cricket ball and goes a colossal height – so high in fact that I wonder they never hit the aeroplanes which dot the sky like stars.

Never before have I realised what vast preparations we have been making for the Big Push. The whole countryside is stiff with guns of all sizes and shapes. General Congreve is reported to have said that 'he wished they wouldn't send him any more guns, as he didn't know where to put them'! and the amount of warlike material has to be seen to be realised, while everywhere are soldiers – French and English – a truly wonderful sight.

I can't get out of my mind the sight of that aeroplane. An aero-plane always seems more like a sentient being than a machine, and to see it come down like a bird sore stricken, fluttering over and over is pitiful to the extreme.

13 July 1916. I am getting this off tonight as our Division attacks at dawn – our Brigade however is in reserve, and has the pleasing job of pushing through as soon as the gap is made, and helping the Cavalry to round up the prisoners and guns.

21 July 1916. For the moment we are getting our breath back after the second round of the Big Push. The Censor won't allow me to be very technical, but I don't think there will be any harm done if I give you an account of our doings in diary form, beginning where my last letter ended:

July 13th. We marched away from our bivouacs just as light was failing, to take our part in the second phase of this colossal battle. The situation then was roughly like this, we occupied the German second line of defence with the Germans some 1500 yards in front, each army entrenched on parallel ridges with a Cumberland dale dividing us.

During the previous days we had really occupied the valley, or at least we had dumped all sorts of stores and provisions in it – really a stupendous piece of cheek to dump our stuff in no man's land. But the plan was successful and helped our attack to be the victory it was.

We marched away then full of hope, with spirits running high, for there is something very inspiring about war. Little electric thrills were running up and down my spine as we moved forward on our great adventure into the valley of death. No one hates war more than I do, yet I wouldn't have missed being there for a king's ransom.

I rode with the Doctor in rear of the Battalion; immediately in front of us were the Mess Waiters. You would have laughed if you could have seen them. In addition to their weapons of offence, one man carried a frying pan and a piece of bacon, another carried a saucepan and sandbag of tinned foods, while bringing up the rear he who acts as butler staggering along under a load of a dozen bottles of whisky slung round his neck. Thus does the British Army go forth to fight. That night we occupied one of the German trenches, captured on July 1st. The German trenches are full of interest and even in their battered state bear the stamp of genius. This particular one was krumped all along – a testimony to the wonderful accuracy of our guns – every few yards a shell had landed in the trench so that now it might aptly be compared to the perforation between two penny stamps. The dugouts however have for the most part escaped, being dug out umpteen feet below the trench level. The one we took for the night is built in two storeys! A flight of steps leads down into an office with a kitchen leading off it, while down another flight of stairs are the sleeping bunks and a long corridor which ends in another stairway leading direct to the trench. I suppose this is a back entrance in case the first one got blown in by shell fire.

It is a veritable work of art and must have taken weeks to dig, being lined throughout with wood. But I wouldn't care to live in it long, for being so deep, little air and less light find their way down. And in addition to this, a deep dugout has a demoralising effect upon its occupants, who must be sorely tempted to remain below in comparative safety rather than come up and fight. As the poet might have said, 'deep dugouts make cowards of us all'.

At 3.45 am on Friday July 14th as dawn was breaking the whole line was to advance to the attack. But before the infantry went forward the German trenches were lashed with a hail of shells – 2000 guns of all sizes barked and roared at once. It was stupendous, the sky was lighted up with the continual flashes and the whole earth throbbed and rocked. Words fail me to describe a tithe of the colossal wonder of it, or to give you any idea of the noise. As the hour of the attack drew near the excitement was intense, especially in our Brigade, for we were in reserve and as we thought were simply waiting for the line to be broken before we poured through towards Berlin.

During the whole of our bombardment the Hun sent up signals of distress to his artillery, who however paid scant attention to their appeals for retaliation. At the moment arranged the Infantry surged forward, and the guns lifted 100 yards behind the German trenches and formed a barrage or curtain of fire to prevent reinforcements coming up.

Soon the whole ridge was in our hands from Longueval to Bazentin le Petit, and at 10 am we received orders to go forward ready to reinforce our Division if necessary.

By this time the Hun was retaliating with his guns which were firing more or less wildly, searching the captured valley. Right at the bottom of this valley we were halted and told to dig ourselves in, which we proceeded to do with great vigour. It is surprising how soon a Battalion can dig itself in under the spur of HE shrapnel, and I don't mind confessing that I was not above picking up an entrenching tool and scratching quite a substantial hole before I was told that a ready-made Hun dugout had been discovered in the side of a sunken road, and taken over by our Headquarters, with whom I live.

This dugout formerly belonged to an Officer of Artillery, as we discovered from the miscellaneous kit which he left behind when the Big Push drove him back. By the side of it were two of his gun emplacements, battered in and, with them, the guns which had received direct hits from our shells. In fact the whole valley is a great testimony to the good shooting of our Gunners. Only a short distance away is another gun pit and gun krumped in with its store of ammunition blown up, and by the side of the road which runs down the valley is a limber full of shells but with its team lying dead all round. At least they were there when we arrived, and from external evidence had already been there some time – I know of no smell more truly awful than a ripe horse, so despite the intermittent shelling we got a squad of men to bury them good and deep.

All that day we waited patiently for news, and continued to dig down for at any moment the Hun might have shelled us heavily. In fact we did have one or two bursts of rapid fire from 4.7 howitzers, and were lucky only to have four or five casualties.

In the evening we stopped in our work to watch enthralled the most inspiring spectacle of the war. Down over the ridge behind us came the cavalry in long lines. First came fierce-looking Indians, their turbans streaming behind them as they cantered past, some with lances with points agleam, others armed with carbine and machine guns. Behind them came our English cavalry, and behind them again more Indians until we thought they would never end. Across the valley they cantered and up the other side, until just behind the crest they halted and formed up into their Troops and Squadrons.

Thousands there were of them, and all mounted magnificently, and absolutely awe-inspiring. After they had disappeared from view we pictured them charging and sticking the running Huns, and our hearts and prayers went with them. Soon after the last of them had passed the crest we heard the German machine guns tapping out their stream of death, but we knew nothing until next morning when the wounded began to come back, some horseless, others still mounted, and from them we learnt that they had charged into rapid fire, and had managed to kill several and capture many more of the enemy before they had to draw off.

July 15th. Spent the day improving our trenches and waiting for news. Went over to a neighbouring Battery and offered to bury two of their men who had been killed by shrapnel. To my surprise discovered that one of the Subs was an old Oxford pal of mine. I didn't at first recognize him under the disguise of a heavy moustache and a three-day's beard but he knew me. When last I saw him he was spare man to the Varsity crew, and now he sits behind a megaphone and gives orders incomprehensible to a layman, but which help to write the world's history.

In the evening our Transport came up with food and other supplies, particularly some much-needed water – of which more in a moment, and unfortunately got in the way of a shell and lost four mules killed, and two men wounded.

The supply of water at first was rather a problem, as the wells had been krumped and the only stream polluted. But this difficulty has been overcome and a regular and fairly plentiful supply has been established. The water is brought up in petrol tins and dumped in a central place, each unit drawing from the dump as its needs arise and getting full tins in return for empty ones. The only drawback to this plan, which in theory is excellent, is that the drawers of water have apparently forgotten that petrol is still a valuable fluid, and are rather lavish in its use. Water tainted with petrol, even when freely diluted with whisky is not a very delectable summer drink! But as a medium for shaving it has many points of superiority over cold tea, which was all we had for the first two days, and with which I managed to dampen my beard sufficiently to make it amenable to my Gillette.

July 16th. I woke up at four o'clock perished with cold and stiff from sleeping on a narrow form in our overcrowded dugout. High Wood, just north of our new line was being heavily shelled and the village of Longueval on the right of our new ridge was on fire, and casting a red glow on the clouds above. A fine rain was falling, which continued all day and made it a *dies non* as far as the advance was concerned. That night I took my boots off for the first time since we came into the battle area.

July 17th. We were still in our valley of desolation, waiting with impatience for the word to advance, and drinking in with avidity such scraps of information as we could gather from the four winds. I busied myself with the burial of the dead who had fallen in the previous fight, and in remarking the wonders of our valley. It presented a most remarkable sight. At the bottom runs a badly wounded light railway, with a few gaunt skeletons of wagons still standing on it; on each side the new-dug trenches were stiff with troops waiting to be hurled at the throat of Brother Hun where and when they were wanted. On the slopes which rise from the valley towards the captured ridge were and are batteries on batteries of guns, so many that it is hardly an exaggeration to say that they are wheel to wheel, with no attempt at concealment and firing all day and night as fast as their limbers can keep them supplied with food for the guns. Halfway down the valley is an old chalk quarry, now used as a Dressing Station and a dump for stores. The quarry is honeycombed with dugouts and passages laboriously dug by our friend the enemy. All day down the valley is a constant stream of horsed transport – ammunition limbers, ration carts, cookers, water carts and the like – which amble unconcernedly up to their unit, discharge their cargoes and amble home again, paying no more attention to the shells (which tho' never very heavy are never wholly absent), than is necessary to cut away a fallen horse or bandage a stricken driver.

After dinner that night we had a great laugh. One of our officers affectionately known as Tigers marched into Headquarters dugout, where we were all assembled sipping rum, and announced that a German prisoner had been captured by our reconnoitring patrol, and was outside. The CO at once ordered him to be brought inside. In marched a sentry with fixed bayonet and behind him a huge Hun, dressed in his overcoat and helmet, and badly wounded in the face. In fact the blood had soaked through his bandage and had caked on the top of the grime with which the rest of his face was covered. We all felt very sorry for the poor fellow, and beckoned him to sit down and gave him a tot of rum while we sent for Brown, the only officer who can speak German to act as interpreter. As soon as he arrived he began jabbering German to the unfortunate man, who seemed to be completely dazed and could only say 'nah pooh' and 'non compree'. It never struck Brown that these were strange replies to receive from a German and he persevered manfully with his questions. Finally he had to give it up, but not before we had all tumbled to the joke and left the dugout helpless from suppressed laughter. Finally the Hun prisoner could control his feelings no longer and completely broke down and simply howled with laughter. It was Bardsley who had dressed up in some of the captured spoil, and had played the part magnificently. It is still a mystery where he found or procured the blood or the art of making up. It was worth pounds to have seen poor Brown's face fall when he discovered how he had been had, and that his valiant attempts to interpret had been in vain.

July 18th. Tears and laughter, grim reality and playful jest go hand-in-hand in this war. Within three hours of the release of our 'Hun prisoner', the Battalion had received orders to advance into action, and within six, poor Tigers was dead, shot in the head leading his company to attack the Hun.

Ever since we gained the ridge, the enemy had been busy digging himself into the northern edge of Delville Wood and in the orchards to the north of the village of Longueval. It was to dislodge him that the Gordons were sent forward, supported by our Battalion. The attack was carried out successfully, and we went forward and started to dig the new line. But we had not reckoned with the Hun artillery which concentrated on our narrow front and simply blew us out of the trenches we had dug.

In twenty-four hours our casualties were 342, and the Gordons nearly 500, though fortunately the great percentage of these were slight. I cannot tell you how magnificently our fellows stood the terrific gruelling, but in the end they had to come back, and our line is still very much where it was before.

I'm not sure that I haven't offended the Censor already, for *c'est absolument défendu* to give information helpful to the enemy, so I confine myself to my part in the battle.

I went up with the Doctor, having received a direct order from the General not to go 'over the top' with the Battalion. We opened our Regimental Dressing Station a few hundred yards behind our trenches, just below the crest of the ridge, near a forward dump of ammunition and water. It was raining a little so to shelter our dressing and medical stores we built a bivouac of full SAA boxes and roofed it with a piece of corrugated iron.

All went well, the shelling was not great, and what there was, was still some distance in front. Early we heard that the attack had succeeded from the few wounded who came back. But about ten am the shelling grew in intensity, and krumps began to fall on each side of us. It was then that we longed for a deep dugout and our longing grew in proportion to the shelling. The stream of wounded grew longer and longer, and reports came through that the battle was going none too well. Things were getting warm, but we were too busy to pay much attention to anything but to dressing the wounded and getting them away.

By this time the Hun was making a strong counter-attack, and was putting a very heavy barrage all along the ridge on which we were, and so prevented the wounded from getting through. It was just at this time that our Doctor was hit by a machine-gun bullet, which went through his neck and came out at his cheek, breaking his jaw and knocking out four or five teeth on its way. Things were looking bad, for without a doctor we were helpless. However, we kept the Aid Post open for the sake of appearances and did what we could for the wounded. I pride myself that I can treat shell-shock cases as well as any Harley Street specialist, a strong tot of brandy, a few kind words are all that are required before packing them off to the Field Ambulance, which is the next link in the chain that binds the front-line with Blighty.

After the Doctor had gone down, the shelling grew in intensity and for a long time no wounded came through, so we sat behind ammunition boxes and waited for the end.

One of the stretcher bearers with me completely broke down and whimpered like a child, and shook from head to foot, and another was so badly shaken that I had to send him back. Finally, I was left with only my servant and two men. Literally the shells fell every-where but on us. It was God's providence that we were not blown sky high, for we waited for eight hours expecting any minute to be killed.

At ten pm I made up my mind to evacuate our Aid Post as no wounded had come through for several hours, so we packed up what little dressings we still had and went back to the quarry in the valley, where I made arrangements with the existing Aid Post there to treat our wounded if and when they came through.

July 19th. After arranging things in the Quarry, I slept with my little band in a German gun pit on a heap of wicker baskets in which the shells are packed. We were all badly in need of sleep and a few hours

An officer of the 2nd Suffolks who met Leonard in the ruins of Montauban wrote: 'I cannot speak too highly of Pat Leonard, Noel Mellish, and "Nigel" Danvers as Padres of the right stamp. These men who moved amongst ALL ranks and were liked by all, both in peace and war, and who really did their proper duty on the battlefield and in billets.'

made all the difference, and I woke refreshed and ready to carry on. But there was little I could do, except to bury some of the dead and give a hand with an occasional stretcher. During the day the Huns heavily strafed the Quarry with krumps and gas shells, and did a good lot of damage to the wounded.

That afternoon the Battalion was relieved and we staggered back to the German trench of which I told you in the earlier part of this letter.

July 20th. A much-needed day of rest in the same trench. For eight or nine days we never had a chance to take our clothes off, and were under the strain of shell fire the whole time, tho' of course it varied considerably in intensity.

In the evening, we saw a most exciting and invigorating sight. It was the downing of a German aeroplane. When we first caught sight of the battle, a German plane was chasing one of ours and firing at it madly with his machine gun. Our hearts stood still when we saw our plane suddenly pitch forward and nose dive several hundred feet, and we turned away to avoid seeing the smash. When we looked again our pilot had regained control of his machine, and the Hun was diving steeply after him. Again our machine appeared to fall, and again the Fokker followed hard on its tail, the Hun still intent on killing our pilot with his machine gun. So intent was he that he never saw another English aeroplane which came up fast and got between the Hun and his own lines, thus cutting off his retreat. Then when the first English machine had enticed his pursuer down to within a few hundred feet of our trenches, he waved his hand, meta-phorically at any rate, and flew away. Before the Hun could realise that he had been led into a trap, our Infantry opened rapid fire at him and brought him hurtling down amid the cheers of our men who stood up in the trenches back here and cheered with delight.

July 21st. I walked over today to see the village of Mamet, or at least to see all that remains of it. Not a single wall is standing, nothing to mark the site of a smiling French village but heaps of dust and crumbling plaster.

As I write my eyes are streaming with tears. The last two hours the Hun has been sending over his latest form of frightfulness – small shells containing some gas which irritates the eyes and nose until the torture is almost unbearable. It is so petty & so useless that one hates the Hun for being such a cold-blooded blaggard.

2 August 1916. It's amazingly hot, the sun beats down upon us with relentless vigour, and we have no shade except in stifling tents. We came out of the line a week ago today and I ought to have made an opportunity of writing to you before, but everything is against it. By day we frizzle, in the evening we are stung to madness by mosquitoes and other small game, and by night we try to recuperate.

We are living the simple life, a few miles behind the line, daily receiving drafts of officers and men, and generally preparing for our next spasm in the battle area [Méricourt, to bivouacs].

The weather ever since we arrived has been most glorious, which is lucky as we are in bivouacs. The men sleep under their ground-sheets and two or three combine to make a small tent-like erection. The ground which we occupy – a sort of orchard near the railway line – to the casual observer with Biblical knowledge would give the impression that the Feasts of Tabernacles was in full swing.

My own home is under an apple tree. I sleep on a stretcher raised on boxes, with nothing between me and the starry vault of heaven but the top layer of my 'flea bag'.

On the branches of the tree hang all my *Lares and Penates*, and at the foot thereof sleeps Spot – my trusty hound and friend.

We eat our meals under the shade of another tree, balancing precariously on boxes of various sizes and stability. Under these conditions you will realise that letter writing has nothing in its favour – yet my job for the last many days has mainly been writing letters of sympathy to the bereaved. In the intervals when the ground got too hard or the sun intolerable, I have formed one of a merry party for a dip in the chalky river which winds its way about 300 yards away. We have found a deep pool below the mill sluice in which we disport and have rigged up a springboard and high dive.

By the side of the stream is a nice shady bit of grass on which we bask without a care in the world. If this was the only side of war I would never grumble. Long may this life continue even if it means our total extinction, or partial mastication by mosquitoes. Since my last letter we had another day of battle, and again lost fairly heavily from a really wicked oblique shell fire. We were really only manning a reserve trench, but in rather a critical corner of the battle line. I went up with the Battalion, and as no dugouts existed, spent much time and more sweat in delving a hole out of the side of a bank in which the CO and I sheltered successfully from the attentions of 5.9 H.E. krumps, and other presents from the Huns.

We had only got back at midnight the day before, when at three o'clock in the morning word came to return so as you can imagine we were all worn out and that day's shelling put the lid on it completely. All that day and night we crouched in our hole waiting for relief to appear. You can hardly imagine the weird experience it is, sitting in a hole in the side of the road, shivering with cold – for the night airs are anything but balmy – and wondering which will arrive first: the long-expected relief or the annihilating shell.

However now that we are out of that stricken valley we will say no more about it but talk about other things. Sunday for example was a great day. I discovered a shady glade in the middle of one of those artificial forests which the thrifty French plant so assiduously [at Mericourt]. There I had two Celebrations, to the second of which some sixty officers and men came. It was a very fine Service and really most inspiring. It was a gloriously sunny day and that grassy glade was as appropriate as any cathedral. The official Church Parade I had in a nice park, with the Brigade formed in a hollow square and supported by the massed Bands. It was the first Brigade Service that I've had the chance of having since I've been out here, for this is the first time that we have been billeted in the same village, and it is only possible now I suppose because we are so reduced in numbers.

P.S. September 25th will soon be here, and I come then whatever happens, as long as I am still alive.

6 August 1916. It is Sunday night, the village clock is just chiming eleven o'clock and peace broods over our little city of bivouacs. Far away I can hear the rumbling of guns and the rattling of the transport on some distant road. I am sitting under my apple tree writing by the light of a flickering candle on a table improvised from a ration box, my seat is the edge of my stretcher bed, and altogether I feel in a tender and reminiscent mood.

Sunday night, especially on a fine summer evening, always brings with it a delightful feeling of rest after labour, when pleasurably tired the body and mind relax from strain and care, and take their ease.

Today has been another glorious example of summer at its best, brilliant sun and blue sky, with a soft zephyr breeze soughing through the tops of the trees. We are still in the same delightful spot, our rest cure nearly completed.

I had my Services as last Sunday in a glade of a plantation of elms, I think. I wish I could make you see it: the nave of my cathedral was the arching branches of the trees, my little altar a vivid splash of white against the background of green, my reredos and east window a vista of mossy grass tartaned by the sunlight shining through the tracery of the avenue of trees beyond, while round the altar knelt the officers and men who came to pay their duty to the King of Kings. This evening we met there again and sang hymns sitting and lying on the shady grass, until the Last Post called us home to camp. War is a fiendish thing, but it has its compensations, and if nothing else, it forces us all to live very near to nature and to truth. I love the simple, almost childlike life, and consequently appreciate all the more occasional jaunts into the old life and way of living.

We had a great day last Thursday. The Staff Captain – one Dinwiddie who before the war was reading for the Scottish Ministry, and is one of the best – and I went into a neighbouring city [Amiens] for a day's outing. We arrived at lunchtime, so repaired at once to the nearest hotel, which was so full of French and English officers that it was almost impossible to get a seat. Even when we had successfully managed to overcome that initial difficulty, it took two hours by the clock to wander from the hors d'oeuvre to the cheese. Incidentally, these were the only two courses that I could spread myself on, for mussels I didn't fancy in any case and ours looked as if they were second-hand, and the hock of a horse, even though it is stewed with those marvellous vegetables known only to the French, doesn't really offer much sustenance to a hungry warrior. However, we managed to fill all aching voids with vast quantities of bread nibbled during the lengthy waits, and sallied forth to see the sights and particularly the Cathedral for which this city is justly famed. The Cathedral we discovered masquerading as a gigantic dugout, all the carving and statues are protected by huge walls of sandbags, as is also the marvellous west end Gothic doorway and facade. Even under this disguise, however, we could appreciate the grandeur and wonderful proportion of this many chapeled House of God, which is by the way the inspiration and subject of one of Ruskin's works. So far the Hun has not succeeded in damaging this Cathedral, but being so near the front there is always a danger of visits from Hun aeroplanes with their load of vandalising bombs.

After drinking our fill of the beauties of the Cathedral we spent some time gluing our noses to the shop windows and replenishing our wardrobes. Later on, sated with sight-seeing we sat in the gardens, watching the crowds and admiring the much-decorated French officers and men. Nearly everyone seems to wear either the *Croix de guerre* or *Legion d'honneur* or both. Nor are they content with the ribbon only but bravely sport the medal as well. As usual we soon made friends with our neighbours on the seat, and talked War with a very voluble old Frenchman who denounced the Kaiser with flashing eyes and passion-laden words.

At 7.30 pm all the officers of the Mess met for a *bon diner* at the most fashionable hotel – and a very *bon diner* they gave us. Our CO very kindly insisted on being our host, and regardless of expense gave us a regular City Fathers' banquet.

In the small hours of the morning we made a move for home, our means of transport – the only one available – was a motor lorry so into it we all clambered and jolted our noisy way home in great spirits, which found vent in the vociferous singing of all the popular ditties.

The village clock is just chiming the hour of midnight and the mosquitoes are eating me alive, so I will to bed.

13 August 1916. I expect the note I sent off yesterday surprised you some. When I wrote last Sunday I little thought that a visit to Paris was in the offing. But the CO suggested it at the Mess one night, jokingly I think, but we took it up and got leave for seventy-two hours, although we were recalled before our time was really up. However we had two whole days in the gay city & a most amusing time. We taxied to the Grand Hotel near the Opera and got rooms without difficulty. Our first activity was to have a bath in a luxurious porcelain one with unlimited hot water, and all modern comforts.

Each room has its own bathroom attached – a great treat to the mighty unwashed.

Dinner in a sparkling salon with gleaming napery and glittering silver & glass was the next treat – an almost overpowering contrast to eating off the grass under an apple tree. Then followed stalls at the *Folies Bergères*, and so to bed.

The next day was devoted to sightseeing – all the well-known places we visited, and were particularly braced by the sight of a countless collection of German war material, guns, aeroplanes, trench mortars, machine guns, bits of Zeppelins and the rest bravely placed on view in the courtyard of Les Invalides. It was a boiling day, much too hot to walk, so we hired a taxi horse-landau and drove about in style, and at an extraordinary cheap rate. It worked out at about two francs an hour. Consequently we had no qualms in keeping the old bag of tricks waiting while we popped in to see the glories of Notre Dame, or to sip the cooling joys of a pêche melba at the Café de Paris or the Dauphine. Then in the evening we went to the Marigny and afterwards saw a little of Paris by night! Next day as we were drinking our early cup of coffee came a telephone message from the APM telling us the sad news that all officers were recalled, so we were robbed of our ride in the Bois de Boulogne, which we had kept as a *bonne bouche*. However, we had time to drive down the Champs Elysées, read the Battle Honours on the Arc de Triomphe, and then take the Metro out to Dauphine and have one hurried glimpse at Longchamps and the Bois de Boulogne before hurrying back to catch our train.

I can't do justice in a letter to the supreme joy of the whole visit, but for two days we forgot all about war, and were absolutely light-hearted and irresponsible.

Of the journey back I will say nothing. Let a veil be drawn – umpteen hours in a crowded carriage, followed by a few hours' sleep on the floor of a YMCA hut.

18 August 1916. We are in again, and have again suffered heavily I am afraid. But the price of victory must be paid. Our Division has been paid a very encouraging compliment by the Corps – our allies asked that a good Division might be placed immediately on their left. The Corps Commander said he would give them the best he had, and so we came back into the line some time before we otherwise would have done.

This time, I am back at the Advance Dressing Station, miles and miles behind the line – a perfectly safe place to be but I don't like it and feel very apologetic to all our boys who come through wounded. It is the first time I hadn't been with them when they have been in action.

As I write, sitting on a pile of stretchers during a lull in the work, I can see the line that we are hoping soon to hold being plastered with our artillery preparation, and the din as usual is prodigious. Oh, here come some cases so I must knock off for a bit.

Later. Here we are again! The cases are dressed first at the Battalion Aid Post in or near the line. Nothing very much can be done there, of course, so they are redone when they come to us, and we then pack them off in motor ambulances to the main Dressing Station; and so the poor fellows go stage by stage until they reach the Base.

My work consists chiefly in carrying the stretcher cases into the operating dugout, and back again and hoisting them into the cars – getting them a drink of tea, or writing a field postcard for them, and generally trying to make them comfortable and buck them up. Any definitely spiritual work – whatever that may mean – is almost impossible here, at least as far as I can see.

Last Monday I had rather an unusual ministry to perform. One of the last draft [Frank Atkinson] wished to be baptised. We were then in bivouacs in a dusty plain, a few miles behind the line, waiting to go up. Under the circumstances it wasn't easy to know quite how to arrange things. Luckily, however, I discovered a disused gun pit with a dugout attached. Here then was my Church – about six foot square and five foot six inches high.

At one end I fixed a diminutive altar with cross and lights, and on the altar I put my font, which in default of anything more suitable or fitting was my chalice.

What a liturgiologist would say to this I don't know and hush – *entre nous*, don't very much care, for we had a most impressive little Service with the catechumen's two pals present to act as sponsors and witnesses.

It was a little scene that I am sure will always remain photographed on the minds and hearts, I hope, of all of us. The same evening the Battalion went into action.

On active service the Chaplain is jack of all trades, and has a finger in every pie – *par exemple* I try to run the Mess, I censor letters,

I organise concerts, sports and football matches – I keep saying 'I'. I should say 'we' for all chaplains are the same. It is not that we have any more experience or skill than anyone else, but simply that we have, or are supposed to have, more time.

On Monday, I tried my hand at a new game – namely judging a Transport Competition. What I know about transport might be written easily on a threepenny bit, but nothing daunted I inspected mules and harness and wagons and the rest, and tried to look as if I had been doing it all my life.

Saturday. I've never been so tired in my life, simply deadbeat. Since Wednesday I have been on duty the whole time and have managed to snatch an hour or two of sleep each night during a lull but nothing more, and my back and arms ache with the continual lifting and carrying. The bearers are very shorthanded, so I have to give them a lift.

24 August 1916. In the last month our casualties have exceeded those sustained by the Gordon Highlanders during the whole of the South African War! That gives one pause to think, doesn't it? Five officers killed & five wounded in the last show. When we came out on Saturday night we had only six left with the Battalion and the casualties among the men were in the same proportion. Consequently I am as busy as I can be writing to the poor bereaved. Now that we have emerged from the peace of the winter and are fairly launched into the shooting season this is a work which never ends.

Really there is nothing to record since I last wrote. We have moved back some thirty miles behind the line [from Morlancourt to Mazingarbe], spending most of the day yesterday on the journey.

I have received today a long letter from [brother] Hal written the night before they 'went over the top' to take an isolated hill near Dorran. I imagine it is the same hill as I see from the papers has been captured by the Allies.

My servant has just fallen down the stairs & hurt his head. As I was writing I was summoned to see him, & found him surrounded by the girls of the village full of pity for the wounded *Anglais*. I think perhaps he would have got better sooner if they hadn't been there! As it was he had the dying-duck expression to the T, and was thoroughly enjoying himself.

'Dear Padre,' wrote [then Lieutenant Colonel] Kentish. 'You have proved yourself a born leader of men and an example for all soldiers to imitate when in action. I can never forget your splendid example of gallantry and cheerfulness during the Battle of the Somme, and thank you from the bottom of my heart for the great part you played in helping the officers and men of the Kings Own throughout that very intense period of fighting – a part which, thanks in no small measure to you and your efforts in the Battalion, they played so nobly and well. Yours ever, RJ Kentish.'

Friday. Yesterday came word of another trek, and now it is a *fait accompli*. We started after an early breakfast to avoid the heat, and arrived here in time for lunch. Tomorrow we repeat the dose, & the history of the day after will be precisely the same. We have had rumours of a rest by the sad sea waves, but by the direction of our wandering I think we are going back whence we came to take our part in the Big Push. But truth to tell, nobody knows anything and plans are changed from hour to hour.

I am sitting at the open window of my billet – a spotlessly clean, red-tiled floored, white-washed room in a picturesque cottage. Through the window I can see a riot of poppies and other brilliantly coloured flowers, mixed up with cabbages & turnip tops – moreover it is raining – softly and silently – and all is peace.

That really exhausts my stock of news if I except the desertion of Spot & his subsequent return.

He has been charged with the following crime: 'While on active service deserting His Majesty's Forces in that while on the line of march he absented himself without leave'. Sentence of the Court 'To suffer Death by being shot'. The sentence however has been commuted to one day Field Imprisonment No.1.

One piece of news I am itching to tell you, but it can wait a little longer [the award of his DSO].

30 August 1916. Ever since I wrote last we have been on trek, and each night our caravan has rested in a different village. For some time the direction of our march favoured the idea that we were going for a rest far from the madding Hun, but one evil day we slewed round umpteen degrees, and are now within measurable distance of the trenches which we learn we are to hold. So after the hurly burly of the Big Push we are coming back to peacetime warfare again.

Well our purple patch on the Somme has not been without interest. I forget if I told you that we saw one day the miracle of Albert Church. The figure on the top of the steeple is the Madonna holding the Babe at arms length. Months ago a Hun shell hit the base of the statue and dislodged it so that now it hangs at right angles to the ground as if asking Pilate's famous question. 'What, will you crucify your King?' Local tradition says that the war will end the day it falls.

Yesterday we stopped at rather an interesting village, very primitive & old fashioned, untouched by the march of labour-saving machinery. In one barn there was an old patriarch threshing corn by hand, and doing it extremely well with a wobbly flail and uncanny precision.

In another place a horse was philosophically walking on a sort of endless platform which worked a small grinding mill. The funny part was that the horse seemed to like its job, and didn't appear to be at all disappointed that for all its walking it remained in precisely the same place. I expect you remember seeing dogs running round in cage-like wheels & working various small machines; as far as I can see most of the churning is done by dog power.

We have got quite accustomed by this time to seeing dogs drawing handcarts especially up in Flanders, but the other day we saw the dog cart de luxe. A top-hole little trap standing about four foot high, drawn by a big dog & driven by a nipper of ten, with his little sister by his side – a most charming turn-out imaginable.

I can't tell you where we are, but I suppose there is no harm in saying that we have left behind us the smiling cornfields and mud walls of Picardy, and are now in country that reminds me of Askam & Barrow – pit-heads and mining villages superimposed on an agricultural district [Noeux-les-Mines]. The illusion is increased by the amount of rain which we have had during the last twenty-four hours. We had got about half-way here yesterday when the heavens opened and the rain came down in torrents to the accompaniment of big guns up aloft which flashed and thundered away for some time.

Did I tell you that the man I baptised and his two sponsors were all wounded in the last show – rather tragic don't you think?

3 September 1916. You could hardly believe how strange it feels to have an address again after having lived the life of a tramp for so long. I am giving the Hun no useful information when I say that 32 Rue de Mazingarbe is an undistinguished looking, rather shabby house, exactly the same as its long row of neighbours, an unimportant unit in a large mining village, and unlikely to be known to history unless it be as the temporary home of Padre Leonard and Roger the Interpreter.

At one end of the street is the town consisting of a few shops, a church, a cinema run by the Division, numberless estaminets, and a Field Force Canteen; at the other end is one of those ungainly mountains of slack or slag which mines always produce in great quantities.

Here for the time being I am installed, and very nice it is too. The inside of the house is much superior to what its exterior might lead one to expect. The landlady is an ex-domestic servant, and so knows how to do things. We have subsidised her to take the cooking out of the hands of our batman, and do it herself; so for the first time since I have been out here my meals are prepared by a female hand.

I didn't tell you of one of our men, an old soldier, who came to me the other day and said he wanted me to accept a trifle towards the cost of some new hymn-books which we have been getting. He wanted it to be a little thank-offering for coming through safely, though he didn't quite know how to express himself. However, he thrust five francs into my hands. It was exactly half of a fortnight's pay which he had just received!

Another little act which delighted me was performed by an old countrywoman. As we were marching through a village she ran out with a large armful of flowers and gave them to us as we swung past. Her graceful action nearly ended in tragedy for the vivid colour of her posy nearly terrified the Major's horse out of his life, and all but put the Major on his bald head.

Another incident of the march which didn't cause me any pleasure, but which amused me nevertheless was a difficult meeting which I had with an APM. The APMs correspond to the proctors at Oxford and the sister universities. I was trotting along with my dog Fido at the head of the column when he pulled up and said 'is tha-tha-that your-your d-d-d-dog?' The answer was in the affirmative, so he said 'We we d-d-do'nt li-li-like d-d-dogs in th-th-the so and so ar-ar army!' I expressed surprise and ventured to say that the dog in question was not a stray. He had other remarks to make, and at the rate at which he spoke, it took a long time, but luckily after he had used a good deal of energy and lost a fair quantity of saliva over the sibilants, he discovered that we were only birds of passage and not in his jurisdiction. So Spot is still alive and still the proud mascot of the Regiment.

11 September 1916. It is so long since I last wrote perhaps a diary form of letter will be the simplest way of conveying my news:

Monday 4th September. Roger – the Interpreter – and I went up to the trenches [14 Bis Sector]. It's a weary long way up an endless and deep communication trench – so deep that you can see nothing but the chalky sides and the narrow duck board along which you walk. You can't even see any distance ahead, for the trench – as is usual with good CTs – winds and twists like a writhing reptile of the baser sort. As you can well imagine three or four miles of this form of exercise are all that one can comfortably manage before the mind becomes unhinged or the body falls exhausted to the ground.

Seriously, I know of no more boring and tiring work than walking up a long deep CT. It's quite the last thing in scientific torture, and should be given as a punishment for wife-beating and blackmailing and kindred crimes.

About halfway up I caught sight of a pal who for the moment owned a dugout a short distance down a branch trench. Into it I staggered, dropped on the only chair and faintly clamoured for water. Luckily he had something to dilute it with, and we went on our way cheered and refreshed.

Up in the front line a curious state of affairs exists. Immediately behind our firing line is an old chalk quarry into which during a former advance they managed to lower a 4.5 Howitzer. The Huns however managed to drive our line back into its present position before the Howitzer could be removed. So there it is now, about a mile and a half in advance of any other gun. The Huns know all about it – otherwise I couldn't have mentioned it, and periodically try to winkle it. Of course they can't get the gun itself, it would want an army of engineers with cranes to get it out now, but they managed once to carry off the sights and the breach block. The amusing part is that we have built a dugout over it, and fire it occasionally through the window!

Tuesday 5th Sept. In the morning and the rain I buried two of our poor fellows, killed by a shell in the trenches and brought down here for burial. Afterwards, in company with the Chaplains of the Division and a London motor bus, we responded to an invitation from the Army Commander [Rawlinson] who decided to meet all the Chaplains in his Army. There must have been at least 200 there when the proceedings opened with a few kind words from the General. After that we all streamed over to his Chateau for tea which was dispensed – is that the word? – to the sweet accompaniment of the Band of the Grenadier Guards. It was a pleasant change, and I met an old pal of mine whom I haven't seen for more than two years, but the more I see of the 'brethren' in mass, the more I like to meet them singly.

Wednesday 6th. The dissipation of the day before proving too much for me, I spent the day in bed. The Major had come down the night before, having been given the post as Commandant of the Divisional Training Schools. During the night a picker-up of unconsidered trifles had put his hand through the open window of the Major's bedroom, and removed his breeches, his cap, and his Burberry which were hanging on a chair just inside. In the morning when the loss was discovered the noise was terrific, and the poor old Major had to go off to take command dressed in a borrowed pair of slacks and a Tommy's cap, looking the most awful rake imaginable. How we all roared!

At tea time the Huns threw two shells into our village which decided me to get up. They shrieked past my window and burst at the end of the street – luckily without damage to life, but near enough to make me feel the disability of being without my breeches and my boots! It isn't often they shell this place, for our system of retaliation is to give them six for every one they have the nerve to throw at us.

I couldn't help smiling at the hurry and scurry of the native inhabitants when the first shell came over. Those who had cellars collected their children and their silver teapots and retired there until peace was restored. Those who hadn't cellars carefully, tho' with nervous haste, locked their front doors and scurried off to take refuge with neighbours or in the vault of the church.

Talking to one of our fellows afterwards I asked him where he was during the shelling. His reply is a good example of the unrufflable humour of Tommy Atkins – 'outside an estaminet' he said, 'but the people never budged', this last in a tone of regret, almost of personal injury.

Friday & Saturday. I spent in bed with a temperature and an ill-formed desire to die.

Sunday 10th. I managed to have my Services, but rode to them in the spring Mess cart and not *à cheval* as usual.

Monday 11th. Feeling better I wrote letters all the morning and did Canteen accounts, and generally dabbled with the clerical side of my duties. After lunch I did some practical work for the Canteen, buying stores here and sending them up to the trenches where our Canteen is now housed. We have got a big dugout in one of the support trenches, fitted up with shelves, well stocked with cigarettes and tinned salmon, cake & Shinio; in fact all that a soldier wants.

From there each day we send hawkers round the front line, soldiers carrying trays of various smokes & foods, who also sell the daily papers to the troops up there. And this is war!

Tea I had with the Brigade to talk over details of this new development. In the evening we had a Guest Night and did ourselves proud, inviting some of the Staff to share our salmon mayonnaise and our jugged rabbit.

17 September 1916. I am enclosing a copy of Routine Orders for September 13th. There is one item in them which may amuse you. I knew about it unofficially some time ago but it is unwise to talk about such things until they are published officially in case of an 11th hour revoke. [His DSO]

17 October 1916. It's over a week since I said goodbye, but except for the short note I sent off from Abbeville, I haven't had a chance of writing.

I actually arrived at the Battalion Headquarters at 2.15 pm on Thursday – over thirty hours after leaving Victoria. Lunch was finished but they found me something to eat, and I then went off *à cheval* with several others to see the 'Tanks', which were on show a few miles away.

I can't of course describe them minutely, but they filled me with confidence, and are a most excellent invention, and safe from anything but a direct hit from a heavy shell. All that the papers say is true, they certainly must cause a certain amount of comic relief when in action. They are bigger than I expected & inside remind one of a submarine, or engine room and gun turret combined of a small cruiser. There are apparently two sexes among the Tanks, males carry two six pounders & machine guns, females nothing but machine guns. And the number of tanks we have is fabulous.

On Friday & Saturday I was busy riding round to my scattered flock arranging for Services and paying calls and doing the hundred and one jobs of work which have to be done each week end.

On Sunday I had a busy morning [at Bertrancourt and Louvencourt], and finished my seventh Service at 1.15 pm!

Roger the Interpreter & I are living in a very dirty & ratty room in a tumbledown house, while across the way in similar quarters are the rest of Headquarters. We Mess in a very draughty & excessively cold hut & I sigh for the warmth of the drawing room fire.

Since we have been here we have had three or four spasms of hate from the Hun, but luckily all the shells have fallen without doing any more damage than to destroy a few turnips and dig holes in a stubble field.

Today we move our quarters to a neighbouring village [Louvencourt]. As it is only a stone's throw away we cannot fathom the reason or the meaning of the move, but much of what we do in the Army seems to be without reason.

I am enclosing a few odds and ends of things which may be of interest – two letters from brother Hal, a menu card of a dinner given at Locre for our gallant Colonel, a map of the trenches at Montauban & Longueval with the Aid Post marked where the Doctor got knocked out, and where the shells didn't quite succeed in blowing us up.

22 October 1916. At 2 am Thursday morning came sudden orders to proceed at 7 am to the trenches, which we did in pouring rain, arriving there up to the ears in mud and soaked to the skin. It was a terrible day, the sort you want to forget, but it was redeemed by the finding of poor Spot who finding himself lost returned to my last billet and spent a restless night there running in & out and crying the whole time, so at least the old girl of the billet told me.

On Friday I rode back to the village I had left the day before to give the Field Ambulance a Celebration, and later in the day went up to the trenches to spend a few days with the Battalion. However no sooner had I got there than orders came that we were to be relieved next morning. This came as a bit of a surprise as we thought we were to stay until we had made the attack. So early Saturday morning we came out again to a village just behind the line, much battered and shelled. There in a very tired looking Chateau we found billets. All round the billets are massed guns and howitzers which fire all day & night and make a perfectly appalling noise – a noise that really hurts – and each time the nearest big gun goes off the whole place shakes, bits of the shattered windows fall jingling to the ground, and another slate or two slides off the already porous roof [Courcelles].

There we have spent today, and tomorrow we go back to the trenches. Nobody knows why we came out, and everybody unites in wishing that we had been allowed to stay in, once we were there. For it is the getting in and out of the trenches, & the constant moving about which is so tiring & incidentally so dangerous.

In the Chateau are crowded practically all the officers of the Battalion, the Colonel & the Adjutant have small rooms, the rest herd in the living rooms & sleep on stretchers or improvised beds. Believing that my absence would be more acceptable than my presence both to the rest of the overcrowded mess and to myself, for I like not the close & noisy proximity of those guns, Roger & I have returned to our old ratty billet – about a mile from the Chateau. We come back here to sleep, but have our meals over there.

We have just got back to our billet, it is one o'clock in the morning & a beautiful starry night.

After dinner we had a glorious log fire built up, and all sat round in a double semicircle, those in front reclining on the ground, those behind on chairs, boxes, and a dilapidated Chesterfield, all very cosy and warm. Outside the booming of the guns, inside sweet melody; we started by having a singsong & ended with feats of strength, including Cumberland & Westmorland wrestling. Quite a jolly and a jovial evening.

25 October 1916. I am in great distress and sorrow of heart for I have just said goodbye to the best CO that a battalion ever had. Colonel Smith who has commanded us since last December and led us to victory every time we have been in action, has been suddenly sent down to the Base for reasons unstated and his mantle has been taken by a Major of the Cavalry.

I can't pretend to understand the working of the Staff mind or to unravel the intrigues of the brass hat and red tab world, but the fact remains that the ideal leader of men who has won the love & devotion of the whole Battalion, and the written admiration of the late Divisional General, to say nothing of the DSO and Russian Cross of St. George first class, has been sent to look after some footling business at the Base, and his place taken by a Cavalry man & a dyspeptic at that. Whether it is because he is a Territorial, or because they are all jealous of him I don't know, but there it is for all the world to see and marvel at.

Quite in keeping with my feelings is the weather. Pause while I compose a diatribe on the weather. The glory of the summer is departed, and the heavens pour down upon us unceasingly and ungrudgingly of their abundance, the whole world shrouded in dampness and depressing dimness.

The roads have become a succession of holes of unplumbed depth full of liquid slime, and the fields a swampy morass. While to complete the discomfort of man & beast there blows from every direction an icy blast which cuts through to the marrow of the best-covered bones.

When I arrived, as I think I told you, I found the Battalion momentarily expecting to go over the top, in which state of tension & expectancy we still remain, for all fighting is held up by the weather,

Extract from KORL Diary dated 24 October 1916: 'The following letter has been received from Brigadier General R.J. Kentish, late commanding 76th Infantry Brigade: "Colonel Smith, officers, non-commissioned officers and men of the 8th Battalion, The King's Own Royal Lancaster Regiment, I desire to place on record my deep appreciation of your conduct in the face of the enemy during the intense fighting you have taken part in, in the great battle of the Somme … you gave proof of those splendid qualities of gallantry, bravery and endurance that has ever been characteristic of the men of the King's Own Regiment" … etc.'

though nothing can stop the music of the guns which continue day and night to hurl great lumps of potential death at Brother Hun.

To feed these hungry monsters there is an unceasing stream of glistening lorries and steaming teams of horses hauling at their rattling rumbling ammunition limbers going up full and coming back empty for more.

The noise round our *soi-disant* Chateau is appalling and continuous, one big gun in particular is the bane of our existence, and goes off with such a vicious bang that it has 'put the wind up' poor Spotty who lies at my feet and shivers. I went out to see it yesterday, and found it masquerading as an apple tree in the orchard. The sergeant in charge told me that in retaliation for fourteen shells which the Hun had the audacity to throw into our village, we threw a thousand into every one of his used for billeting purposes, and moreover only took ten minutes in which to do it. All our guns in the neighbourhood joined in the merry game and sloshed them in at the rate of a hundred a minute – I'm mighty glad I'm not a Hun!

31 October 1916. I am still in my ratty billet at the cross roads, but very comfy and above all very central for visiting the various parts of my scattered flock. Here I stay each night and write my letters and keep my *lares & penates*, and incidentally have my breakfast & drink deeply of excellent French-made coffee. I am sitting at this moment by the side of a very comforting stove, on all sides of which hang shirts & socks and handkerchiefs, for my billet keeper is a washer-woman and the mother of two small girls – Yvonne and Gabrielle – who are playing round my feet & making the divil of a noise. But their baby voices are nothing to their mother's who is having a heated argument with a French Interpreter who has come over to try to recover some washing of an English officer which he says the good woman has lost – such a din! Both going together & the air seems full of waving hands!

Outside the sun is shining for the first time for days, but the ground is still a saturated solution of mud and chalk, and the roads quite unutterably bad.

By day a journey by road is quite an adventure, but by night it's a complete odyssey, especially these dark moonless nights, for if you escape the Scyllas of the muddy holes which swallow the unfortunates who step into them, you fall foul of a Charybdis of lumbering lorries or straining limbers which never cease to make their tedious way to the front. However I seldom walk, for it is always possible to board a passing lorry & ride if not in comfort at least in less danger than when on foot. It is really like a very up-to-date London motor bus service, for lorries go everywhere and at all times, and if you don't mind being bumped about like a pea in a whistle, you can travel where & when you will.

One dark night when you couldn't really see two yards in front of the bonnet I marvelled how the driver kept his lumbering lorry & load upright on the road & avoided crashing into infantry or the horse transport which suddenly loomed up out of the night, for of course no lights are allowed so near the front. We were suddenly stopped by a block in front, and an officer came to the side of the lorry & said 'Are you one of ours?' to the driver. As it happened he wasn't. 'What are you then. Heavies? 'No sir,' replied the man, and then after a pause, 'As a matter of fact, Sir, & begging your pardon I mustn't tell you.' So what we had on board I have no idea – something very mysterious anyway. I was quite glad to get off without being arrested as a spy or a conspirator.

It really is astounding how much goes on under the cover of darkness, when the back of the front really begins to move; unending lines of transport of every sort, & of helmeted men, and puffing grunting caterpillars hauling guns from one place to another, and everyone knows where to go & goes there like clockwork.

5 November 1916. On Saturday, between the showers, the Gordons and the Suffolks held some inter-regimental sports, the *bonne bouche* of which was a tug-of-war between the Regimental Cooks. Cooks on active service certainly have an unenviable job standing all day over smoky open fires, and must find it almost impossible to keep clean. Anyhow they always bear very evident marks of their profession on their clothes & persons. They are like the men in the picture in last month's Punch – 'it isn't as 'ow they don't wash, but they dries dirty'!

But of all cooks, the ones who lined up on the rope to do battle for their respective Regiments were the dirtiest set of ruffians you ever saw. The spectators regarded their exertions as a species of unintentional buffoonery, as indeed it was, for their evident seriousness and grim determination made it a thousand times funnier.

· For some time nothing happened despite their frantic and audible exertions, the rope remained stationary until in one hapless moment the Gordons all collapsed together and let go of the rope, except the end man who in an excess of keenness had inextricably wound himself up in the rope. The Suffolks being country men and holding tight to the instructions they had received that the winners had to pull their opponents right over the mark, proceeded stolidly to drag the luckless endman by his neck through the mud, and refused to stop until he had finished the course, despite the orders of the umpire and the evident signs of suffocation displayed by the writhing Gordon. How we screamed with laughter. It was quite the funniest thing I have seen for ages.

Chapter 6

'If I fall, we shall meet again'

The Somme – the Attack on Serre,
November 1916

12 November 1916. This week has been letter-writing week par excellence, for I have in hand the collecting of subs from all officers of the Battalion, for an engraved silver salver for our late CO – Colonel Smith. The great majority of those who have served under him are now in Blighty, sick, wounded or convalescent, to all of whom I have had to write. However that work is nearly done now and most of the money collected.

The middle of the salver is to be engraved with the Regimental Crest and Lion, surrounded by the Battalion Battle Honours – The Bluff, St Eloi, Longueval and Guillemont, while all around are to be facsimile signatures of all contributing officers. So it will be vellum and parchment book and presentation rolled into one, and will be, I hope, a reminder of the respect, admiration and devotion which we all have for him.

This morning from 6:30 am to lunch time I was busy with Celebrations and Church Parades, all of which were particularly impressive for we go up to the trenches this evening for the long delayed Big Push.

By the time you get this it will be all over I hope, and we shall be out again resting. I am afraid I hate these shows more and more, for whereas ignorance is bliss, knowledge is just the reverse, and I have seen too much now to have any feelings of elation.

The majority of the men, I think, are the same. The spirit of willing sacrifice is there just the same, and there's hardly a man who

119

isn't ready to give his life, but the horror of war grows on one and makes it increasingly difficult. I almost envy the men who fell in their first engagement. It isn't that one is afraid of death, however sweet life may be, but it is more or less a physical feeling of revulsion at all the blood and mud and noise and diabolical horror of modern war.

I can hardly imagine that there will ever be another world war as long as the memory of this one remains with those who have taken part, either actively in the field, or more still, passively waiting and praying at home.

The attack is to be at dawn, on a very wide front, and the Tanks, bless their mechanical hearts, are to go with us. If things go well there should be a lot of prisoners and guns captured, so keep your eye on the papers: we are in front of Serre, and our Brigade has the job of taking the northern half of it.

I'll write again as soon as we are out; I am going to be in a very safe place this time, so there is no need to worry darlings, and anyway if I fall, we shall meet again.

16 November 1916. I got back to my billet at 3 o'clock this morning, looking and feeling like Rip Van Winkle! The show is over but the Battalion is still in the line, but I have come out since the stream of wounded has ceased, and I have a lot of letters to write, not only to the bereaved, but also to the wives and mothers of the wounded, who have given me a pocket book full of messages to send. However, before I tackle this work I must get a line off to you so that you may know that all is well with me.

It is now 2 pm, I have just had my lunch-breakfast, had a bath and a shave and feel as fit and as cheery as can be. From the time I went in on Sunday until midday today, I hadn't a wash of any sort or description, for the little water we had was too precious to use in removing the mud, which submerged and permeated everything. I am glad you didn't see me when I got back – a four-day growth of beard bursting its way through a mask of dried mud and dirt, a mass of unkempt hair also caked with mud, and an outfit of clothes, as it were starched with a mixture of clay and chalk. The attack as a whole has been a great success, you will have seen the papers that Beaumont Hamel and St. Pierre Divion have been captured with several thousands of prisoners, and the usual quantities of war material, but I am sorry to say that our efforts ended in failure – we were on the extreme left of the attack, and made no progress. It was a thick mist in the low-lying ground over which we advanced, and the mud was so deep that the men could not advance at anything more than a snail's pace. In fact, burdened as they are with all the paraphernalia of war, it was a superhuman effort to drag one foot after the other. The result was they got hung up and lost direction, and got into our own barrage, and generally had a bad and unprofitable time; but our sacrifice and efforts have not been in vain for the main object of the attack, i.e. on the south of Beaumont Hamel, has been achieved.

I spent the first twenty-four hours at the Advanced Dressing Station, about 1500 yards back, but afterwards went up to the Battalion Aid Post, which was in a very deep dugout in the front line. There I lived in perfect safety but in the midst of an unceasing and deafening roar of bursting shells.

A deep dugout is a real luxury, you feel so absolutely safe and yet you are on the spot to miss nothing.

Our casualties were not heavy, I am glad to say, not to be compared with what we had on the Somme before, probably about a quarter, but the numbers are not definitely known yet.

Our dugout – to return to it – was a wonderful feat of engineering – about thirty-five feet deep in the clayey bowels of the earth. I call it dugout, but 'tunnel' or 'tube' would describe it better, for it is about 180 yards long, running along parallel with the trench, with five or six stairways leading down from the trench to it.

Hundreds of men live there and shelter during heavy shelling, and can pop up into the trench as soon as the shelling ceases, or the time for action arrives.

This tube is about six foot wide and six foot high, so that it is quite convenient, and you don't live in a state of perpetual bentness. The only drawback is that a hurricane of a draught blows down it, and anybody wanting to get from one end to the other has to walk over your feet – which is a bit unpleasant after you have had your boots on for ninety-six hours and your corns are beginning to join in the general craze for strafing.

We lived near one of the stairways, which had been specially adapted with a slide, up and down which the stretchers were dragged by a rope and human donkey engine. Life in such a tunnel is really very weird. We were in the middle more or less, and both ways we could see an endless succession of flickering candles which lit up the faces of the men grouped round. Between each little candle-lit group, utter darkness.

Now I am out again and in comfort and safety, I can afford to look back on that tunnel with a certain amount of sorrow and regret. I really enjoyed my time there – tho' the word 'enjoy' perhaps sounds rather heartless, seeing that we were surrounded the whole time by an endless stream of maimed and broken men.

Thank you so much, Father dear, for your long letter which was waiting for me when I got back this morning, and which I devoured with avidity and much joy. I can't tell you how much your letters mean to me. I simply live for letters from home.

[He got Mentioned in Dispatches during the period he covers in this letter – Mentioned in Dispatches, but not in here!]

17 November 1916. I wrote yesterday but forgot to mention one or two things, so write again this evening, although my fingers feel like so much lifeless meat. If I say it is cold I understate the truth, it is perishing in this mud-walled scullery which I call my billet. I am back again in the same old ratty house of the washerwoman, sitting by the stove, surrounded by her brazen-lunged and sabot-booted infants. Quite the family man.

As if to mock us at our failure in the mud last Monday, Jack Frost has appeared with his icy blast and his all-embracing vice, and the ground now is a petrified ocean – the waves of mud are turned to stone and our marrow is frozen hard. Today, for the first time, I have donned my woolly waistcoat which you had washed for me when I was home on leave – very warm and comforting it is, but my nose and ears and finger-tips ache under the lash of this bitter wind.

Had we attacked today, I am certain we would have got through to our last objective without much difficulty, but such is the fortune of war, and even our Staff can't order the weather to suit the occasion.

22 November 1916. We are now out of the trenches for a week, and I am still in my same old billet [in Courcelles]. I've never been so long in one billet since last June. It is a comfort to get your roots in somewhere and unpack your traps and leave your things about for a change. I think it is likely that we may settle down here for the winter, holding trenches in the ordinary way, week in and week out.

The victory at Beaumont Hamel is still bearing fruit, and prisoners continue to dribble in. Yesterday I saw a large party of about 300, being marched off on a road-mending fatigue – fine-looking fellows, and not at all the degenerates of Beach Thomas and Co.

Certainly when you see them on their way down from the trenches in which they have been captured, they do look rather pitiful, but then so do our own fellows, for it is hard to look dignified even as a victor, when you are dog-tired and coated in mud.

Our casualties in this last show were 105 all told, of whom more than three-quarters were wounded; but we came off best in the Brigade for once in a way.

The DSO has at last appeared. Perhaps you have seen it. Colonel Smith sent me a copy of the Times, and I send it on to you, in case you haven't.

I expect you will feel what I felt when I read the recommendation. What on earth did (he) mean by giving me the DSO? Helping the Doctor and carrying in stretchers is what every Chaplain does. You will see that quite a few Chaplains have got Military Crosses for doing much more than I did.

28 November 1916. Christian Shairps has written to me from Town. She is now war-working at the War Office apparently. It's really rather fine the way the girls of England are doing their bit. We are gradually waking up I think, but the War isn't over by a long chalk, and really I don't yet see the end. Roumania is taking it in the neck, and Germany shows no sign of exhaustion. Apparently she is as strong today as ever she's been. Well we haven't learnt our lesson yet, so we must bear a little longer with this madness, but, my hat, how I wish I was a civilian again!

The Battalion went up for a week in the trenches yesterday [north of Serre] and I follow them as soon as I have coped with my really gargantuan correspondence.

I have on the table on my side forty-three letters that I have answered, and thirteen still to tackle, so you will forgive me if my letter lacks the essential ingredients of news and sparkle. Anyway you know it brings you all my love, and a thousand thanks for all your sweet letters and parcels.

6 December 1916. Just after I wrote last week we heard the sad news that Harry Saxon, who has been Brigade Bombing Officer for some time, had been killed by a shell in the front line. He was a splendid boy, absolutely fearless and good all through, everybody loved him and his death has cast quite a gloom over us all, callous and hardened veterans though we are. Had he lived he was hoping to take Orders after the war, and he would have been the ideal priest.

We buried him in a little military cemetery at Courcelles with full honours: all the Battalion and most of the Brigade Staff came to the Service; I have never seen such infinite care and such evident desire to do honour to the fallen at any funeral before out here. He really was a most lovable and charming boy.

On Sunday I had a full day, starting with a Celebration at 7:15 at [Louvencourt] a village three or four miles further back where the Field Ambulance is at present. The ride there and back was some-what of a trial as the roads were coated with ice and poor little Niger could hardly stand.

At 9 am I had a celebration here [in Bus] in the cinema for the Transport and Details. Then rode up to a village [Courcelles] about halfway between here and the front line, for a Church Parade and Celebration for the Engineers. We had it in a new hut which they have just built, and moreover had a piano, umpteen years old and very decrepit, but which under the skilful hands of a pukka organist, led the hymns with great éclat.

Then came lunch with the Engineers, the CO of whom is an old Rossallian and a very charming man. After lunch I paid a pastoral call on the Brigadier and Staff, all of whom were speechless with colds. Then on to another village of ill-repute [Colincamps], and the dumping ground of tons of German iron rations. All day long they shell it, and little is now left except the cellars in which the men live.

The Advanced Dressing Station lives there in some splendid dug-outs, and thither I went, saw some wounded, and had a little Service for the bearers and nursing orderlies.

The dugout in which they live is so small that we all had to sit on the edge of their bunks round the table which fills the greater part of the low space. Here in the dim light of a flickering candle we had evensong, and I tried to give them an Advent message. Quite like early Christians in a catacomb!

On Monday all the Senior Chaplains of the 4th and 5th Armies met at Amiens for a Conference. We are some distance away, but managed to borrow an ambulance which ran us there in a couple of hours.

The Conference was to settle the part we could play in the National Mission. Canon Cunningham came out from England to tell us what had happened there and to give suggestions. It was a splendid meeting, and for once a Clerical Conference didn't live up to its reputation of being the body of Antichrist.

Quite a lot of well-known people were there – the two Talbots, Father Waggett, Bishop Gwynne (the Deputy Chaplain General), and a host more – about sixty all told.

We lived in an hotel in the hall of which we held our meetings and our Services. The Conference lasted from tea-time on Monday to lunch on Tuesday, and we were hard at it the whole time. Nothing definite was settled as to dates etc, for we are at war down here and dates are on the knees of the gods, but we were unanimous on making a big effort, and certain details were arranged. The chief aim of the Conference was to think over and clarify the Message, and personally I have come away very much helped, encouraged, and inspired, and am going to begin at once to have informal meetings in the billets and ask for the cooperation of officers and men. As in England it is to be a National Mission, and the keynote of the Message, the 'Call of the Kingdom'.

9 December 1916. As far as we can foretell the future we shall be out of the trenches for Christmas, so we are hoping to be able to arrange a bit of a treat for the men.

These last few days I have busied myself in starting a Brigade Canteen on wheels. I've bought a country cart which I have swapped for a four-wheeled baker's van – a real big one. The door behind I have had divided so that the top half can be opened revealing a small counter at which the troops can buy cigarettes, salmon, chewing gum, chocolate, candles, Dubbin, writing paper, and a hundred and one other things.

The outside is gaily painted with 'Brigade Canteen', and looks very fine. This Noah's Ark does a daily round ringing a bell as it goes and dealing with the men in their billets. In addition to this retail business I am also preparing to do wholesale transactions with the Battalions, and keep the Regimental Canteens supplied with stock – quite the complete business man!

14 December 1916. The last week has been composed of a series of minor troubles and disappointments, most of which are not without their funny side. The first was on Sunday morning when after much spiritual labour I sufficiently overcame the body to get up at

6 o'clock in the cold and dark, and rode three or four miles with all my Communion things on my back through the rain. I found that the bulk of the Ambulance had moved suddenly and no Service was possible. All day long the Services seemed to go wrong, the Battalions had to find working parties, and so only a few could come to church, and so on. In the evening I went up to [Colincamps] a very unhealthy village, or to be more exact to the site of a village, and had a little Service in a dugout for some stretcher bearers. After the Service, when I came to mount my horse, Niger was gone. Once again he had managed to break away. However he hadn't a very long run for his money as a soldier on point duty arrested him within 200 yards of the dugout, for having no visible means of support, or being without a licence. Anyhow when I asked him if he had seen a stray pony he produced Niger and I rode home safely.

Next day, Monday, was devoted to getting the travelling Canteen into proper working order, and I was chiefly occupied in setting it off on its first pukka daily round.

It did a good day's work, and did splendidly, but unfortunately got stuck in the mud coming home and got properly torn, almost a total wreck – for the front carriage with the two small front wheels, was violently wrenched away from the main body – and only reached port with great difficulty. Here was a tragedy for you if you like! However for the time being the old bus was propped up and became a stationary Canteen, until such time as it could be mended.

On Wednesday the Battalion moved up to the trench area, and I rode over to a big Canteen Depot some miles back to try to make arrangements for getting a regular supply of stores, for nowadays some things are almost unprocurable. My mission was entirely successful, and I made friends with the Manager man, who stood me lunch and promised me first option on everything he got in and I have given him a weekly order for 2000 francs which he has promised to make up however short of things he may be.

I have also arranged for a lorry to go in and bring the stores out. This is easily written but you have no idea how much work and persuasion it entailed.

On my return, feeling very well satisfied, I was met by my batman, who broke the news that I had been turned out of my billet, so I had to set to work to find a new one.

Incidentally the Major who took my billet was an ill-conditioned ranker who objected to my servant taking my canvas bed away

126

with him, and who rudely said he would report me to the Brigade for insisting on taking it against his orders. However as the bed was made for me by the Engineers, the bed was mine and still is. Moreover as I am very much in with the Brigade, I am glad to say he will get no change out of me there. However, I dislike scrapping even with a choleric Major.

The only billet Roger and I could find was a small room in which a mad woman who throws fits did her cooking. When we suggested we would like to do our humble cooking there too, she raved, and stormed and became almost inarticulate despite the soothing attempts of the local mayor. So homeless and hungry we faced a cruel world and wondered what to try next.

Roger however had still a trump up his sleeve, took me off to see a family of refugees from Paris, who are eking out a miserable living by selling postcards and chocolates. They were perfectly charming and gave us a splendid meal, *figurez vous* an eight-egg omelette, with eggs at famine prices, a dish of salmon – from a tin certainly – *pommes de terre à la rôte de chambre*, dessert, coffee and cider – all for six francs!

After dinner the two girls got out their violins and played all the old favourite airs for us. Never did expectations fall so pitifully short of the realisation. It really was a magnificent evening's entertainment. That night I slept on the disputed bed in the billet of the Senior Chaplain, and so was on the spot to take the Celebration for the Chaplains next morning.

In the afternoon I got a peremptory order to move my Canteen from the gateway where it had found refuge. It was still a wreck, and so the moving of it was a superhuman effort, which was eventually managed with the help of the Divisional Band. The new site however blocked somebody's ancient lights, and it was chased away. Again it came to rest, and now after three or four chasings it's fixed near the church and I hope will remain under the shadow of the Pope until the repairs are finished.

21 December 1916. By the time this arrives Christmas will have come and gone, but I hope the peace and quiet joy of Christmas will remain. I shall be thinking of you all very much at my many Eucharists, and will be with you all except in body.

This last week has been full to overflowing, and I still have an appalling lot to do before Sunday. The Canteen has taken a lot of my time – too much I'm inclined to believe – however it is going well and proving very acceptable. It is still out of action, for it is almost impossible to get men on to the job of mending it. Everybody is so busy building stables and huts that the Canteen must wait. Meanwhile it still stands under the shadow of the church, and I have had to put my groom into harness as Assistant Canteen Manager to cope with the rush of orders [in the village of Bus].

Since writing I have changed my billet again, the mad woman was quite impossible. For the time being, I hope I am now permanently settled (this is a trifle Hibernian) in a large stone-flagged room with Roger the Interpreter.

All available floor space is stacked with cases of salmon & cigarettes, biscuits and candles, and we live in an atmosphere of shop. This is my stores and general dump from which I feed my Noah's Ark, and the Regimental Canteens.

Tuesday and Wednesday I spent with the Battalion in the trenches. They went up last Sunday, and have had a hard time, for the weather has been as bad as bad can be, and the trenches sloughs of despond. One little bright ray of satisfaction was the capture of two German prisoners. The trenches are so bad, & such a maze of shell holes and mud, that these two wandered into our lines by mistake. They were the postmen of the Battalion opposite to us, and were laden with Christmas mail!

The Christmas parcels of sausage and cake got no further than our front line, but the cards and letters have been sent back for the Staff to read and digest. There may be some useful information, or at any rate an indication of the public morale.

Yesterday I tried a new experiment, which I intend to repeat. I posted notices up in the Field Ambulance calling for a Debate on the subject 'How and why the Church has failed', and fixing time and place. Last night I rode over and found about twenty men waiting for me, so round the stove in their billet we tried to find the cause of the apparent apathy of the masses for what we feel is the very foundation of our life. I opened the debate by explaining that we chaplains felt that we had a pearl of great price which we wanted to share with all, but were astounded and perplexed that so many were not only unwilling, but were absolutely unconscious of the need; and appealed to them to tell me what they would do in my place. Of course we had to listen to the tales of erring parsons and the scandals of formality, but on the whole it was a great help and at any rate we broke new ground. Quite a lot of the men commented on the fact that it was a sign of the new era that the church should come as it were to the working man and ask his advice.

28 December 1916. I am afraid you will have thought that I have let Christmas pass almost unnoticed. I certainly feel that I have neglected you shamefully, but the flesh has been so busy that the spirit really hasn't had a look in.

I had the whole Brigade out of the trenches, billeted in villages behind the line, so really the greater part of the days was spent riding from one to the other.

At 8 pm we all sat down, packed like sardines in the HQ Mess room, for our Christmas dinner. The dinner was excellent and of traditional dimensions and of traditional fare.

After dinner everyone had to give of his best – make a speech, sing a song or dance a dance. The fun of it was that the last performer had the joy of nominating his successor. Later on in the evening, or rather early next morning, the Brigade Staff and other old friends came in, and we kept things going until the sma' wee hours.

2 January 1917. I am sitting in my billet – a large stone-flagged room, rather gloomy and very cold for it boasts no fire-place, and the only means of heating it is my little oil stove, for which paraffin is necessary but unobtainable. Tonight however is very mild, and my own blue blood keeps me warm. Facing me whenever I look up is a wall of packing cases – my stores, from which I feed my travelling Canteen. At the moment there are twenty-one of them.

I have nothing else to write about so I'll tell you what they contain. Wild Woodbines of course, in tins and in packets, Goldflake and Players likewise, also various makes of tobacco from John Cotton to plug, tins of milk, writing pads, Butterscotch, HP Sauce, candles, biscuits, tins of pineapple chunks, a case of sardines at a franc a tin, matches, bachelor buttons, Quaker Oats, chocolate plain and cream, salmon and lobster both in the ubiquitous tins, soap of various kinds from carbolic and Sunlight to Wrights Coal Tar and Pears, tinned tomatoes, bootlaces, button brushes, Soldiers Friend and Ginger-breads, to say nothing of chewing gum and slabs of cake. I am fast becoming the complete shopkeeper and go off in a lorry or limber to the neighbouring towns to think nothing of spending 2000 francs at a time, coming home again with boxes and cases by the score. It's a great game. Our daily turn-over at the Canteen is about 500 francs, but it varies in proportion to the length of time since last pay day. If all else fails me, I shall start a General Stores at Raughton Head and shall expect your patronage.

I don't suppose you will be surprised when I say that Niger is lost! I tied him up to a telegraph post outside Brigade Headquarters yesterday afternoon while I went in to see the General and took tea off him. When I came out an hour later Niger had broken his head rope, but was grazing about ten yards away. As soon as he saw me he threw up his heels and scampered off, for all the world as if he had been waiting for me to come out in order to show me what he thought of me. It was getting dark but I managed to follow him, and he let me get within about five yards of him before he gave three bucks and with a final high kick went off at the gallop. When I last saw him he was making for the sea, and at the rate he was going he ought to have arrived by this time. Anyhow I have seen nothing more of him, and incidentally got very tired and dirty sloshing home through the mirey mud.

On Sunday, the last day I actually possessed a horse, I had to walk to Courcelles, the site of a village near the line because my lord Niger lost a shoe on his way from his stable [sic] to my billet. Consequently I was a trifle late and arrived steaming, and my back nearly broken under the weight of 500 hymn books which I had had to hump along as best I could. The Congregation – bless 'em – having been fitted into the old barn with a shoe horn, couldn't move about or stretch their legs while waiting for their tarrying parson, but they seemed to bear me no ill will when I did at last arrive, and we had a most delightful Service, with the drums and fifes wheezing out the hymns outside.

The barn is used as a men's billet, and has been fitted up with two tiers of bunks, rabbit-netting over a wooden framework. These bunks occupy the whole floor space so my congregation had to sit packed like sardines in two layers the whole time. Fancy saying the Creed or singing 'The King' sitting like a tailor!

10 January 1917. Since my last letter we have moved back from the front area to rest billets [at Halloy], about twenty miles behind the line. Here we are, as we fondly hope and pray, for six weeks rest and training in a sleepy little village out of sight and sound of the guns. The billets on the whole are good; I share with Roger the

Interpreter a large bedroom in a little cottage owned by a mother and daughter whose total ages are 160! Mother for ninety-five is extraordinary active and has all her faculties but no hair! And both are extremely kind and hospitable.

Niger is still missing, I am afraid I must give up all hope now of finding him again. I am awfully sorry for he suited me down to the ground, and was a really excellent cob. In default of a pony I am working Shank's Mare to death, and my boot bills will go up alarmingly!

Spot I am glad to say, is still faithful, and refuses to let me out of his sight. He is developing a great taste for mud baths. Nothing pleases him so much as a stone thrown into the middle of a deep muddy pool. In he goes with a running dive, and for the next few minutes you can hear nothing but snorts and grunts and snuffles, until he reappears triumphant, but oozing mud from eyes and ears and nose. The next stage in his ascent to bliss is to roll himself dry on my blankets or to sit dripping on my bedroom slippers.

14 January 1917. We are fast settling down in our new homes [near Halloy], and are already beginning to forget what war is like. The whole Brigade is billeted in two little villages separated by a railway. The General and his Staff are in a little detached red brick villa, the four Battalions are in barns and outhouses, with the officers thereof finding beds in cottages and farmhouses. Our Field Ambulance is also here, likewise the Engineers, the Trench Mortar wallahs and the Machine Gun Company. Personally it suits me down to the ground, for I have my flock all round me, and as I have lost Niger, I am lucky in being able to walk round my parish in about half an hour.

Here we hope to remain for a month or six weeks, 'resting' as the Army facetiously calls the course of training which it has mapped out for us. However it is a great relief to be out of the liquid mud area, and to be safe from the ever-present strain of a shell dropping at your feet as you walk abroad, or bursting under your bed as you take your ease.

Since we arrived, except for the day I spent in bed with strange and grievous pains, and a highly developed spirit of unrest, I have been 'all out' trying to improvise a Church, a Recreation Room and a Canteen.

Absolutely nothing existed when we arrived. The village doesn't even boast a paraffin and postcard shop, nothing but two small

131

estaminets. My Canteen cart is the only place where the men can spend their money with the result that the day's takings average about 600 francs.

As soon as I can get the place I am going to open up on a much larger scale. There is a three-roomed cottage at present filled with soldiers, which the Brigade have promised me, and there my great enterprise will blossom forth. One room will be the Canteen, where everything that Tommy needs will be purchasable at cost price. The next room will be a Tea Room and Coffee Bar, tastefully decorated with red curtains and coloured prints. There also on Sundays I mean to have my Celebrations. The third room is *très petite*, and will be used as a storeroom and a Barber's Shop! However all this is still in the air. What is an accomplished fact is my Church [sic].

I managed with great difficulty to beg or borrow a small marquee yesterday, and had it conveyed to a small piece of waste ground near the station. There with the help of twenty strong and hearty men we erected it – no small feat in itself for a marquee is an awkward thing to put up until you know the way, and I must confess my ideas on the subject were a trifle vague and misty. Next thing was a visit to the Engineers who undertook to put up the pews [again sic]. They are planks nailed on the top of stakes driven into the ground. At the same time they built me a reading desk and pulpit – an elaborate piece of furniture! – a framework of wood covered with green canvas, and big enough for three Cabinet Ministers to give election addresses from at the same time. However this time yesterday there was nothing but a piece of waste land, and today I had a simply ripping Service there.

Unfortunately it is all too small and when the Battalion arrived in full strength for Church Parade, it was impossible to get them all in. I suggested then that those who didn't want to go to church should take a pace to the rear, and was frightfully pleased when the vast majority stood firm, so we simply packed them in as tight as we could, men standing all round my canvas erection, and all down the central gangway and clustering round the entrance. The Band was also squeezed inside and we had one of the very best Services I can ever remember having.

Apart from these organising and building activities the week has been marked by the arrival of the Christmas parcel post. Each day the poor Post Sergeant staggers into the Mess, red of face and short of wind, under the weight of bulging sandbags. *En passant* I may say that the one thing which a sandbag never contains is sand, hence its name. Could a sandbag tell its life's story, it could proudly assert that it had clasped in its hempen arms coal, yes coal certainly, sugar, tea, candles, bread, dirty socks from the Trenches, all manner of tinned rations, the Royal Mail, the Padre's hymn books, RE stores, bombs and I know not what else besides. Everything that has to be carried is carried in sandbags. It is the soldiers' portmanteau and string-bag combined. For quite a long time I never could understand why the sugar out here was always flecked with tea leaves, and full of wirey hairs. But I solved the mystery one day when I saw rations being issued at the Quartermaster's stores.

The men who come for the Companies' rations produce a sand-bag into which is poured the day's issue of sugar, the bag is then tied, more or less securely, round the middle with a piece of string, and then on the top is poured the day's issue of tea, again a piece of string seals the mouth of the bag, and any remaining space is filled up with candles or tins of plum and apple.

The hapless bag is then carried umpteen miles on the shoulder of a more hapless man, and unless there is a special providence to look after sandbags, the string is sure to come undone and the sugar and tea join hands, and that's the reason why you always eat dry tea on your porridge!

This morning, in the dark early hours when I arose, I looked out like King Wenceslas onto a world where the snow lay round about, thick, and white, and even. But the thaw has come, and all is dripping. White patches still remain in the shadows, which with the red tint in the sky and the blue numbness of my fingers, speak with insistent and patriotic voice of the red, white and blue of old England, and of *la belle France. Vive l'entente, c'est la guerre!*

22 January 1917. Today is the day to which I have been looking forward most ardently, as I hoped to get away on leave this morning, but my leave is off. I now count on the Battalion roster, and so have to wait my turn. We are sending one officer on leave every eight days and there are ten who go before me, so as far as I can see I have little hope of getting away before the beginning of April.

On Tuesday morning I set off on the front-seat of a motor lorry with my pockets bulging with money for a day's shopping in Abbeville. Halfway there I was so cold that I stopped the lorry and clambered in behind, preferring to be jolted to death, to death by

133

freezing. After a two hours' journey we arrived at 10.30 and at once started buying largely biscuits, chocolate, & tinned salmon. The Brigade Interpreter, Leo, went with me, and shared my labours and my lunch. Until 5.30 we practically never stopped, and by that time we had filled the lorry, so after a cup of coffee to keep us warm we started back, and arrived triumphant. Everything that we most wanted we managed to find, except good English beer, so the day's work was much appreciated by the various Canteens and Officers' Messes for whom we went shopping.

Just in case I should find time hanging heavily on my hands, I have been appointed Brigade representative on the Committee of Recreational Training, and went to a meeting at Divisional HQ on Friday. While we are out resting, we are going to have great football competitions, ditto boxing, bayonet fighting, cross-country marathons, and I know not what else. The football is already in full swing, and we, the King's Own, play the French Mortar Battery *cette après midi*.

Yesterday between my fifth and sixth Service, I went off with one or two more to find a course for the cross-country run, and walked umpteen miles over frozen plough and snow-covered stubble, and mapped out a three mile course which will take a good man to complete. The winner will have to be nothing less than a superman.

The country round about is very much like the Westmorland moors, and hares and partridge abound. Yesterday in the course of our two hour tramp we put up at least ten hares, and killed one which we found snared. And as for partridge, our Mess cart killed one on the road, ran clean over its head!

5 February 1917. The cold weather still continues. Personally, I never remember such a spell of frost before and we will feel that it is being wasted shamefully. What a time we could have at home skating and tobogganing.

Out here, we can make no use of it at all, and with draughty billets and a shortage of fuel, we are already beginning to think mud and rain are preferable as long as it is warmer. It really is perishing cold. I have a stone-flagged bedroom, which is like an ice-house. Each morning my water is frozen in its jug, and all my hairbrushes, toothbrushes, sponge and soap frozen to the top of my washstand and my towel is stiff as if it had been starched. I go about looking like Bairnsfather's Alf with a balaclava helmet and a sheepskin and a pair of socks over my hands and sleeves. Even then, I feel cold. The only thing to do is to keep moving.

9 February 1917. We are no longer in a Chateau and we are not very comfy. Yesterday we moved again about ten miles to a village which before we arrived had ten times as many soldiers in it as its original population, so you can imagine that our billets are not the best. The majority of the men are in open barns with broken walls and no doors, bitterly cold and open to all the winds that blow. Tommy is an absolute hero, how he sticks it beats me. He really is the most patient long-suffering man. He gets the tail-end of everything except the fighting and does it all for a very problematical shilling a day. That's one of the paradoxes of the war – danger and pay, discomfort and recompense go in inverse ratio.

From the munitions worker who enjoys all the comforts of civilisation and home life, works fixed and regular hours, and doesn't know the word danger, to poor Tommy Atkins who enjoys nothing but the glow of satisfaction at playing the man, works all day and all night and is shot at dawn if he takes a day off, and doesn't know what it is like to feel safe: the pay is graduated from pounds to pence. In other words the nearer you are to the Hun, the less you get, either in pay or decorations. The ASC and similar Safety Corps get all the former, and the Staff and Chaplains get all the latter. Poor old Thomas, God bless him.

With that grouse off my chest I feel better. Yesterday we did rather a record march in the face of a cruel east wind; the Battalion came along in great style and all finished with the Band. But it *was* cold. We started with the wind on our left ear, and before we had gone a mile we were all suffering the initial stage of frostbite which doctors tell us is intense pain. The second stage is loss of sensation, but we never had the luck to get as far as that. I've never known such a cruelly biting wind, it seemed to sting like a lash from a whip. Everybody marched with their tin hats and heads on one side and with their left hands grasping their ears [to Wanquetin].

Chapter 7

Success in Action – and the Cost

The Battle of Arras, the Scarpe, April 1917

17 February 1917. Every Division, the Corps, and Army out here has its Schools of Instruction in which young officers are taught bombing, or musketry, or machine gunning, or physical jerks. Every branch of the service in fact has its School in which its own particular art is taught, so it was only right that the Chaplains' Department should have its School of Instruction too. It caused great amusement in the Mess, however, when the Senior Chaplain came along last Monday and asked me if I would like to go for a week's course at the Padres' School which had just opened at St. Omer. I jumped at the idea, though none of us had the very slightest idea of what we were to be taught to do, or what the week's course would be like. I confessed my chief motive in coming was the desire for a week's holiday, leave being napooh, out of the sound of the guns.

The School, so-called, is housed in the house of an Avocat, as I learn from the brass plate outside, but what has happened to him, or where he lives now I know not. It is a large house in the square near the cathedral – the Place Victor Hugo.

Here we are for a week, and having a really very good time. The word 'School' is a misnomer, but necessary to satisfy the Army Authorities.

There are twenty-five of us here, all good fellows, nearly all from the Front, though one or two from the Bases. We have a daily Celebration, and the Daily Offices, and a couple of lectures, but apart from that our time is our own. Yesterday we had a quiet day, and another one tomorrow. The joy of the whole thing is meeting other fellows and exchanging experiences and picking up tips, and really for a bunch of Padres we are quite a merry crew.

The chapel is rather nice, and it is a joy to visit after pigging it in barns and dirty huts for so long.

26 February 1917. For some reason unknown and unknowable, we were not allowed to go the shortest way to our destination, but sent round on a circular tour. It's a way of the army, when wishful to proceed from Aldershot to London, to choose the line of advance which includes the most changes and to approach London from the east, touching Dover and Margate en route. That's analogous to the journey we were ordered to take. All Friday we spent in the train. Luckily we had a nice, large and airy first-class carriage, really a small saloon, in which seven returning Chaplains, including a Canadian Bishop, lolled at their ease. The shades of night had already fallen when we reached the outskirts of Boulogne, and all was peace when suddenly came a terrific crash and we all pitched onto the floor; even the slowest witted grasped the fact that we had left the line, for we bumped along over the sleepers amid a terrific splintering of glass and grinding of breaking iron and woodwork. As we lay huddled inextricably on the floor, we were subjected to a bombardment of packs and water bottles and other hard and knobbly articles from the racks, then the floor began to slope up until it was an angle of 45°, and we all slithered down to the bottom end, everyone saying 'keep cool' and trying to get a spring off each other's face or tummy towards the top-end and safety. Imagine all this going on in the pitch dark. The only funny thing about the whole adventure was the speed with which the Bishop got through what was left of the window!

When at length we managed to crawl out of the wreckage, and to get a light on the scene, we found that the bottom end of our coach was within a few feet of the canal, into which five or six luckless fellows jumped in their eagerness to leave the train. They all said afterwards that they thought it was a hard white road, and got the shock of their lives when they disappeared in the icy stream.

The compartment we were occupying was the middle one of three. The ones each side were absolutely cut off, they simply didn't exist, and the poor fellows in them were badly mauled, and one or two were pinned under the wreckage, groaning and shouting for help.

It was a beastly experience. It was miraculous how our compartment escaped being reduced to matchwood, and its seven occupants emerged untouched.

Of course, to complete the story I ought to be able to say that the seven Chaplains were all reading their Bibles, but as a matter of fact we were playing card tricks when the crash came!

Our coach was the only one which jumped the rails, and being the front one of all, it was concertinaed between the engine and the weight of the train behind, which coming on after the engine stopped, pushed us out of the way and then flung one end in the air.

When all was over the remnants of our coach was at right angles to the rest of the train, one end perched up on the next coach, and the other end trying to paddle in the canal.

After a long period of hanging about, wondering what to do next, we were marched back to Boulogne, and got rooms for the night in the Hôtel Meurice.

It was rather a quaint feeling, being in Boulogne. So near the leave boat, and yet not for leave. You can picture me wistfully looking seawards and thinking of what might have been.

Sunday morning later, I found my way up to the Battalion, stopping at the Divisional HQ for lunch, and the Brigade HQ for tea. The Battalion I found in billets in a city [Arras], which lies, *mirabile dictu*, within half a mile of the front line.

It is perfectly astounding how this city has escaped the fate of Ypres. On an ordinary light night, no-one would imagine that it wasn't a peaceful and prosperous city, untouched by war. Daylight however reveals the scars of shells, broken houses, roofless sometimes, windowless often, but still occupied by the hardy natives. Life here is an entirely new sensation. All day long the streets are empty, bullets whistle down them, and shells scream overhead and burst occasionally on some house. At night-time however the city comes to life, cafés open, and soldiers surge everywhere. And 800 yards away is no man's land, and the hateful Hun!

Here, we live in a furnished house, the best billet we have ever had, carpets on the floors, pictures on the wall, fires in our bedrooms and all the luxuries of civilisation.

Certain parts of the city are of course very unhealthy, and are simply levelled to the ground, but as a whole the city still stands and lives.

It's like nothing else on earth, or at least on the Western front. I can't describe the extraordinary sensation of living in a civilised house, and walking down city streets and thinking that any moment the Hun may throw a shell at you at short range.

As you walk abroad, you run into a party of French women, dressed up in all their Sunday clothes going to Mass, and the next minute you find barbed wire across the street with a machine gun emplacement at the corner, firing at the Bosch trenches – indirect fire of course.

Last night I went to Church in a topping chapel fitted up in a large hall over a Soldiers' Club. The place was packed and we had the most church-like Service I have ever been to out here. We sang the psalms and the chants. I can say no more than that, but it just makes all the difference.

This morning I took advantage of the daily Celebration which is held in the chapel, to offer up my very heartfelt thanks for my miraculous escape from the train wreck. Halfway through the Service some guns in the courtyard below and in the garden next door started blazing away – an awful din, made worse by the echoes thrown from wall to wall. There was a local raid on, which I am glad to say was entirely successful, and several prisoners were brought in, eyes gaping at the strangeness of their surroundings. The Huns apparently came over without any show of resistance, and our casualties were, I am told, only eleven wounded!

6 March 1917. One evening a party of us went to the opera house – a perfect gem of a place inside, and quite untouched. A Divisional pierrot troupe perform there nightly, and the place is packed. And all within fifteen minutes walk of the front line!

It's funny how safe one feels there too. I think there must be some ostrich blood in there somewhere. At Longueval, I remember, some extraordinary minded person pitched a tent just near our Dressing Station, and it was almost ludicrous to watch the fellows crowding into it, when the Huns started shelling. Even the piece of corrugated iron or waterproof sheet which often forms the only roof in the trenches, gives one a supreme and satisfying sense of security.

After all, that's the main thing. It's not being killed which is annoying or alarming, but the fear of being killed, which puts your wind up.

Last Friday, being March 2nd and the anniversary of the Bluff victory, our real baptism of fire, and the first nail we had the chance of driving into the coffin of the Germans' hopes, we had a little Thanksgiving and Memorial Service to which the surviving members of the Th' Owd Eighth marched, led through the streets [of Wanquetin] by the Band. The Church Army Hut was packed, and we had rather a nice little Service, and we took a resolution to love the things which our pals died to protect, and to hate with a bitter hatred the things which brought them to their death.

This afternoon we had a visit from the C-in-C. The Battalion was drawn up in fighting kit in a neighbouring field when Sir Douglas arrived with umpteen other generals. It was rather a pleasing sight to see a small fleet of five spotless cars draw up and disgorge their loads of resplendent brass hats, red tabs, and glittering field boots all complete.

The good man had only fifteen minutes to spare us, so the inspection was soon over, but I think even a fleeting glance of our Commanders is good for the morale of the troops.

12 March 1917. Last night we had a discussion to which a big crowd of fellows came. The subject was 'A soldier's religion' and we had quite an instructive time, not unmixed with humour.

It's a great help to the clergy to know what exactly Tommy believes and why he doesn't like church Services. They all seem to have a great dislike of dogma or creed, and a real grasp of the fact that Christianity is a life, and a fellowship.

19 March 1917. Big things are happening. The Hun is falling back in front of our sector, burning villages as he goes. We are out resting at the moment but expect any minute to be rushed up to join in the hunt.

Last night wires kept coming in, another village evacuated, then another, the Cavalry through etc. It *was* exciting. And everybody except your humble optimist, slept in his boots ready for the call, but here we are this morning still unsummoned. We are some twelve miles back, so of course are missing the thrill of occupying without a shot being fired the trenches and villages at which we have peeked wistfully, day by day.

Hal writes from Birkenhead. Poor kid, I'm afraid Salonica has taken a great deal out of him, and he confesses his nerves are not too good. I can sympathise with him. This war is a *guerre* one hates more and more. Time, so far from deadening or soothing one's nerves and fears, only intensifies the physical horror and terror of high explosive and sudden death. How Tommy sticks it is an ever-present marvel. Bless his honest patient soul.

The other day, the non-combatants of the Battalion, the Doctor and myself, were invited by the Anarchist, or in other words the Bombing Officer, to have an afternoon with Mills hand grenades and revolvers.

Bombing is a great game, when there are no plans to hit back. We spent a very amusing hour, crouching behind a sandbag breastwork, and throwing live bombs into a pit beyond and listening to the bang. As a revolver shot I'm something of a marvel, and hit the target with commendable frequency.

The next day, we marched back here for a fortnight, training in preparation for the Big Push. On some downland nearby are dug a replica of the trenches which we are going to attack, but which have meanwhile passed into British hands without bloodshed. Rather amusing *n'est-ce pas?* What our next move will be I know nothing, and cannot even guess.

I am supposed to be in training for a boxing match next Monday – a week today. After much persuasion and against my innate sense of self preservation, I have been matched against a Captain of the ASC, who a few years ago was a Public School champion or something of the sort. I've tried to reduce my smoking and have sparred two or three times with our Adjutant, the Orderly Room being emptied for the purpose. The chief results of this being a very sore head and the conviction that I can never last three rounds. However, we shall see.

Meanwhile, I must write umpteen more letters. We had our first and I hope our only case of suicide the day before yesterday, and I have to break the news to the poor fellow's wife.

22 March 1917. Yesterday we played a soccer match against the local Field Hospital. Great was the rivalry and somewhat bitter was the feeling especially among the onlooking partisans, who vied in taunting their opponents and encouraging their own side in the same breath. 'Play up the soldiers' was a nasty knock in the eye for the non-combatant RAMC and cheered the King's Own immensely. The medicals caught it every time, and wilted away under the ironical cries of 'well done the body snatchers' or 'play up the Number Nines'. Number Nine being the designation of a pill, very much employed by Medical Officers for every ill poor Tommy is heir to, and which is chiefly noted for the disturbing influence it has upon the patient's night's rest.

2 April 1917. The journey back to the line took us two days. We marched off from rest billets last Thursday morning in the pouring rain, and were soon soaked to the skin. To add to our miseries the road was full of transport, and the checks and blocks frequent and lengthy. We arrived eventually at the village where we were to spend the night, and found that our billets were in huts, which had only been finished that morning, and that fuel did not exist. As you can imagine, we spent a somewhat comfortless night, and the joy of putting on damp breeches and boots is a thing apart.

Next day, as we were not to march until the evening, we bought a tree – a good big one – and with incredible labour cut it down and sawed it up into firewood, and so managed to dry our clothes before we started on our last stage back to the war. Again the road was filled with transport and soldiers, and the seven miles took up from 6:30 pm. until well after midnight.

The men were billeted in the cellars with which this city [Arras] abounds, while we, the officers, found refuge in an empty house in the Rue de la Paix. That night our valises went astray, likewise our Mess Cart, and it wasn't until the sma' wee hours that we got a meal and retired to our fleabags. However, we made up for it in the morning and had our porridge and bacon at about the time you were eating your midday meal.

We soon discovered that things are not always what they seem, and the Rue de la Paix was anything but what one might expect, so we sent our new Interpreter to find more salubrious quarters which he did just in time, for no sooner had we moved out than the Hun put a krump just outside the dining room window, and transferred most of the pavement onto the hearth rug.

Our new billet is a most delightful house, the home of a doctor, of taste and means. Where he is now, I know not, but his oak panels and his tapestry remain intact and delight the eye, and prove a counter-sedative to the incessant noise.

The three weeks which have passed since we were here before have made a great difference to the appearance of the city. Things are quite evidently boiling up for the Big Push, and the Hun artillery is more active than before, and life consequently more precarious. I can see that we shall soon be constrained to forsake our tapestry room permanently for the chilly security of the cellar. The most wonderful part of this strange city is its underworld.

There is a vast system of tunnels and sewers leading from anywhere to everywhere else; and connecting the city with vast caves in the bowels of the earth. In one of these caves is housed my Field Ambulance, so on Sunday I went to give them their Communion. A long gently sloping tunnel leads from God's fresh air to the caves and galleries cut out of the living chalk, seventy feet below. On emerging from the dark tunnel lighted only by the flickering candle which every man carries when he becomes a mole, into the electric-lighted main cave full of Nursing Orderlies and Doctors and the glittering instruments of their profession, gives one the sort of shock which Aladdin must have got the first time he said 'Open Sesame'. I wandered about mouth agape, charmed beyond words with the beauty and the strangeness of this hospital. In every direction rough-hewn galleries run off opening into caves and more galleries, so that one gets continually new and entrancing vistas of distant lights and moving figures.

13 April 1917. We have just got back from earning another clasp for our war medal [Serre], and very hard work it has been. On the evening of Easter Day we took up our position in our assembly trenches, attacked at dawn on Monday, and have been fighting and advancing without a rest or a pause until Thursday morning at 5 am when we were relieved and got back to some dugouts in the German position we had first captured. At 4 pm that afternoon I had my first wash and shave since Sunday morning, which made as wonderful an improvement to my general health, as it did to my facial appearance. Now after a good sleep, I feel quite fit and strong despite a heavy cold I can feel coming on.

Holy Week and Easter came and went almost unmarked. Everyone was too busy preparing for the great advance, and as we were all in cellars and sewers under Arras to avoid the death which the Bosch kept throwing into the city, it was almost impossible to get the men together for Services.

Yesterday, however, I did manage two Celebrations, one in the big cave at 7:30 am, to which many of the Bearers and Nursing Orderlies came, and the second in our HQ Mess, the tapestried and oak-panelled room of which I told you – to this about forty officers and men came. I used the oak sideboard as my altar, and very well it looked with a carved reredos all complete. After lunch we moved out into the trenches, going up the whole way by an underground tunnel, and took up our position ready for the attack at dawn. Battle Headquarters were in a deep dugout leading off the tunnel. In this tunnel, or at least in rooms leading off, were housed everybody but the actual assaulting troops, such as Brigade HQ. Here we spent the hours of darkness waiting for the moment of assault. Zero was fixed for 5:30 am and as the hour drew near the bombardment became more intense, and the tension of excitement quite indescribable. In any case Beach Thomas has painted this picture *ad nauseam* so there is no need for me to attempt it.

At the same moment our Brigade, with other Brigades right and left, left the trenches and crossed no man's land, creeping up behind the curtain of our shells, and carried three lines of trenches without difficulty or loss of time. Then came a short pause while the barrage lifted and annihilated the next system of trenches. During this time the prisoners began to come back, in many cases carrying wounded men, both their own and ours. The next attack was equally success-ful and more prisoners came in. Again a short pause, and intense gunfire before the next Brigade came through us and advanced the assault of the third German system, including the battered village of Tilloy, and the strong point known as the Harp, from the shape of the trenches.

This was regarded as one of the strongest positions ever pre-pared, but such was the accuracy of our gunners that the forest of barbed wire was cut to ribbons, and all the concrete and machine gun emplacements were knocked in, and our fellows captured it with ridiculous ease.

Soon afterwards the third Brigade of the Division came through to attack the next line – some two miles further back, while we went forward to consolidate the Harp.

It was a wonderful sight as we streamed down the hillside to see the fellows in front advancing up the other side of the valley, with the Huns just topping the far crest. The feeling of elation was almost painful, and we almost felt as if the war was already won.

You must read the great Beach Thomas to know what a battlefield looks like; but so intense had been our artillery preparation that we failed to recognize the Harp, and began to dig in in the wrong place. The mistake was soon discovered, and we got to work to clear the captured trench and prepare it to resist a most unlikely counter-attack. We made our Headquarters and Aid Post by the side of a stranded tank which had failed to clear the trench and had slipped back with its tail in the entrance of a dugout and had stuck there. Meanwhile, the cavalry had come up and were waiting for the last line to be taken, in order to break through and clear up the guns and the retreating Germans. It was exhilarating to see the masses of Cavalry and the lances stuck in the ground in little groups, but unfortunately they never got a chance to get forward, as the Hun managed to hold on to their last line.

As soon as night fell we went forward in artillery formation to reinforce the Brigade which had been held up. Unluckily the message to move was delayed owing to the heaviness of the ground, and the difficulty which the orderly had in finding us amid such a featureless wilderness of mud and krump holes, and so we were not in time to take part in the attack itself but were in time to fill a very awkward gap in the line and dig ourselves in.

14 April 1917. To resume after another move:
When the Battalion moved forward, I unheroically moved back with a wounded man, whom I helped to carry to the Dressing Station in the cave. The Caves I have since discovered are really chalk mines, from which all the building material of Arras has come for many years.

The cave was full of wounded by this time, and I stayed there until three o'clock Tuesday morning, talking to the wounded and to a German Sergeant Major, with whom I exchanged views in French. He had heard nothing of America's entry into the war, hated the Kaiser, thought we were responsible for the war, expressed a strong dislike for the Tanks, and was of the opinion that peace wouldn't come within the next twelve months. After reassuring him on the contrary, I made my way back to the Battalion, and found the Headquarters in a German dugout attached to one of their late gun positions. Here also the Doctor had his Aid Post. All Tuesday we remained there in reserve, bitterly cold and not a little hungry. Between orders and counter-orders to stand to arms, the Doctor and

I prospected round and found another German dugout. The two pukka entrances had been blown in by shells, but we found a way in down the ventilating shaft. It was rather a jolly little place inside, and it was evident its late occupants had left in some hurry. I was rather intrigued by their names, marked over their lockers. Franders I pictured as the leader, mainly because of the breezy way in which he had written his name. Eggers must have been fat and sleepy. Schramm I think was the architect and carpenter, while a fourth man, whose name I have forgotten, had a feather mattress and a pretty taste in coloured prints. Finding plenty of firewood, we lit a fire, and smoked ourselves out, but suffered haddocking as a change to frostbite. Up and down the slippery and muddy shaft we clambered as each false alarm to fall in was given, but eventually we got word soon after midnight to advance at 4:30 am to the Brown Line, which was the name given to the system of trenches on the far crest captured during the day. Once more we went forward in artillery formation, and arrived at the crest just as dawn was breaking – a few minutes too late unfortunately for the Huns saw us against the skyline and shelled us pretty heavily. It was here I had my narrowest escape, and the Doctor did an extraordinary gallant deed.

The part of the trench in which we were was packed with men, when the Huns landed a 5.9 shell plump in the trench, and converted it into a regular shambles. One poor man's leg was badly shattered, and the Doctor, without paying the slightest heed to the shells which continued to fall thick and fast, carried out a most masterly amputation. I'm hoping he will get a DSO for it; we have put his name in, and right well he deserves it, for this is but one of the many gallant things he has done.

Later that morning we were ordered to attack the village lying in the valley beyond. Over the top we went and down the slope under a very galling fire from hidden machine guns, and the usual shellfire.

Before we could gain our objective, our attack was held up, and the remnant of the Battalion went to ground in shell holes, harassed all day by these cursed machine guns and snipers, who took a pretty heavy toll of the poor old Battalion. Later in the day, a fresh attack was ordered by another Battalion which suffered the same fate, and the survivors joined us in the shell holes.

The Colonel and the Adjutant had the supreme good fortune to take cover behind a mound, round which they crawled and found – what do you think, the mouth of a dugout fifty foot deep! Another

Hun gun emplacement. Here we made our Headquarters and Aid Post, and here the Doctor found a German helmet and I a German officer's greatcoat, which I at once donned, having parted with mine earlier in the day to a wounded officer of ours, whom I helped to carry back to the Advanced Dressing Station.

That night we got the welcome news that we were to be relieved, and at midnight staggered back over the snow to some dugouts in Tilloy. Tilloy by this time being almost out of range of shells, and the Germans who built the dugouts being Sybarites, we thanked our stars exceedingly. At five o'clock Thursday morning we got there, and knew no more until that evening.

15 April 1917. Sunday evening. I hope this bare uninteresting and untechnical account of the part we played in the battle of Arras hasn't bored you. One or two incidents stand out in my mind, both tragic and pathetic. In one of the trenches of the Harp I came across a German and a Jock facing each other, advancing from opposite ends of the trench with bayonets fixed, squaring up for a scrap. Before they could engage a shell had burst near them and killed them both. When I saw them they were both on their knees, with their rifles still in their hands, their heads within a few inches of each other, stone dead.

Another wonderful but pathetic sight was the Cavalry trying to get through, troop after troop galloped into a village held by the Germans – we could see them from the hill above – disappeared from view in the smoke of bursting shells and dust of crumbling houses, and after a pause back came the riderless horses.

However, last week has been really a wonderful time and the Huns have taken a pretty shrewd knock, which may prove to be the beginning of the end.

Now we are back again in 'our city', which is already thronging with returning exiles, shops are opening again, and beautiful women are once more seen in the land.

Where last week we walked in fear and trembling, Brass Bands play popular tunes today. Yesterday the first passenger train arrived since the beginning of the war, and drew up in what was once the station – now little more than a heap of twisted metal work, broken girders and shattered stones.

Leave is reopening; four men went today from the Battalion, so again I live in hopes.

21 April 1917. Since I last wrote we have remained in 'our city' though we have moved billets once or twice. I am writing this in the attic of a house near the Station. On the ground floor is a hatter's shop – as yet unopened for the sale of silk hats & gents' boaters. On the first floor is our Mess Room and Orderly Room, on the floor below me sleeps the Colonel and Major, while I share my little room with the Interpreter. It's a nice clean little cubby, but suffers from the same drawback which all houses in Arras have, the total absence of window glass, which makes it a bit chilly at nights.

I am writing at my table by candlelight, while my bed reposes on the ground by my side – a spring mattress salvaged from the remains of the house next door. Spot keeps me company and is making free with my pyjamas as his couch.

All this week I have been busy writing my letters to the bereaved. It is my usual mournful task after a strafe. In the moments of relaxation I have been meeting old friends. I am becoming quite a celebrity for yesterday I received a large blue envelope with a heavy piece of paper inside asking me to write a short biography of myself for insertion in Who's Who, and suggesting leading questions 'How many sons and daughters have you living?', 'Who is heir to your title?', and ending up with a space for Motor car number, publications, clubs and size in collars!

Incidentally, it may amuse you to hear that the General asked me a day or two ago, whether I should prefer a bar to my DSO or a Military Cross. I certainly don't deserve or want either when the men who do the fighting and get all the kicks go unrewarded. However as he insisted, I plumped for a Military Cross. No harm is done however as I'm sure the recommendation won't go through.

Apropos of the men who fight, rather a pretty little story. A very mud-stained and war-worn Jock bringing down an equally battle-scarred Hun prisoner passed a Military Policeman, glittering with Nugget and Shines – 'Hallo Jock, some fight!' – 'Aye' replied Jock 'and some don't!' with a withering glance at the immaculate MP.

You will see from the papers that we have pushed the old German back some miles, but we are still within range of a naval gun which fires off occasionally, and of his aeroplanes. A day or two ago a Hun plane came over among the clouds and dropped a bomb just down the road, which put our wind up very much and smashed the water main. These stray shells and bombs are really much more alarming than a real heavy barrage in the front-line trenches, mainly I suppose because there you are ready for them, while in the back areas they come unexpectedly.

However, my nerves are very much better than they were. I've come to the conclusion that a real-life battle is a stimulant and an excellent nerve tonic.

This afternoon I have been busy trying to salvage a much-battered concert hall and convert it into a church for tomorrow. With the help of a fatigue party we have succeeded tolerably well, but our comfort tomorrow will depend largely on the weather.

Most of the roof was on the floor and balconies, and very little where it should be. We managed however to dig out sufficient seating accommodation, and discreetly to hide the most obvious defects in the walls with pieces of scenery and wings left derelict on the stage.

Yesterday my Canteen van broke all records, and the man in charge, Private Reading, handed in as the day's taking 855 francs and £2.4.6, roughly £33 in all. The difficulty is not to find buyers, but to find supplies. If I could only get a regular supply of biscuits, chocolate and cigarettes in unlimited quantities, there would be no limit to my business.

29 April 1917. All this last week the Battalion has been up holding the new positions won, and has had a bad time. The Hun I think realises the gravity of the situation, for he has made strenuous efforts to win back the ground he has lost.

I think I can best tell you what we have been doing and enduring if I stick to a diary form of narrative:

Monday 23rd. The Battalion went up into the reserve trenches under cover of darkness [NW corner of the Harp], while I stayed back here to finish my letters, joining the next day.

Tuesday 24th. We were heavily shelled for about an hour, being unfortunately sandwiched between two Field Gun Batteries, so that we got the 'shorts' aimed at the Battery behind us and the 'longs' aimed at the Battery in front. While we were there, we lost a few men killed, including one topping little Sergeant who was a great pal of mine and a regular Communicant.

That night we went forward and relieved one of the home Battalions in the front line. Our HQ was in a cellar in a village, much mentioned in the papers [Monchy]. Three weeks ago it was a flourishing smiling village crowning a small hill, now nothing remains but scattered brick dust. All day and every day the Hun pounds it with heavy shells raising great red clouds of dust, but doing little damage luckily to the deep cellars. The cellar was a very small one, and the number desirous of finding refuge there a big one, so at the Colonel's request I retired back here – and I'm honest enough to admit that I wasn't altogether sorry. The Battalion meanwhile dug itself in some little distance in front of the village, and had a good number of casualties from the incessant shellfire.

Wednesday 25th. The shellfire, if anything grew in intensity, and one of our best and oldest officers was killed – a Company Commander, who had been all through German West Africa untouched. Poor boy he was another good pal to me.

The shell that killed him wounded the remaining officer in his Company, and so the command was taken over by the Acting Sergeant Major – the famous Paddy Moylin – one day I must write that man's life. He is the most astounding figure out here.

I heard all the news from another Sub, who got a bullet in his elbow, and who got down here safely during the night. I was in bed at the time when I heard two fellows stamping about the landing, opening and shutting doors. Half-asleep, I heard one say 'That's him, for there's his dawg.' Spot has his use after all, and acts as my identity disc in the world of darkness and blankets. Realising that they were after me, I enquired their business. It was an urgent message from Mr Millbank – the wounded Sub – who wanted to see me at once in the Hospital. Imagining him to be dying, I dashed into my breeches and British Warm and rushed off to the Officers' Ward and tiptoed into the room to be greeted in a strong loud voice 'Hello Padre, how are you?' then followed a long graphic account of what it feels like to be wounded. I could hardly believe that it was to listen to this that I had been urgently summoned from my bed at 2:30 am, and finally asked him what it was he wanted to see me about. 'Oh,' he said, 'I don't want to see you about anything in particular, I only wanted you to look in if you were passing.' The poor fellow got the shock of his life when I told him the time. This just shows how little one notices the passage of the hours out here, day and night means nothing, and all artificial divisions of time go by the board, and the only thing that matters is when is the next meal.

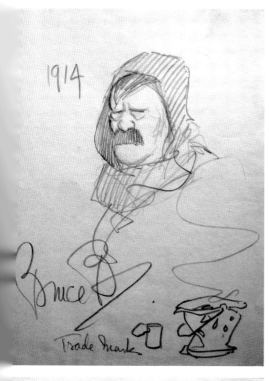

Cartoons drawn for Leonard by artist Bruce Bairnsfather when they met in the Trenches. They illustrate an increasingly cheerful Tommy Atkins. (*The Leonard Family*)

Family portrait of
Leonard (3rd on the
right) and his siblings.
Note that Hal (on the left)
also served on the Western Front
until he was wounded in 1918.
(*The Leonard Family*)

Temporary Chaplain to
the Forces 4th Class,
M.P.G. Leonard DSO.
(*The Leonard Family*)

Leonard and his dog 'Spot' in the village of Eecke. Both dog and village are much mentioned.
(*The Leonard Family*)

Leonard at war end. (*The Leonard Family*)

Colonel Smith – popular commanding officer of th Battalion, the King's Own Royal Lancaster Regiment. (*King's Own Museum, Lancaster*)

Bishop Gwynne, Deputy Chaplain General. (*From Ray Mentzer's* Photos of the Great War)

Leonard's stole and medal ribbons. (*The Leonard Family*)

One of Leonard's field services. (*The Leonard Family*)

Revd Tubby Clayton, founder of TocH, outside Talbot House, Poperinghe. (*TocH archives*)

Artillery spotting. (*From Ray Mentzer's* Photos of the Great War)

Leaving the trenches 'over the top'. (*From Ray Mentzer's* Photos of the Great War)

Wounded back in the trenches. (*From Ray Mentzer's* Photos of the Great War)

Massed Indian cavalry. (*From Ray Mentzer's* Photos of the Great War)

Boxing match. (*From Ray Mentzer's* Photos of the Great War)

By bus to the front. (*From Ray Mentzer's* Photos of the Great War)

RFC crew being debriefed after a sortie. (*TocH archives*)

The giant Handley Page bomber. (*From Ray Mentzer's* Photos of the Great War)

A German Taube aircraft – mentioned frequently. (*From Ray Mentzer's* Photos of the Great War)

The Upper Room Chapel in Talbot House, Poperinghe, 1917. (*The Leonard Family*)

The Upper Room as it is today. (*TocH archives*)

During the operations near Longueval on July 18th 1916, Pte T. Lindsay shewed magnificent courage & coolness, throughout a very intense period of fighting.

While acting as orderly, he came through an exceedingly heavy barrage to the Regimental Aid Post, which was at the time being severely shelled. While waiting there, a dugout some fifty yards away was blown in and several men buried — Without a moment's hesitation, & with utter disregard of his personal safety, while others held back, he rushed across the open, and was the means of saving many lives —

Apart from this, his gallant & fearless bearing was at once a sedative and an inspiration to all who saw him.

M.P.G. Leonard C.F. 42 atty 8th Kings Own Regt.

One of many letters to bereaved relatives. (*Written by Leonard*)

The army issue notebooks
containing the original letters.
(*The Leonard Family*)

Cover of trench map that
prevented shrapnel from
hitting Leonard's back. Known
by the family as 'the holey
map'. (*The Leonard Family*)

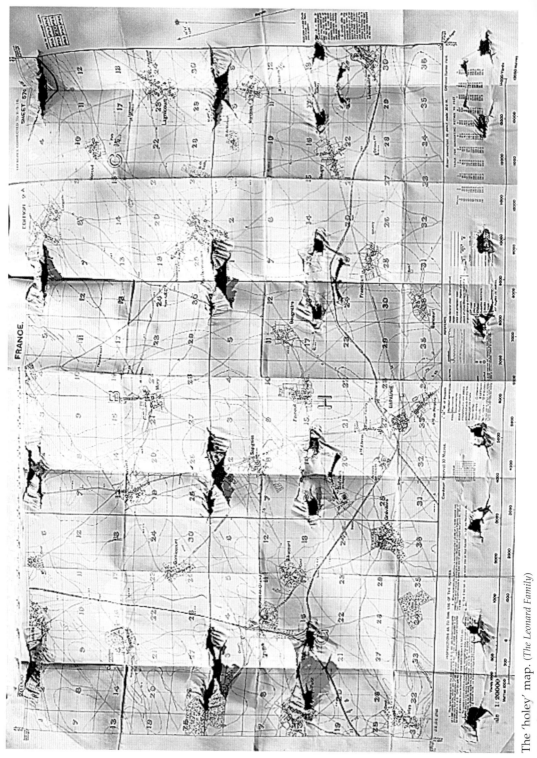

The 'holey' map. (*The Leonard Family*)

Thursday 26th. While we were having 'brunch' about 11 o'clock we were startled by a most appalling crash and roar which shook the whole place and rattled down a few of the remaining slates. We all thought the Hun had started to shell our city with a seventeen-inch, and dashed into the street to see the damage. The air was full of a cloud of dark brown smoke, rising in one huge pillar umpteen feet high. It turned out to be a dump of our shells which had been hit by a lucky shot from 'Whistling Rufus' as Tommy calls the high-velocity naval gun which occasionally fires a round or two at us. No great damage was done, and nobody was hurt, but one's nerves dislike that sort of thing after eighteen months' of war.

Friday 27th. I went up to the Battalion and stayed with Brigade Headquarters, which were in a chalk cave under the remains of a farm a few hundred yards from the Battalion HQ. This farm and the village were storm centres of every conceivable size of bursting shell imaginable. The Hun having occupied the ground for so long has every inch of it taped, and consequently he doesn't waste a shell in the wrong place.

I got to within a couple of hundred yards of the farm and lay in a shell hole waiting for a lull in which to do a sprint for the opening to the cave. It's exciting work, but once inside you are as safe as can be, it's getting in and getting out that is the tricky part.

That evening the enemy counter-attacked in force, but our fellows were ready for them and let them get within a few yards of our trench before they opened up on them with rifles, machine guns, bombs, rifle grenades, and every other form of offensive weapon imaginable. Not many got back to their own lines again. We captured a few prisoners into the bargain, and altogether the Battalion had its tail well up. It was rather interesting seeing the prisoners being brought in to Brigade HQ for examination. They were Prussians & fine looking fellows – not a bit beaten men. One in particular – an NCO – behaved just as I hope I should behave if I was captured, with a quiet dignity and natural courtesy. When he was brought before the General he clicked his heels and bowed slightly and addressed him in German as 'My General' and was perfectly polite, but refused to give away any information, and in a dignified way commented on the hammering they had given our village that afternoon. Not at all what you would expect from a prisoner, and as we fondly hope, a beaten army.

That same night my groom volunteered to come up with the pack ponies bringing up the rations, and so relieve one of the other men, for each night the Transport has had a rough journey and come in for a lot of shelling. It was just like Mather, who was one of the best men who ever lived, a real Christian gentleman. Poor boy, he got a shell right on top of him and was killed outright. I can't tell you how much I feel his death. He married such a pretty girl just before the war, and they were devoted to each other.

I came down last night and we buried him back here in the big military cemetery. The whole Transport turned out, and I knew they all felt as I did that we were saying goodbye to one of the very best friends any of us had had, and a really gallant fellow.

I suppose it's partly this, and partly all the other good men we have lost. Anyhow, I feel frightfully down in the mouth. This last show seems to have knocked all the heart out of me and I don't care how soon the war ends.

It is a never-ending marvel to me how Tommy stands it. This is the seventh day that they have been up in that hell, and they can't have slept a wink the whole time. My word, they are heroes all. You can't imagine the horror and the misery of one tenth of it, and I'm glad you can't. You think I have a rough time, but it's not within 100 miles of what the fighting men have to endure, and it makes me feel an unutterable worm to wear a DSO while they have nothing to distinguish them from the skulkers who have only got into khaki when they were forced to. Forgive me, I'm only a bit downhearted. If we get out for a few days and this lovely sunshine continues, we shall all get our spirits back and feel fit for anything again.

2 May 1917. The Battalion came back from the advanced position this morning, shortly before dawn. They've had a tough spell, seven days ceaseless shelling and sleepless tension, and they are all naturally frightfully tired. A long sleep and a shave however will work wonders, and help them to forget the nightmare they have been through.

I told you about the chalk cave under the farm in which the Brigade HQ was this time, but I didn't tell you the sequel. While I was there the constant pounding on top brought down a bit of the roof, but after I had gone they had a much worse fall. A German 5.9 burst in an old Hun bomb store on top and gave the place such a shake that a few tons of the chalk roof came hurtling down, and I'm afraid caught some of the orderlies underneath. Luckily the walls of the cave rise into natural arches, and so the majority of the fellows were saved by being under the lee of the sides. For a few minutes however it must have been a nerve-wracking experience for the Staff, who had to go on directing affairs by telephone and writing out messages and drawing up plans.

Of course, in all these underground funk holes, the fear is that the entrance will be blown in, and the people below trapped like rats in a cage. It is to prevent this that all dugouts now are built with two separate exits.

This reminds me of an extraordinary story, which I just heard from a Gunner Major. Tilloy, the village we captured on Easter Monday, and which today is five or six miles behind the front line, is full of dugouts and cellars which are occupied by our troops in reserve and by the gunners and anti-aircraft people, and all the hundred-and-one people who go to make up the army of today. You can imagine the surprise then of these people when the earth in one place began to move, and the head of a German officer appeared, shortly followed by his body and seventeen other Huns. It was a German Quartermaster and his staff, who had gone to shelter in their dugout when our bombardment started nearly a month ago. Apparently a shell or number of shells had fallen on the mouth of the entrance, so blocking it up that we never even suspected its existence. For three weeks at least, those luckless Bosch had lived in their dugout wondering why no one came to dig them out. Lucky indeed for them that it was the Quartermaster's store, for they were able to live on the supplies accumulated there. Finally, when their food was finished and all seemed quiet above, they dug their way out to discover themselves prisoners, left miles behind by the tide of war.

You ask about my narrow escape. It was simply the nearness of the shell which fell in the crowded bay of the trench and gave the Doctor his chance for earning the DSO, for I happened to be in the self same bay at the moment the shell burst, and was the only one to escape untouched. But out here a miss is as good as a mile, and the shield of faith is still mighty to save.

Leave, I'm afraid, is a rumour and at the moment I think the allotment is two per Division, per day, perhaps, so I don't imagine the U-boats will get a chance of sinking the transport I'm on.

9 May 1917. I had rather a good day on Sunday. The morning I spent down here in 'the city', having Services for the Field Ambulance, for our Transport and Details. After lunch I wandered up towards the front, over the lines and lines of old trenches captured on Easter Monday and now occupied by the Divisions in reserve. In the foremost of these [at Tilloy] I found one of my Battalions, and my Field Company of Engineers. As I had brought my books with me and the afternoon was sunny though windy, I soon fixed up Services for them. At both of them the fellows sat round the sloping sides of the biggest shell crater I could find, while I stood at the bottom. I suppose there were about 100 or 150 at each Service, but they were packed so tight that had I asked them to stand up I'm sure they would all have slipped to the bottom in a seething mass and smothered the parson. So I let them sit the whole time. After all, it is no bad thing to make them realise that the position of the body isn't vital to the right attitude of the spirit. Afterwards I had tea with the Brigade Staff, who incidentally came to the second Service and shared the dangers of a landslide with the men, while Dinwiddie our Staff Captain led the singing. I am exceedingly lucky in the Brigade Staff, from the General down they are all most charming and encourage and help me all they can.

Dinner I had with the Battalion up in front, and home by midnight to my little bed here.

I've just got to run off now and buy some stores for my Canteen and then I'm going up to the Battalion for the afternoon. The old Canteen cart broke all records on May 2nd, the day we came back from the front line into support. The day's takings were well over 1000 francs!

The weather still remains gorgeous, a small thunderstorm three days ago cleared away the sultry oppressiveness and laid the dust very successfully.

15 May 1917. It will doubtless surprise you to hear that we were put over the top again on Saturday evening. It seems that sometimes a brass hat removes the General from the realm of common sense and out of touch with human nature and the limits of human endurance. Our Battalion, reduced to 350 rifles by three weeks' constant shelling and sniping, was hardly strong enough to do the work allotted to it, even if the men were fit and fresh; but with them all dog-tired and worn-out with endless strain and want of sleep, with swollen feet – not one had had his boots and puttees off for umpteen days – and shaken nerves, it was suicidal to put them in for another fight.

However they went over with stiff upper lips, and undismayed spirit, and would I think have taken the Bosch trench had it not been that they were caught in our own machine-gun barrage as they topped a rise in the ground. That put the finishing touch on, and when they came back to our own line again under cover of darkness, the whole Battalion numbered 167!

It is only fair to say that the blame does not rest with the Machine Gun Corps; but the situation is all so uncertain and mixed up that it was small wonder that they didn't realise that their fire, directed quite accurately on the Hun trench, should in its passage sweep the crest over which we had to pass.

We were relieved in the early hours this morning, and came back a few miles to a rest camp behind the line. Thank goodness our troubles and weariness are over for a bit at any rate, and we shall soon be hard at work reorganising the Battalion and training recruits and new drafts. I came down yesterday, had a bath and changed my shirt – but without altogether foiling my persevering little friend – got a few hours sleep, and was ready to meet the poor old Battalion when it staggered down the long road this morning. I went so far to meet them, and as they came limping along in ones and twos tried to cheer them up with the prospect of the tea and bacon waiting for them in the original no man's land that we bounced over so gaily on Easter Monday.

It really was a pathetic sight to see them trying to smile through their masks of mud and matted beards. Gad they are heroes, every

From the KORL War Diary dated 17 May 1917. 'Following letter received from Brigadier General G.L. Porter, commanding 76th Brigade: "Please make known to all ranks under your command how very highly I appreciate their gallant conduct in front of Monchy during the recent operations. Their steadfastness and gallantry in taking up their line on the night of the 24/25 April and beating off the heavy attack of the enemy on the night of 27/28 April, are yet another example of the splendid fighting qualities of all ranks of the Battalion ... I most deeply sympathise with all ranks in the loss of so many gallant comrades sustained by them."'

one! And if they don't all adhere always to the so-called Christian code of ethics, they are at least very wonderful and lovable pagans.

After they had had their first hot meal for a week, we got them into motor lorries, and away they came here. This is peace indeed, and as I write the sun is shining brilliantly out of a pure blue sky, the trees are all in their tender fresh green coat which is the joy of spring, and poor tired Tommy snores to his heart's content. Later in the evening the great cleaning process will begin, and by tomorrow they will all look again like the men they are.

21 May 1917. Only a couple of lines this time, because this time next week I hope to be in Blighty and on my way home. After many false alarms I think I'm to get some leave at last. The Staff Captain – my good pal Dinwiddie, known to all as 'Mac' – has arranged a seat for me next Sunday night in a Divisional car to Boulogne, and all being well I cross Monday morning, and will travel up by the midnight train arriving in time for breakfast on Tuesday.

Chapter 8

God and Man on Active Service

The 3rd Battle of Ypres: Zonnebeke, September 1917

11 June 1917. Back once more in harness after a perfectly topping leave refreshed in body, mind, and spirit & certain that the war will end in September. Such is the power of thirteen days in Blighty to change a weary, jaundiced pessimist in to a buoyant cheerful optimist.

I had a good journey across, tho' the Channel was very foggy, and we had to endure a perfect concerto of foghorns and sirens. Luckily I caught a train from Boulogne the same evening, and after travelling all night in a packed compartment with a hilarious flying man who insisted on sitting on the rack, we eventually arrived here – back in our own city – the same old place in time for breakfast.

I found we are still out of the line, Glory be, and were having swimming sports, so yesterday afternoon I spent timing races and judging high dives. Today so far I have been trying to cope with the fifty-three letters which were awaiting my return, all from bereaved or anxious parents. So I'm plunged at once, and look back on my leave now only as an exceedingly sweet and pleasant dream.

21 June 1917. My last letter I wrote on Tuesday afternoon; in the evening we went up into the same old position again where we had had such a rotten time before I went on leave. But the three weeks that had passed since we were there before had seen a great improvement, and everything was much quieter.

Extract from the KORL War Diary dated 21 June 1917. 'The following letter received from Lieutenant General A. Haldane, commanding VI Corps: "The Corps Commander is now in possession of the full facts of the German counter-attack on our trenches, east of Monchy-le-Preau on the morning of the 8th June ... Thanks to the gallant stand made by the 76th Infantry Brigade, the attack of the enemy was checked and completely disorganised, heavy losses being inflicted on his troops. It is a source of particular satisfaction to the Corps Commander that the troops of the 3rd Division held their ground during the very severe test which they underwent with their customary gallantry and resolution. He wishes to remind them that, by doing so, they maintained their proud record of never having lost a trench to the enemy both while under his command and that of General Deverell."'

When we were first there after the successful Easter week push, we simply held a line of shell holes, which by degrees we connected up to form a trench, but we had no communication trenches or dugouts. During our tenure we did as much as we could to improve things, but the constant shelling gave us little chance.

After we went however and the Messurier battle began, things quietened down, and when we returned to our old haunt on Tuesday we found a regular trench system, with proper trenches and dugouts. The greatest improvement of all however is a light narrow-gauge railway which now runs up to within about a mile of the front-line trench. It's a most quaint little affair, rather after the style of the 'Little Giant' which dragged sightseers round the grounds of the Franco-British Exhibition. An electric tractor and a few open trucks in which passengers and rations and shells huddle *corps à corps.* The line runs through a house, two or three back yards, orchards, through a cemetery and so on, winding its way over the captured country, avoiding as far as possible the favourite targets of the Bosch gunners.

I went up on this little train and took up my abode with Head-quarters in a cellar in Monchy. Six weeks ago it was a pleasant village crowning a gentle slope, now nothing but heaps of dust and the reek of dead horses. The whole village is blotted out and it is impossible now even to trace where the streets were, or to find the site of the village church. However our cellar was deep and large and comfortable. There for the last seven days we have lived, by the light of a candle stuck in an empty bottle.

I daresay you read in the Daily Mail of an attack on a certain hill. The reporter called it a Two Minute Victory and described how our fellows suddenly sprang out of the trenches and rushed across no man's land to the surprise of Brother Bosch and captured two lines of trenches. Anyhow, whether you saw it or not, that was our little show, and the Brigade is very popular with the High Command as a result.

The actual taking of the hill, after four other Brigades had failed, was rather a triumph in its way, but it wasn't half such a test as holding it afterwards which we had to do for five and a half days until we were relieved.

Early last Monday morning the enemy counter-attacked after a very heavy bombardment and all but succeeded in winning back the lost position. In fact they did overrun the first line, but a small party of seventeen men under a Sub held on until our counter-attack relieved them. The Officer by the way is being put up for a VC and all the men for Military Medals.

Altogether it has been a hard week, second only to the first time we were there. It was a shock to be so suddenly plunged from the honey pot of leave into the seething cauldron of bloody war, but we are out of it now & back in rest.

After waiting all night for our relief, we got away about five o'clock yesterday morning & returned to our city for breakfast & bath. I came down by the Monday express of which I told you; the return journey is quite exhilarating for it is mostly downhill, and the little train buzzes along at a good ten miles an hour!

After breakfast I lay down on a mattress & slept solidly for four hours, until I was wakened by Spot licking my face and wagging his tail. Feeling stronger I made my way to the Public Baths & simply wallowed in oceans of hot water & shaved my beard & emerged again feeling a perfect gentleman.

The same afternoon we received the first fruits of our latest success; for instead of marching back to our rest area we were taken back in buses! It is only the third time that the Battalion has been treated thus since we've been out here, and we all appreciated the ride immensely. Just as we arrived at our destination the heavens opened

& a solid sheet of water descended upon us. Nobody grumbled however for rest billets are rest billets for a' that [Halloy].

I am in a farm house with the Doctor, and am amazingly comfortable with a table at which to write my letters home, & the new crop of letters to the poor bereaved.

I wonder if you would send me out the map I left behind by mistake – not the one with the bullet holes but a paper one folded plenteously – Arras & the country east of it.

26 June 1917. Life in rest billets is peculiarly happy. If only we could make war entirely mechanical, and eliminate the slaughter of the innocents, I shouldn't be in half such a hurry for peace to be declared. Apart from the killing and maiming of one's pals, life on active service has much to be said for it; it is a free easy picnicking sort of existence, with all the advantages of the communal life, and with none of the bugbears of a settled civilised existence, no rates and taxes, no butcher's bills or sanitary inspectors, and no Mrs Grundy to show the whites of her eyes if you choose to walk ahead in your pyjamas or play football on Sunday afternoon.

However, its advantages end there, and we all miss our home life and our womenfolk more than we like to own, and to the tidy ones of us – myself for example – it is a bit of a bore not having fixed places in which to hoard our *lares and penates*.

I sigh greatly for my rolltop-desk and a chest of drawers, for it is a nuisance to have to use one's library as a bolster, and one's clean linen as a mattress. You never quite know where you will find your one and only clean handkerchief if you are in a hurry; you may find it in the toe of your Field boots, or you may not discover it until you have turned your flea bag inside out.

2 July 1917. On July 1st last year we entrained at St. Omer where we had been resting and travelled down to Doullens where we detrained and whence we marched to take our part in the great Somme offensive. Precisely a year later we again entrained, but it is at least encouraging that this time we boarded our train at exactly that point at which last year we left it, and we were carried along past the scenes of our triumphs and our failures; and saw again in safety and in comfort the places which a year ago had filled our hearts with terror and our knee joints with water. It was a most interesting journey, and we all craned our heads out of the windows to pick out the most notorious and ill-omened spots, now so peaceful and harmless. The most abiding impression is the speed with which nature obliterates man's handiwork. What had been a howling wilderness of mud and craters was now hidden under a coat of green, even the trees which our shells had blasted and all but uprooted were trying to hide their scars with their leafy exuberance.

The line ran past our old rest billets, along the track we used to follow on our way to the war, beside the old communication trench, over the maze of trenches, through the mangled remains of our barbed wire entanglements, out into no man's land, then across the German old front line, and straight ahead into Hunland. You can hardly imagine the strange joy of seeing from a train & without fear of sudden death, what we had so often & so timidly viewed by periscope from the limited view point of our front trench. It was also a revelation and an impish satisfaction to see how thoroughly our guns had strafed the Huns, not only in their trenches but in their back areas of which we knew nothing. Miles back behind their lines we could see the effects of our shelling and could picture the rotten time they must have had.

Once through the belt of desolation we came out into the part that the Germans had evacuated at the beginning of this year, and saw with our own eyes the wanton destruction of which the Daily Mail had told us; fruit trees cut down, houses and barns shattered – not by shell fire but by charges of guncotton touched off inside – everything done to render the country unfruitful & uninhabitable.

We got out of the train at the remains of a big station [Achet le Grand] and marched along one of the national avenued roads to our camp [Bihucourt], a collection of tents and bivouacs in the middle of a rolling down. Every tree of that long avenue was cut about a third of the way through on the side nearest the road. I suppose with the idea of finishing them off at the last minute and so blocking the road against our advance. However the Huns never had time to finish their fell work, and now each tree has its bandage of tar and sacking round the injured trunk.

I believe we will remain here for a day or two, and then move up to hold the line for a spell as a change to the active fighting & assaulting which has been our lot since the beginning of April.

On Friday in the morning there was a ceremonial Parade & distribution of ribbons to the men who had won Military Medals in the recent fighting. In the afternoon a Brigade Transport Show.

Never have I seen the horses and the limbers look so clean; as the Transports marched round they glittered and flashed in the sun as if they were straight from the makers' hands. It was a very braw show and I think the King's Own were unlucky not to have got 1st place instead of second.

In the evening the Welsh gave a concert in their orchard to which they invited me, and afterwards a very wonderful dinner of umpteen courses, served on immaculate china with flawless glass and silver – all looted I understand from Arras.

9 July 1917. The day after I wrote my last letter we moved about eight miles [to Le Bucquière] and are now lying in support just behind the line. All the villages are obliterated, each building being blown up from the cellars, so we live the simple life in bivvies and rough-made huts, but as the line is extremely quiet we don't grumble at our removal from the comforts of civilisation.

My billet is a tarpaulin thrown over three walls of a kitchen – all that remains of a French cottage.

Yesterday unfortunately it rained torrentially all the morning so that all my Services had to be cancelled, as for want of a roof to cover us they had to be out of doors. In the evening however it cleared up and I was able to have two Services – one for the Engineers, and a voluntary one for my two Battalions. This last was held in the ruins of a large Chateau which the Huns blew up.

The Bosch, dirty dog, left a time fuse & a big charge in the cellars when he departed, and five days later the whole place went up in smoke. Fortunately knowing the Hun, no-one had occupied it so his trick didn't come off. But I'm getting off the point. About 400 men sat about on the lumps of fallen masonry, and Williams the Welsh Nonconformist Padre and I took turn about – the poor victims endured it manfully & we really had quite a nice Service.

This evening I am getting up more boxing, a novices' competition and a match against the East Ridings. I've just been weighing in the competitors on a spring balance suspended from a nail.

13 July 1917. I am writing this in our Headquarters in the line, where we have been for the last two days. If you could peep in now you would re-adjust your estimate of the hardships of active service, for you would see your son and heir sitting at a table writing in comfort in a nice little bungalow built with its back in the side of an embankment, which runs parallel to the trenches and acts as a buffer between us and German shells. Along the whole length of the front side of our bungalow are long narrow windows which look out onto the scene of rustic peace and beauty, for the floor is sunk about five feet into the earth, so that the turf just comes to the lower edge of the window. Inside, walls and ceiling are lined with green canvas on which are printed multitudinous maps and aeroplane photographs of our sector and of the Hun trenches immediately in front of us. On the table in a stone jar are about fifteen arum lilies culled from a garden in a neighbouring blown-up village, whence also come the redcurrants & the raspberries, and the cabbage & new potatoes which regale us at dinner. It is a beautiful sunny day & a perfect blue sky, flecked with puffs of drifting white. All is peace except for an occasional shell wailing overhead, and the warning whistle which tells us that a Hun aeroplane is overhead, and that all movement outside must cease.

So far the Hun has not discovered our whereabouts so we have lived in peace, but if and when he does shell us, we retire into a deep dugout through an opening in the back wall. This dugout is the usual type of long narrow passage, strongly timbered, with sleeping bunks in tiers all along one side. We only want window boxes with geraniums in front of the windows to make our Headquarters as comfortable a little crib as exists on the whole front.

Movement by day is not possible for fear of Hun observation, so we sleep and idle through the hours of sunshine, but as soon as dusk falls stern business begins, officers visit their posts, ration parties carry up food and hot tea to the men in the front line, fighting patrols go out to find the Hun and do him bodily injury, working parties dig new trenches or improve what already exists, and tear their clothes and spoil their tempers putting up barbed-wire entanglements in the dark.

I think I told you that our Doctor has gone for a change of air to the Field Ambulance. He has done his full whack of regimental work and has earned a safer billet with the FA. In his stead we have a new man who I think will worthily fill Doctor Wallace's shoes. A good fellow of the name Uttley, who got a wire yesterday that he was the proud father of a second son.

On Wednesday Wallace and I had a very jolly day together. He managed to borrow a car, and we went off after breakfast to visit Albert and do some necessary shopping. Albert looks very much what it did last year, when I saw it first, except that there is now a complete and satisfying absence of bursting shells. The famous statue of the Madonna and Child still remains in the same extraordinary position, bending over at right angles from the top of the battered Cathedral spire; and little has as yet been done to efface the ravage of shells. Although it is now miles behind the line, I was surprised to find that very few of the civilian population has come back, and that apart from our troops, life is practically at a standstill.

We went to shop but found very few shops open, except our own ubiquitous Expeditionary Force canteens which sell everything from gumboots to shrimp paste; and from sevenpenny novels to Coronas. We soon grew tired of the limited joys of Albert despite the pleasant little lunch we had, so set off to renew old memories of the Somme battlefield. Leaving Albert we crossed the old front lines and no man's land and then bearing off to the right went past the site of Contalmaison, of which not one stone or brick remains, between the two Bazentins, along the north-east edge of Mametz Wood, and so along the ridge which we captured a year ago tomorrow to Longueval and Delville Wood. Then we got out of the car and wandered about trying in vain to pick up old landmarks. It is quite impossible to describe the utter difference which a year has made; not a stick or stone remains of Longueval, and Delville Wood like all the other famous woods which saw so much bloody fighting last year, is now nothing but a few gaunt blasted trunks. Even with a map it is difficult to reconstruct the scenes of a year ago, for the whole lie of the land seems to have altered and everything is buried and covered in knee-deep grass and weeds. Even the existence of shell holes is hidden, and walking about is not only difficult but extremely hazardous.

With great difficulty I found the little quarry where a year ago I had the Aid Post. Since then, as the tide of war flowed forward it has been used as a horse standings, and is now deep in ripening oats.

Of Longueval, the village we fought through, there is nothing left. Nothing even to mark the site except a weather beaten notice board, half hidden by luxurious chickweed, 'Dangerous deep well here', and the twisted iron bedstead thrown up and caught on the stump of a tree. The road which had got worse and worse as we came along, soon afterwards disappeared altogether and was merged in the petrified sea of mud and krump holes, so we had to turn the car round and retrace our steps until we hit once more the main road from Albert to Bapaume. Gangs of men were working on it and it was in first-class order, so we bowled along past the site of Pozières, where General Birdwood has just unveiled a monument to the Anzacs who fell in the taking of the village, past La Sars and the Butte of Warlencourt and all the other sites of famous villages and woods.

The Butte which held us up so long is an insignificant slag heap, very much battle-scarred and with two crosses silhouetted against the sky. It stands some little distance from the road so we didn't go over to see it. Had we gone, I daresay the impression of insignificance would have given way to one of awe and wonderment at its potential defensive value.

Just as we were nearly at Bapaume we saw a huge cloud of red dust and black smoke spurt up into the air, though the noise of the engine drowned the boom of the explosion. The Huns were shelling the town through which we had to go. It was no good stopping so on we went with hearts thumping very near the top of our throats. Just as we got to the crossroads we suddenly saw the traffic man on point duty and a little knot of soldiers scatter like greased lightning and dive for the side of the road; we could hear nothing, but the next minute down came a shower of bits, and the pall of smoke showed us where the shell had burst some way down the road we had just come. However, we got through and out into the country again without further thrills, and so home to the comparative safety of the line.

18 July 1917. We are still in the trenches where the only things that happen are just what the censor doesn't approve of me writing about. Things are a little more lively than when we came in, but it is what we expected and absolutely our own fault. We always stir up trouble for ourselves wherever we go; it is now a tradition of the Division to transform peaceful Hun trenches into a hornets' nest with as little delay as possible [Louveral Sector].

On Sunday, the only Service possible was a Celebration in our Headquarters. Our little bungalow was transformed for the time being into quite a pretty little chapel; the altar with its lights and lilies and its Union Jack frontal looked quite nice. Unfortunately not many were able to come, only eight all told, but many I think were present in spirit who could not be present in body.

During our stay here I've had one or two funerals. We have a little cemetery just behind our Headquarters; it nestles in a little hollow, and there we have laid our dead just as dawn is breaking, with our own guns firing the last salute over the open grave. Rather impressive in its simplicity, with the little crowd of comrades standing round in the dim light [Frémicourt].

In the same little cemetery lies a German Sergeant Major who was challenged while scouting behind our lines in a destroyed village nearby. Brave man that he was, he refused to surrender and so was shot.

Much as I hate the Hun ideals and the Hun method of waging war, I have nothing but admiration for their fighting men, and I take off my hat every time to their courage and devotion. The papers which describe them as degenerate scum get my goat every time, besides paying a very poor compliment to our army which drives back these 'degenerate' Germans with such difficulty.

25 July 1917. Since I last wrote we have been out of the line for six days, but came in again last night. As we cannot move about by day for fear of giving our positions away to spying 'sausages', we are more or less tied to our dugouts, and thus I get my chance of writing to my family.

We were relieved soon after midnight and started our eight mile march back to camp in a fine drizzle which soon developed into a real live thunder storm, and so we trudged along in the dark wringing wet with our boots squishing & oozing water at every step. We got to our destination eventually to find our camp under water, but some hot tea & cold tongue waiting for us in our HQ Mess.

While we were having our second dinner, or first breakfast, the rain stopped and we went outside to watch the dawning of the new day. It was the most perfect dawn I have ever seen. The purple storm cloud seemed to roll back revealing the higher clouds above touched with all the glories of the rising sun, & tinged with every conceivable colour from the palest pearl grey to the purest saffron. It was indescribably beautiful. If I hadn't been so wet I could have watched it all day.

31 July 1917. After lunch with the Welsh I caught a lorry down to Bapaume where the Archbishop of York was holding a Confirmation. I had only two candidates, one an ex-Congregationalist who, did I give him rope enough, would hang himself on the pinnacles of Catholicity.

The Confirmation was held in a Church Army hut, and in addition to some 100-odd candidates were umpteen Chaplains, nearly all of whom had the privilege of shaking hands with his Grace the Archbishop. I was astounded to see how the last few years have aged him. His hair is as white as driven snow, and if it hadn't been for his firm handshake I should have thought his age was nearer seventy than fifty.

4 August 1917. There is little to record except a recrudescence of Auction Bridge in the Mess, and a ride on Mary – the Colonel's two hundred guinea hunter – over to my Field Ambulance to pay a pastoral visit and to arrange for a Service tomorrow.

The Celebration I missed on Sunday last I gave them on Monday, and I think the majority who waited in vain came the next day and bore me no ill will.

Sunday *après midi.*: No it was too much to expect. It was a foolish presumption on my part to attempt to write letters on Saturday. I might have known it was simply asking for trouble, and ought to have foreseen that it was an invitation to my underlings of the Mess and Canteen to come and produce accounts & demand moneys for the carrying on of the good work.

By the time I had got things straight and had found the necessary money it was time to pack up & get mounted. The RC Padre and I arranged to swap bedding again for the night so yesterday afternoon with my Communion bag slung in a pack on my back and my razor & toothbrush in my pocket I hiked me over to the Field Ambulance in time for tea followed by a short Service of preparation for Communicants and a Confirmation class.

This morning I had thirty-one communicants at the 7.30 [at Braulencourt] which tho' far from good is at least a little better than it has been. Afterwards I bicycled back to camp for Church Parade & Celebration for the King's Own.

10 August 1917. On Sunday night after I scribbled my last letter to you, I rode up to the village among whose ruins my Field Company of RE's live and had a Service for them under the cover of a bivvy sheet which seems to collect all the heat & oppressive closeness of a very sultry afternoon. After saying good-bye to them I walked across the fields to the sunken road in which Brigade Headquarters live [at Morchies] and had a Service for them in the half-finished new Mess Room. The General and all the Staff came and a good number of clerks, orderlies, and signallers. Dinwiddie – the Staff Captain – as usual acted as Precentor & led the singing while I said the special prayers for the Third Anniversary of the Great War. Having finished our orisons, I stayed to dinner with them, and then played two games of chess with the General and so home by bicycle in the sma' wee hours the five miles to my camp & fleabag.

This afternoon I went for a stroll with the Brigadier, combining exercise and fresh air with a thirst for knowledge of the Hun back area. From an observation post behind some fallen timber we looked far away behind his line and with the aid of a telescope became very intimate with the Bosch in rest.

We could see a village behind his trenches in which stray orderlies moved about, while out in the open fields we saw one fellow wandering about quite unconscious of our gaze. He seemed to be looking for mushrooms for from time to time he bent down to pick something up from the grass.

It is a strange feeling to be brought so near and to be so intimate with Brother Bosch in his wild state.

19 August 1917. On Monday, the RWF were having a concert and were giving a home-made sketch so I stayed down to see it, and then in the pitch-blackness biked my perilous way along the bumpy shell-torn *pavé* road which leads from Blank to Dash [Ypres to Menin]; the former being in our hands, the latter still in the Germans'. For short we call it the B.Dash Road, and a very much quieter one it is than the road from Arras to the same place that we knew so well at Monchy.

It was an inky night and had it not been for the occasional Very lights and star-shells going up in front, and the even more occasional flash as one of the guns fired which momentarily lighted my path and revealed the gaps in the sets, I think I should have had to get off and push the old bike. Through two devastated villages I wended my way meeting less and less transport as I neared the front, and then branched off along a muddy track to my destination – the dugouts in which the Brigade HQ are housed.

Had I carried on along the Dash [Menin] Road I should have passed our old Battalion HQ in the side of an embankment, on through another deserted village – deserted because in abject ruin – up a long gentle hill past silent figures in posts each side bristling with machine guns and primed with bombs until I ran into the barricade which marks the limit of our domain.

The other side for 1000 yards is no man's land, over which patrols roam from both armies looking for each other, playing a sort of Blind Man's Buff in which the bandage is the darkness and the penalty for being caught is generally death.

At Brigade HQ we almost forget about the war, and when the wind allows, and the Bosch sausages are not looking, play heated games of badminton.

I wonder if you ever thought what an unpleasant sensation it is to feel that a pair of eyes are always watching you from an observation balloon hanging lazily a foot or two above the far horizon.

If you have read The Thirty Nine Steps you will remember how the hero felt when he tried to escape among the moors of Scotland, and was spotted by the aeroplane which always appeared circling above in wide sweeps – a feeling of impotence and that nasty sensation when you wake up knowing someone is in the room.

The next day the Hun had a bad liver attack and pasted one of our Battalions for all he was worth. The Battery was not far away, so we watched the 5.9s bursting in salvos all over the gun pits. More than three hundred shells they threw over and exceedingly accurate shooting they made, but the total damage done was two men killed, one wounded and one gun temporarily damaged, and much earth displaced. The ground afterwards looked as if some long handicap giant had been learning to use his mashie and had neglected to replace his divots.

24 August 1917. The Battalion goes up again shortly. I shall go up for a day or two but am then hoping to get a few days' leave to Rouen to see my old Colonel and friend Colonel Smith, who is still there running a Records Office and eating out his heart in longing to be back with us again.

2 September 1917. I applied for leave to take and present to Colonel Smith the silver tray which the officers who served under him had made for him as a token of devotion and affection. The leave warrant however took so long to come, that in despair of it ever anticipating the declaration of peace, I sent the precious tray off by post. The very next day the warrant arrived! It would of course, wouldn't it?

169

So last Tuesday I set off by lorry to a certain town not far away and there after a short wait on the roadside, chatting to the man on traffic control, I picked up an empty Rolls-Royce going my way and jumped inside. Before I had fully digested my good luck I was at Albert, where I reluctantly parted with the car and continued on my journey by a local French passenger train. It was getting dusk before we made Amiens where I had to spend the night. My train left at 6 am, so I dossed down in a YMCA bunk near the station. About twenty of us in one room packed in tiers of three with a couple of army blankets each – quite all right as long as you didn't sit up suddenly in the night and butt the fellow sleeping above you. There also I had a couple of cold hard-boiled eggs and a cup of cocoa.

The journey to Rouen was uneventful and I fetched up at the Grand Hotel de la Poste in time for lunch. The rest of the day was devoted to finding Colonel Smith and telling him all our news and hearing his. He is in charge of a vast Records Office where the military history of every man is kept – a kind of gigantic Who's Who.

The pride of the office is a card-index system which they have elaborated. Each man has his own card, which is arranged alphabetically. It was an eye-opener to me when I saw the area occupied by these tightly packed cards. The whole of the upstairs floor seemed to be stacked with row upon row of them, until I could hardly believe that we had so many men in the army.

Rouen is the first Base I have seen excepting my periodic and fleeting visits to Boulogne en route for Blighty via the leave boat. Rouen is a city I knew and like – Rouen as a Base I loathe. It is full of soldiers, the majority of them waiting to come up the line as reinforcements. But there is more than a fair sprinkling of healthy young fellows who have dug themselves into soft jobs, and mean to stay there for the duration of the war. Having been shamed or coerced into khaki, they have forsaken their entrenched position in England and have taken refuge in Rouen. On leave, I have no doubt, they talk largely about the war, when their leave is up speak about going back to the front and get the required adulation and admiration from their doting aunts and cousins; but for all they see of the war or know of its hardships or its dangers, they might as well be in Aberdeen or Harrogate.

Colonel Smith, who has been trying to get away for the last six months, won't have any but wounded officers in his office, and they apparently are the only ones who won't stay. One fellow there who has already lost one eye, and still has a piece of shrapnel in his throat, took exactly three days to decide that it was no place for men, and he applied to be sent back to the line.

No, the conscientious objector is a man compared with some of these Base people. He does at least brave the scorn of all right-minded folk, but these other puppies who masquerade as soldiers have a still smaller intention of behaving as such.

However, there is a brighter side of the picture, and that is the WAAC or Brownies as they are called in Rouen. If the male Briton got my goat, the female Briton got my undivided admiration and respect every time. They are fine-looking girls, clean and healthy, and look uncommonly businesslike in their brown coats and broad-brimmed hats. Their clothes are sufficiently uniform to distinguish them as belonging to a Corps, but the dress regulations are elastic enough to preclude any idea that they are playing at soldiers or aping their male relatives in the firing line. Some wear the blue-and-white brassard of the trained signaller and telephonist, and indeed they are all specialists in their various branches of clerical work.

9 September 1917. Of news this week, I'm afraid I haven't a plethora. Chief however is the arrival of a new horse for the Padre. Quite unexpectedly I got a wire asking for my height and weight. I thought someone wanted to arrange a boxing match with me, and was very agreeably surprised when I got another chit authorising me to draw a horse. This time I drew a prize, a topping bay pony which answers to the name of Sunny. He's aged, but has been well cared for, and is very full of life and spirit. Short of my old Niger I know no pony I should prefer.

The joke of the week was a trick played on Davies, the Brigadier's ADC. He's a jolly good fellow, and a great Knut. His hair is always immaculate, so one day the Brigade Major and Dinwiddie the Staff Captain posted sentries all round and then replaced the unguent in Davies's hair-oil bottle with pure ration lime juice. For two days he used it on his hair, and didn't even smell a rat when he found his hair in a state of crystallisation. It was only when the stuff began to ferment and the stopper blew out pop, that he tumbled to the trick that had been played upon him.

Thus, despite the war, we manage to keep young. I'm just off on my new pony to take evensong in the Rest Camp run by my Field

Ambulance; and I shall probably stop to dinner with them; so if this letter is to catch the mail I must get it off before I go.

14 September 1917. Last Wednesday, four lorry loads of King's Dragoon Guards – our CO's old Regiment – came over for the day [to Barastre], bringing with them nine boxers to meet our nine doughty champions. All Tuesday I spent making arrangements, and having the stage and ring built in the middle of the camp.

The Divisional General, the Brigadier and crowds of brass hats came – an illustrious and notable company. From our point of view the boxing was disappointing for we were beaten in seven of the contests and only won the remaining two. Four of our men were knocked out in the first or second round. Tho' beaten we were not disgraced for our boys fought well and were simply outclassed. The Cavalry man is not only bigger and taller than his foot-slogging brother, but he has better opportunities for training and keeping fit. In nearly every case we had to give away a few pounds, and in every case except the heavies, our man was two or three inches shorter. In the heavies our man had to meet Corporal Mann, twice champion of India, and did well to stand up two rounds against him, swapping blows the whole time.

After the boxing we had a Concert and broached the main splice; there was great hilarity in the camp and it was with the greatest difficulty that the officers of the KDGs could collect their flock and shepherd them into the lorries for the return journey.

The officers having cars stayed to dinner and a singsong in the Mess afterwards. As the poet has it, 'we really had a most delightful evening'.

Today and tomorrow I am running a Brigade Boxing Tournament – I'm becoming quite a promoter of boxing – and between writing a few lines of this letter, rush off to see how the ring is getting on, or to interview judges, referees, or competitors.

17 September 1917. Yesterday we had a visit from Bishop Gwynne, the Bishop of Khartoum and boss Padre out here. The whole of the Brigade Group attended Church Parade [at Barastre]. The site was on a piece of grass between the trees of a destroyed village, and the barbed wire of an old German line. There must have been between three and four thousand men packed *à la sardine*, forming three sides of a square. The fourth side was occupied by the Divisional Band and a goodly array of Generals and Staff.

It was a beautiful sunny morning – ideal for an open air Service. In addition to the Bishop there were the Senior Chaplain of the Division (Danvers), the other Brigade Chaplain and myself. I took the Service, Danvers read the lesson, Vischer gave out the hymns, & the Bishop preached, each in turn standing on the sugar box behind the piled drums which formed the pulpit-reading desk-lectern.

Afterwards we had a Celebration in the marquee which houses my Canteen; empty biscuit boxes & wooden crates formed the pews and altar, and it was almost unbearably hot. A new innovation was a portable harmonium which Danvers has had sent out.

19 September 1917. I wrote my last letter after everything had been packed, and I was all dressed up and nowhere to go. While waiting for the hour of assembly we were all surprised by the arrival of a large draft who joined us just in time to fall out and fall in again, and to retrace their steps the seven miles to the railhead with the Battalion. It was a night march for we didn't leave camp until half past one. I marched as usual at the tail of the column with the Doctor. Soon after the first halt a figure came running back, appearing suddenly out of the darkness. He had foolishly left his gasbag, or box respirator, by the side of the road where he had been sitting. I knew he would never find it in the dark. So I went after him with my electric torch. Even with its aid, the Battalion had vanished in the night before we found the missing gas mask, so we had to follow as best we could, and succeeded in finding the Battalion again just outside the siding at which we were to entrain.

Our camp is in the home paddock of a typical Belgian farm [near Watou], with the buildings clustering as close as possible to the ubiquitous and evil-smelling manure pit, which occupies the whole of the courtyard.

The farmer here in addition to his other activities grows tobacco, and at the moment has it drying behind a palisade of straw. You would laugh if you could see the coarse large leaves, more like cabbages than tobacco, and yet he has got this palisade all round and he himself sleeps inside with a loaded gun to protect his precious vegetables from pickers and stealers. It's a regular obsession with him poor fellow.

Chapter 9

Loot in the Hymn Books

8 KORL *distinguish themselves at Zonnebeke and move; Leonard joins 9 Squadron RFC*

22 October 1917. The Battalion left the Ypres Salient during my absence. The Brigade did extremely well, and everybody was frightfully pleased with the way they crossed the Hennebeke and captured Zonnebeke on the morning I left for Blighty – September 26th [the day when the King's Own flanked by the Gordons and the 50th Australian Imperial Force [AIF] did 'hold on at all costs' in the very heavy fighting].

We were relieved in the trenches [by the 34th AIF] on the night of last Thursday/Friday, which means that the Battalion arrived in camp here [Mory] at 3 o'clock on Friday morning. It was a bitterly cold night and black as ink, and hanging about waiting for the latecomers was anything but pleasant. This time we got out without having a shell within miles of us.

I think my transfer to the Flying Corps will come through in a day or two now, but meanwhile I am busy writing letters to the bereaved of the gallant fellows who fell in the taking of Zonnebeke. Luckily our casualties were not very high, in fact, much less than usual. It seems to have been such a good show that I almost regret having missed it!

All Saints Day, 1917. Nothing very much has happened lately, for we have been in the trenches [at Bullecourt] and the sector is commendably quiet. Our chief enemy is the weather, which makes the trenches fall in and submerges the duckboards under a greasy glutinous veneer of mud. Our trenches run through a village that saw a lot of desperate fighting early this year, and the grisly harvest of war still remains in places. Hands and feet stick out of the parapet or trench side in a disconcerting sort of way. Personally I'm not so squeamish as I was, but I must own I hardly understand the mentality of one of our Sergeants who, patting a protruding skull, said 'You've done your bit old man anyway'.

The honours list for the Zonnebeeck stunt have been published, and we find we have snaffled 13 Military Medals [plus a DSO and two Military Crosses]. The man in the firing line is at last coming into his own.

Yesterday morning a sad catastrophe befell the Battalion. We had a man winkled! He was on sentry duty in the front line, and had just been relieved and was making his way to his shelter about twenty yards down the trench, when on turning round a traverse he apparently bumped into a German raiding patrol who had crawled across no man's land and hopped into our trench. The front line is impassable in places and is held by posts at intervals. The Bosch had cleverly picked their point of entry carefully between two posts, and were lying doggo waiting for someone to come along.

They either hit him on the head or stuck him in a fleshy part of his anatomy, for the people each side heard a shout of surprise and a groan, but when they dashed to the place the Huns and their prisoner had scrambled out and got clear away, discouraging pursuit with a couple of bombs.

We are all very sick and ashamed, for he is the first man we have ever had winkled, and we always pride ourselves that Th'Owd Eighth has no depot in Bosch Land.

Did I ever tell you the story of the hymn books? I arrived one day to take a Church Parade for the Royal Welsh Fusiliers with my box of hymn books, and as Dixon my henchman and churchwarden was in the trenches with the King's Own, I supervised the distribution of books myself. A Sergeant from each of the sixteen Platoons stood round to receive their dole while I undid the lid and exposed to their incredulous view as fair a piece of loot as was ever seen. Embedded among the books was a really chased bronze fruit dish, beautifully embossed with prancing horses and fair maidens. Joseph's brothers weren't half so surprised at finding their money in their bags of corn as these worthy Sergeants were at finding their Padre secreting his loot in his hymn books. I couldn't in self-respect explain that it was my servant.

It is now 1 am, all is peace except an occasional whomp of a shell somewhere in the distance. Luckily the Huns haven't found our Headquarters yet, and in any case our dugout is deep and well timbered.

13 November 1917. The Brigade moved into the [Bullecourt] trenches again last night and as there is rather a squash in the HQ dugout, the Brigadier has invited me to take up my abode at Brigade Head-quarters. So here I am installed in a very nice little 'baby elephant'. A baby elephant is Tommy's name for a shelter made of curved corrugated iron, arched over so that it forms a semicircle. The appear-ance from the outside is something like an elephant's back, inside it reminds one of a tunnel or a London Tube. The great advantage is that it is splinter-proof, and has no central pillars or supports to get in the way.

Well here I am with a nice warm stove crackling merrily, and an excellent canvas bed on which I slept last night.

The Battalion has avenged the loss of the winkled man. The following night a stout-hearted Sub, MacLean, went out on patrol with three men to see if the Bosch wire was cut sufficiently to allow the passage of a raiding party of thirty men which was rehearsing a stunt for the next night. MacLean, finding the wire cut, thought he might as well see what the trench was like, so crawled through and leapt lightly into the Bosch front line. While there, a Hun suddenly appeared round the traverse, so MacLean closed thrusting a revolver in his tummy. The secret of a successful *coup de main* is silence, and MacLean wanted to coerce him out without letting off his revolver but the Bosch was so surprised that he let out a yell and seized the revolver. In the struggle, the thing went off and Bosch went down with the bullet in his groin.

That of course raised the whole garrison of the trench and bombs began to fly in all directions. Our three men remained on top to keep MacLean's retreat open, but unfortunately they all got wounded and had to crawl away. MacLean was left in the trench trying to persuade the wounded German to come along. The Bosch unable to move kept saying 'Pardon, Pardon' which annoyed MacLean immensely.

Things by this time were getting pretty warm, so he did the only thing possible by seizing the Bosch shoulder-strap, wrenched it off and scrambled out of the trench and dived into a shell hole. The Bosch were by this time out on top searching for him and throwing bombs at every shadow. The three men managed to regain our line and reported MacLean was captured, but he wasn't and just as dawn was breaking he came in, covered in mud, but with that tell-tale shoulder-strap in his possession.

The value of the shoulder-strap is that it bears the number of the Regiment, and the one thing which both armies always want to know is the identity of the people opposite.

A prisoner qua prisoner is of little value, the identification is the main thing.

MacLean will probably get a MC out of it, and has already gone on fourteen days' leave. The three men too have been given the £5 and fourteen days' leave promised by the General to the obtainers of the first identification.

On Saturday, I arranged with the Concert party of the Field Ambulance to give the King's Own a show in the theatre barn. Except that performers and spectators nearly froze it was a great success; and the stage looked excellently well with a backcloth composed of green canvas on which the regimental crests of the Battalions in the Brigade were painted large.

After the concert, the Officers of the HQ Mess were invited to a musical evening in the Sergeants' Mess. They had got hold of the fact that I was leaving the Battalion, and very kindly drank my health and said nice things to which I had to reply. Rather an ordeal; I had no idea I had so many friends, and am now very sorry that I'm going even for three months. It is my firm intention to come back again when my time is up.

On Sunday after my Church Parades I had the joy of Baptising one of our Sergeants – one of the original Battalion, who, hearing I was going, screwed up courage to confess he had never been Christened and asked if I would baptise him before I went. I was delighted for he is a splendid fellow who won a DCM at the Bluff. The Colonel promised to be Godfather, and the Company Sergeant Major stood as the other sponsor. The Colonel's hut was requisitioned and with the help of a Union Jack, a cross and a pair of candlesticks, was made to look as much like a church as possible. Having no font I used my chalice and baptised Thomas George [Harrison] in the form provided for those of riper years. A very touching little Service.

25 November 1917. The great upheaval has occurred and I am now with my new unit, No. 9 Squadron RFC. On Wednesday November 14th I was up betimes and started with the General at 5.15 am to do a last tour round the trench. Early morning is the best time, for everybody is standing to, waiting for the Bosch if he attacks, and for the rum issue. Also the Hun gunners are generally in bed at this time and peace reigns. We went all round our system and were on the point of leaving the front-line for home when one of the new draft came haring down the trench & in a hoarse whisper announced that 'Johnnie was coming over'. So we hopped up on to a fire step and saw the cause of our young friend's alarm. Four Bosch were wandering about in no man's land as if looking for half pennies – I suppose they thought the ground mist would hide them, but we could see them distinctly. It was too good a chance to miss so a Lewis gun was turned on them & three were killed. War is a ghastly business, it seemed such cold murder & after all, Huns I suppose are somebody's darlings. It's got to be done though and killing Bosch is the only way to bring Germany to her right senses again.

We got back to Brigade Headquarters again at 11 o'clock, having been on the go the whole time and having covered a good nine or ten miles.

I see from my diary that I played chess with the General in the evening and beat him for the first and only time.

That evening my movement order came to report forthwith to the RFC.

Sunday I had my last Service with the King's Own and my other units, and after dinner had a little farewell party in the Junior Mess. On Monday I said goodbye and went off in the Mess cart to Bapaume with all my kit, my dog, and my servant.

Four days I spent on the journey north and at 9.00 pm on Thursday arrived at Poperinghe where I detrained and made for Talbot House. Here I found a bed and an old friend, Padre Clayton who runs the place. On Friday I rang up my new unit who sent a tender for me and brought me and my belongings to 'here' where I now am [Proven].

Everyone is charming & I know I shall be very happy. All the same I miss my old friends and especially regret having to leave before I had got into working order the chipped-potato shop which I had just started in connection with the Brigade Canteen.

My new billet is an Armstrong hut, canvas and wood, very *bon*. I shall make myself very comfy and snug. The Adjutant is a Captain May of the Borders, exceedingly friendly & nice, who lost his leg poor man out here & wears a wooden one very cleverly.

28 November 1917. I'm fast settling down to the new life, and am enjoying myself immensely. My parish consists of four Squadrons, two here and two about three miles away [7 and 9 Squadrons at Proven, and 21 and 23 at La Lorie].

In each Squadron there are between fifty & sixty officers – Pilots, Observers, and Ground Officers – and about 250 men so I spend my time getting to know new people and trying to remember their names. So far everybody has been perfectly charming and cheery to me, and tho' many of the younger ones drink more than is good for them, they are good fellows all.

I can hardly believe I've been here since Friday – five days – I seem to have grown up among them.

On Saturday afternoon I turned out to play rugger for the Squadron. It was a 'dud' day for flying so we went off in tenders to play some Gunners a few miles away. The ground was like nothing on earth, long furrows all down the length of it, with a metalled road behind one goal and a light railway at the back of the other. However we had a great game tho' they beat us by a goal and two tries to a try. After the game we all had tea together in a French farm house, and so back to the aerodrome in time for the evening Concert.

This Squadron runs an exceedingly clever Concert Party and has fitted up a spare hangar as a theatre. The stage, curtain, scenery & lighting are simply above criticism – as good as any provincial theatre, and the standard of the performers exceptionally high.

The next day, Monday to wit, I went off to a neighbouring town [Poperinghe] which I knew of old from the winter of '15–16. It is the Town in which is Talbot House and the dear little chapel I told you about and tried to sketch.

I have been roped in as the House Manager of the Concert Party and am therefore responsible for the advertising and sale of tickets. My trip to this town was primarily to see about getting some posters printed, but I took the opportunity of calling in at Talbot House to see Padre Clayton and to buy some wafers. In the afternoon I went to a third Squadron, introduced myself & took tea off them, and again found everybody charming.

Today I went over to my fourth Squadron to say how d'you do, had an excellent lunch with them and arranged Services for the future. On my way back I called on a Labour Company to offer my services – as usual I found they were nobody's children & had never seen a Padre before. So I've fixed up something for them too.

So you will see that I'm fast finding my legs and am not finding time hanging heavy on my hands. I'm very happy indeed tho' naturally I'm a bit homesick for my old crowd, who however have softened the wrench of parting by writing me umpteen letters. You will be pleased to hear Mother that in the RFC I am a Ground Officer; that means it is not part of my job to fly so don't torture yourself by picturing me flying over the line chased by Huns & strafed by archies. *Terra firma* is the scene of my ministration, and on *terra firma* I will remain.

5 December 1917. Looking back I can't remember anything of a newsy nature. I've done a certain amount to make my hut snug and cosy, particularly and chiefly have I managed to procure – a most useful and popular word in the army – a little stove. A canvas hut is apt to be a chilly home when the east wind blows and the ground is frozen, unless it boasts a stove.

I've also put up a few shelves, a picture or two culled from the Christmas numbers, and generally made a little home for my *lares and penates*.

Apart from my domestic labours I have held a few Services, played a few games of rugger, and got on with the work of making friends in my new parish.

There doesn't appear to be such a need or scope for a Padre as in the infantry – or rather I should say work isn't quite so easy to find, and people continually ask me what I do all day and how I manage to fill up my time.

I find it rather harder to get in touch with the men. They are always busy and being specialists are a good deal scattered plying their various trades. Unfortunately there are no trenches to wander around, where men are only too ready to have a crack to fill up a slack half-hour.

On the other hand there is plenty of work to be done with the young Subs. They are nearly all kids, the average age is about twenty, and easily led.

The trouble in the Flying Corps is that there is so much waiting. They have to hang about waiting to go up. If the weather is 'dud' they have nothing to do but sit in the Mess playing auction and drinking whisky or cocktails, and waiting for the weather to clear. Even if the day is fine, as soon as they have done their job of work – three hours' flying – they have nothing else to fill in the remaining twenty-one; and they can't get away in case they should be suddenly sent up again.

On really 'dud' days we play rugger on the aerodrome which helps a bit, but the majority do nothing.

In my own Squadron I am now quite at home, and rag them if they swear or drink more than is good for them & generally keep them in order. In my other three Squadrons, as yet I am a carefully and punctiliously treated guest and stranger. However I'm gradually finding my legs, and enjoying the change of air and scenery.

8 December 1917. On Saturday last I went to Cassel by car to meet the other RFC Chaplains at the ACG's office. We wanted to divide the work more satisfactorily according to territory rather than Army Divisions. This we did and I came back in time for a game of rugger on the aerodrome.

The Squadron has taken to Boxing, and we are hard at work training for a competition. I have been pushed in to run it; accordingly last night I got some of the officers to come over to the hangar where we have fixed up a ring. I had no intention of boxing and went over in a pair of gumboots. However the young wanted encouraging so Walker, who is a big heavy rugger forward, and I put on the gloves for three rounds. Naturally I couldn't afford to mix it with him, and did a good deal of skipping about in my stocking feet. Result a huge blister on the ball of my toe – very painful and crippling. Today I'm going about in a felt slipper, like a gouty old gentleman, much to everybody's amusement. However it's all part of the game, and for the good of the cause.

The night before last our searchlights picked up a Gotha(?), and at once all the beams which before had been swinging backwards and forwards across the milky sky came together focused on this little silver moth.

Twist and turn as he would they held him, and at once all round the sky was stabbed with little flashes – our Archies getting busy; then machine guns from the ground joined in the game of Bosch-baiting.

I think he was probably too high to be in danger of bullets, but it added to the spectacle to see the tracers streaking upwards.

It was a topping sight and I was spellbound, when suddenly the machine seemed to burst into a blaze of flame, he'd been hit – well done our Archies, and all the ranks of Tuscany could scarce forbear to shout or cheer whichever it is.

But what's that? A green flare, and then the truth dawned on me, it was one of our own machines, firing Very lights to establish his identity, and so dazzled by the light that he didn't know what he was doing.

The minute the searchlight men realised who he was, they switched off so suddenly that you could almost feel the darkness, and began their methodical swinging backwards and forwards again.

14 December 1917. The last few days I've been collecting money for the British Red Cross. There is a collection being made all through the Army I believe. One of my Squadrons [21] raised 760 francs which everybody thought was splendid. That fired the spirit of rivalry in No. 9, and we got together 850 francs. Altogether from my four Squadrons we have raised close on £100. Just a voluntary whip round the Officers' Messes, with a small contribution from the men. All the winners at auction or pontoon give their winnings which I thought was rather a brainy idea though I say it as shouldn't.

I've taken under my wing the Labour Company who live about half a mile down the road. They are all of alien birth, with German or Austrian names. The great majority of them are intensely loyal volunteers, but some are a bit doubtful, and for that reason although they are all of military age they are not allowed in the trenches and are made to work on the roads, or to do jobs like levelling the aerodrome.

I gave them a Service last Sunday which they seemed to appreciate, for several have asked me since to make it a weekly affair which I shall gladly do.

Monday and Tuesday are kept as Sunday by two of my Squadrons [21 & 23], so on each of these days I go over to them, take meals off them and give them Services. Three Sundays in each week is *très bon*. I wonder if I'll get clergyman's throat?!

A great after-dinner game here is 'Stand to your horses', in other words pickaback wrestling. A lad called Watson and I challenged the Mess. Our challenge was accepted by the Major and the Recording

Officer – as the Flying Corps call their Adjutant. It was a mighty fight but the Church was triumphant amid scenes of great enthusiasm. Card players had their tables overturned and the bar supporters forgot their drinks in the excitement of the moment. They are really a very cheery crowd and I like them all exceedingly – I'm duly grateful.

21 December 1917. I keep on heading my letters 'France'; as a matter of sober fact I am in Belgium, but only a mile or two over the border – and a very frozen Flanders it is too.

For the last four or five days we have had intense cold and a bitterly cruel east wind. The ground is like granite with a thin carpet of glittering frost crystals. The sky looks heavy with snow, but as yet none has fallen. Occasionally the sun manages to break through but for the most part the countryside is enveloped in mist. The Flying Corps rejoice for it is 'dud' weather and no machines go up.

Last Saturday I had my first flight out here; about an hour's joyride which I enjoyed immensely though hush not a word to the Flying Corps – it made me feel very sick. How far this was inherently due to flying and how far to my Pilot's desire to show off, I'm not quite certain.

We had a casualty the other day. One of our machines was attacked by five Huns who managed to hit our Observer with an explosive bullet in the arm. Rather a nasty wound, but he is doing quite well now. I went to the CCS to see him once or twice. The third time he had just been carried into the Hospital train whither I followed him. It was a revelation in comfort. Beautifully fitted up with flowers and fresh-picked nurses. I could almost wish for a Blighty One for the pleasure of travelling in a Hospital train.

The same day one of my other Squadrons had a casualty but much more serious. Three Huns attacked from above, and while our machine was fighting them, another Hun came up from below and fired a burst into the petrol tank. At 4000 feet they burst into flame, but managed to get the fire out or at least under control, until they had got down to 500. Then the flames burst out again. The pilot, poor fellow, jumped out and was of course killed. The observer stayed in the machine and was killed in the crash – a vertical nose-dive from 200 feet.

Somehow or other this seems much more tragic than a casualty in the trenches. Here a couple of fellows go out in the morning full of life & good spirits from comparative civilisation, white tablecloths and toast and marmalade and never come back. Up the line everybody lives in an atmosphere of sudden death. It is almost a normal thing, and so death doesn't seem to be so terrible. But here we seem so far away from war that death begins to have all the vague horrors which it brings with it in peacetime.

Boxing Day 1917. Yesterday all the cooks, waiters, and batmen had the whole day off. They had their Christmas Dinner and their Concert. Luckily from the Flying Corps' point of view the weather was 'dud' and so their festivities were uninterrupted by work. We all waited on ourselves and had 'cold collations' – whatever they may be – and did the washing-up and all the rest.

Tonight we have our Christmas Dinner proper, turkeys and our plum puddings. Afterwards I fear there may be some dirty work at the crossroads, for these flying boys are apt to be overindulgent in the consumption of firewater.

New Year's Eve 1917. Christmas with the Flying Corps will always be a happy memory: after spending two Festivals in the trenches, you can imagine how my soul and spirit blossomed in the joy of having Christmas back here in peace and comfort. I enjoyed all my Services immensely despite the distraction of having to keep one eye on the watch the whole time. I had them all in nice warm huts, and the men had forms to sit on instead of standing and kneeling in mud as so often happens up the line.

The Concert in the evening was a great success. The second half was an amateur singing competition in which the audience did the judging. The object of the competitors was to stay on as long as possible, and the method of rejection was by a snowball barrage from the judges. The winner's time was one verse and half the chorus, and he won easily! The great majority didn't complete the first line before the audience took a dislike to them or grew tired of them and pelted them off the stage.

The boy I took to Hospital afterwards in the small wee hours of the morning, I'm sorry to say died two days later. Tears and laughter go ever hand in hand out here.

The following day we had our turkeys and plum puddings – a wonderful feast for the third year of war. Unexpectedly I found I was called on to make a speech, so had to gag some time before I could think of a text, and finally proposed a silent toast to Absent Friends. The only silence we had during the whole evening! After dinner the tables were cleared away and we danced to the music of our little orchestra – the dancing however soon degenerated into a Rough House – 'Stand to your horses', High cock a lorum, jig jigging, rugger scrums, and many other forms of violent exercise and feats of strength. Late in the evening somebody suggested wrestling; so I challenged the world at Cumberland and Westmorland, and threw the CO after a titanic struggle.

10 January 1918. Last Saturday we had an extraordinarily interesting lecture by a flying man who managed to escape from Germany after being held prisoner there for eighteen months. The story of his experiences there was full of interest and he told his tale well.

There is something very fascinating in hearing what goes on the other side of the line; and natural curiosity to have the veil lifted, which he gratified fully. The interest of the lecture was increased for me for his partner in escaping and sharer of his experiences was none other than Johnny Evans, who was up at Oriel with me, and of whom I had had no news since the war started, except that he was in the Flying Corps.

The lecturer confirmed in the fullest possible manner the hungry state of the mass of German people and their utter fed-up-ness with the war. He also encouraged me by saying that Germany's internal economy isn't the perfect machine and picture of organisation that we were pleased to imagine it.

Sunday being Epiphany was duly observed by the faithful and I had my Services as usual. On Monday we had a very unpleasant and unhappy tragedy. An Observer went up with his Pilot in the morning, but hadn't been in the air for more than five minutes when he either fell or jumped out. The machine was then about 500 feet up and the Observer was of course smashed to death when we found him. I'm afraid it was suicide, for he had been very strange for some time and had been drinking hard, and much resented my word of remonstrance a day or two before.

A Court of Enquiry is being held and doubtless the cause of his trouble will come out in the evidence. As you can imagine such a thing cast a greater gloom over us than a casualty in the face of the enemy.

185

The next day – Tuesday – we had a new fall of snow about six inches deep. I was just finishing lunch when the Squadron who live the other side of the Aerodrome [7] rang me up to say they were coming over to raid us. At once the alarm was sounded and everybody dashed off to prepare for the fray. A few minutes later a straggling mass sallied forth to do battle, shouting and laughing, garbed strangely but suitably in rugger jerseys & flying caps – this of course in addition to breeches, boots & puttees.

So sudden was our blow that it fell on the would-be raiders as they were leaving their own quarters and so the battle was fought not in our territory but in theirs. When everybody's hands were frozen, and clothes were a saturated solution of snow, we broke off the scrap and decided to play a game of old English football.

There were no rules but each Squadron defended its own side of the aerodrome, trying to force the ball down and across the far side. Imagine 100 strange-looking wild creatures whooping and scrimmaging about the snow-covered prairie, kicking a rugger ball whenever it came near them, but for the rest sufficiently pleased if they could avoid being cut-off by the enemy & ignominiously rubbed in the snow.

Yesterday I tried a new experiment. The great thing it seems to me is to give these young sparks something to do to fill in their spare time & keep them away from the firewater. As there is a Hospital not very far away, I thought a dance might prove a diversion, so I hired the village school, arranged for a dinner, got an orchestra & invited some nurses. The result was a great evening's entertainment. We ate the dinner off the desks put back to back. Incidentally it was an infants' school & we all got cramp. Afterwards we cleared decks, put some French chalk on the tiled floor & set to work. The dance qua dance wasn't anything striking, or at least the standard of dancing wasn't very high, but everybody enjoyed themselves & if you weren't lucky enough to get a nurse for partner, a small man made an excellent substitute – and the orchestra was great – worthy of a better floor & bigger dance. Everything except the orchestra was makeshift. The lighting for example was supplied by four headlights from the motor transport, the mural decorations were the remnants of our Christmas decorations carefully patched and dusted. You would have smiled if you could have seen us carrying the trifle along the slippery road from our Mess to the schoolroom. The villagers managed the soup & the joint, we supplied the fishcakes & the sweets – also the drinks which we carried down in state.

16 January 1918. Until yesterday morning I thought I should have to wait until I went back to my old Battalion before I could hope for any leave. Since then the Wing Adjutant has rung up and seems to suggest that I may get away any time now. The trouble is that I am not on any roster here. After more than three years of war there is still no Chaplain on the establishment of the Flying Corps. I believe shortly they are to be placed on the establishment, but for the present the few Chaplains attached to the Flying Corps are officially unrecognised and therefore no allotment of leave is made for them. I'm entirely dependent on the goodwill of the Wing, but as the Wing have more leaves at the moment then they really need, apparently they are thinking of giving one to me. Don't be surprised therefore if I suddenly arrive for probably I shall get no time to warn you.

What extraordinary weather we've been having – the whole gamut of climate variations: thick snow, a thaw, hard frost, thaw and rain, slush everywhere when we went to bed, a white world when we got up the next day, thunder and torrential rain, with fog, mist and sunshine thrown in. I shudder to think what the next move will be – tidal waves or sandstorms!

22 January 1918. Yesterday I got orders from the Wing to report at once to another Brigade RFC down south, and with the movement order a chit cancelling my leave. I at once rang up the ACG of this Army and asked what the sudden order meant. Apparently Neville Talbot who got me originally to the RFC and who moved south before my arrival in his old area here has applied for me to follow him south. Tomorrow I am going to see him and try to get him to surrender his claim on me for I have no wish to leave my flock here, among whom I am beginning, I think, to get a hold, and begin all over again with an entirely new set of Squadrons.

18 February 1918. It's nearly a month since I last wrote a numbered letter; how the time has flown & what a lot has happened.

The sidecar ride to St. Omer to see Neville Talbot to let me stay here, then my leave warrant's sudden reappearance & my absolutely priceless fourteen days in England, and all that that means now in happy memories.

Anyhow here I am once more in harness and my stride, and quite settled down & in full swing.

I've been back a week now and am picking up the threads more or less. I arrived back to find that one of my Squadrons [23] had departed for another theatre of war, and that my Labour Company had moved out of my parish & had been replaced by another. I have had three new Squadrons [29, 65 & 70] added to my cure, so getting to know them and the new Labour Company will take all my time for the next few weeks.

Chapter 10

Of Boxing and Praying, Dogfights and Dances

German advances in the South

20 February 1918. I continue to wander around my parish taking meals off all and sundry. Last night in addition to an excellent dinner I relieved my hosts of fifteen francs at auction. The Major, Christian that he is, heaped coals of fire on my head by sending me home in his own luxurious car instead of the usual bumpy sidecar in which I generally do my travelling.

This same Major – Major Gould to wit – gave an exhibition the other day of a new form of communication between aeroplanes & the Infantry. It consists of throwing out different sorts of paper balloons, Christmas decorations and tinsel, each of course meaning something according to a prearranged code.

One of the signals consisted of throwing out a paper bag containing about two pounds weight of silver stars. The bag is supposed to burst in midair and the silver stars descend in a pleasing torrent, or glittering cascade. The bag didn't function properly, however, and came down whump within two feet of an Air Mechanic who was walking across the aerodrome. It thoroughly put the wind up him for there was no reason to connect it with the aeroplane which by that time had flown away. You could almost see him making up his mind to give up drink, for the rest of Lent anyway.

On Monday we had a Confirmation in the chapel of Talbot House to which I took four men from my Labour Company. The Bishop of Khartoum confirmed about seventy officers and men. These active service Confirmations are always very impressive. There

189

is something so real about them, no taint of cant or humbug. Among the candidates was a black man – a true-blooded Jamaican, who I believe is hoping eventually to take Orders.

I have had letters from my old Colonel and from my old Brigade both asking me to go back to the King's Own. I don't quite know what to do. Colonel Hunt's SOS has touched me very much; on the other hand everybody here is pressing me to stay, and certainly there is a lot of work to be done with the Flying Corps. It is hard to know what is the right thing to do. I am hoping that something may turn up to show me where my duty lies.

25 February 1918. The war can offer no nicer billet I imagine than that of a non-flying officer with the Flying Corps. The halo of their glory shines upon you, and for all you know of dangers or discomfort you might as well be at home. In fact I think in many ways life is more comfortable or at any rate less vexatious for we have no ration cards or food queues and no domestic worries or servant troubles. How much longer my conscience will allow me to enjoy this peaceful existence, I'm not quite sure, but I see no signs of having to go back to the line yet awhile.

Today I am off to spend a week with one of my other Squadrons. An occasional afternoon and evening for Services and a meal is not sufficient. At present I know one Squadron very well, and the other five a little less than more.

Spot is very sorry for himself. He joined in mortal combat and came off second best, and with only three serviceable legs. When we arrived we found another dog in possession of the roost – an elderly gentleman soured with rheumatism and heavy with age. For years he has been Lord of the Mess and is known to all as Square Dog, from his shape and truculent bearing. Spot dethroned took an instinctive dislike to him, and in the few passages of arms in which we allowed them to indulge, seemed to have the measure of him with something to spare. However in the last encounter Square Dog undoubtedly won and Spot in consequence is crying very small beer. I didn't see the fight, but Spot has worn all his fangs away over his everlasting stone-carrying fatigue, and suppose couldn't get a decent hold of Square Dog's hide.

At the moment he's lying in front of my stove looking very disreputable, for somebody has spilt a liqueur over his head and thoroughly gummed up his hair with a not inconsiderable portion of the mud of Flanders.

4 March 1918. I had a very happy time with No. 21, though it was cut short by the telephone message from No. 9 that they were standing by to move at twelve hours' notice. I came over at once to see what was doing, and to have what I thought would be a farewell meal with them. That night they made me stay, and as my kit was all over at No. 21 I slept in the flea bag of a Flying Officer who was on leave. The next morning I went over and brought my stuff back from 21 and set up house again in my old Armstrong hut where I still am. Nothing further of the move has been heard, but everything is packed and the Squadron is hard at work grappling with the problem of what to leave behind, for transport is insufficient to carry all the kit and paraphernalia which mysteriously accumulates during a long stay in one place. I am hoping to re-furnish my hut with the abandoned furniture and fittings!

All the same I am very sick that No. 9 are moving, for it upsets all sorts of plans and particularly do I regret the breaking up of my Confirmation class. However if they go where I think they are labelled for, I know the Padre there – another son of Oriel – and he will finish their preparation and present them for their Confirmation.

Apart from the move the week has been much as usual – Services, visits, meals and football being the record of most days. On Wednesday (Feb 27th) one of our giant aeroplanes [Handley Page] landed on the aerodrome and caused a furore of excitement. From every conceivable side crowds surged out to see the monster. The Censor would very rightly blackball me if I gave you any particulars, but this I can say that in my wildest flights of imagination I had never pictured such a super monster. By the side of it our ordinary machines looked too silly for words – flies by the side of a Death's Head butterfly would be about a true comparison. Or to give you another idea of its size a hangar which holds six or seven of our two-seater machines, and which would easily hold a Battalion on parade, is nothing like a big enough dock for this airliner. I walked all over it, and was immensely thrilled and indeed for the next few days it was the sole topic of conversation. So huge was it that we watched with incredulity when the crew had had their cocktail in the Mess, and it was time for them to take off. I think everybody felt it couldn't

191

possibly fly, but it left the ground like a bird and then zummed like a skittish old lady. Once in the air it soon lost its gigantic size and the last we saw of it it was flying off merrily towards its home. The marvel of the whole thing is that I believe we have still bigger fellows somewhere up our sleeves.

Yesterday I had a pretty full programme, five Celebrations and four sermons – eight Services in all but the sidecar is a great help in getting about and more than halves the anxiety of being and keeping up to time.

This afternoon (March 4th) was played the Rugger Cup final between 21 and the Squadron who share this aerodrome with us, and who beat us in the semi-final.

It was a titanic struggle, very keen fast and hard, but commendably clean. I was one of the touch judges so had an excellent view of the game. Both Squadrons turned up in force to watch the match and made the day hideous with klaxon horns and hooters and rattles and gongs, while every try was greeted by a barrage of Very lights and rockets. You never saw such excitement. I'd have given anything to have been playing, for except for a slight mist which made it conveniently 'dud' for flying it was a perfect day for rugger. The final score was 11–0 for the Squadron who beat us [No. 7 Squadron], and right well they earned the victory. Tonight they are celebrating the event; it will be a regular Mark 1 binge. I'm invited, but being wise for my years I shall not be there.

9 March 1918. Yesterday afternoon on a visit to one of my Scout Squadrons I found the CO about to take equestrian exercise and he invited me to mount the spare nag, which I very gladly did and much enjoyed a hack down the side roads and a canter in the Chateau grounds. It was good after so much mechanical transport to feel my legs astride a horse even though it took me all my time to sit tight and look dignified.

There has been a good deal of aerial activity lately – the shooting season is beginning. Two days ago we had our first casualty this year – a Pilot wounded in the leg; and today an Observer was hit.

Two of my particular flock, both of whom had asked me to call tomorrow morning in time to take the 7 am Celebration were up on a NF patrol. A NF patrol is for spotting enemy gun flashes and recording the position of the battery for future attention by our own guns. So interested were they in locating what they thought was a

Hun battery that they failed to notice six German Scouts who dived on their tail and let them have it from about fifty yards.

The first burst hit the Observer in the leg and set his stock of flares on fire. Thinking they had set the petrol tank alight the Bosch fell back a little, which gave the Pilot time to manoeuvre away and the Observer to master the flames. The Scouts however being much faster than our two-seaters dived again and hit the Observer in the arm and shot away some of the control wires. However the Pilot managed to get away and to land safely.

The poor old Observer looked like an imitation pepper castor, about eight holes in his arm and leg, but luckily no bones broken and I hope no permanent damage done.

15 March 1918. No. 9 are still unmoved, so I am still with them and inhabiting my little cosy hut. Even when they go, I'm having my home moved bodily *à l'américaine* to its new site at No. 21. Meanwhile everything remains *in statu quo ante*, except my letters.

In the afternoon I went up to the CCS to see Taylor, the wounded Observer of whom I told you. He was looking very much better and was in surprisingly good spirits. Tea I took with the Sisters in their Mess. Each Sunday afternoon they are 'at Home', and their Mess is always thronged with guests, chiefly from the Flying Corps, for no other units remain in the same place long enough to allow them to get to know them.

On Monday we had another dance. This time at No. 21. Rather more ambitious than the one I got up at Christmas time. Old Lord, the Recording Officer at 21, being a married man, had volunteered to go around inviting Sisters from all the neighbouring CCS. As the time drew near however his courage began to fail him, and he stipulated that I went with him. Eventually it ended by him going with me; I had to do all the interviewing and inviting while he stood outside trying to look like a patient.

Seventeen Sisters promised to turn up and indeed when the night came seventeen Sisters arrived. It was a great success for although the flautist persistently played a semitone flat, and the wooden floor was made in sections which didn't fit very levelly, yet everyone was out to enjoy themselves and certainly the refreshments were *sans reproche* – fruit salad from their native tins, sandwiches, claret cup, champagne cup and lemon squash.

The dancing as such being of a rather primitive standard we eschewed foxtrots and stuck to the dear old Valse & Lancers.

Next morning I had to dash off to Army Headquarters for an RFC Chaplains' meeting. The meeting as usual settled nothing and decided nothing, but it gave us an opportunity of having lunch together at the Sauvage where we were much entertained by the hysterical behaviour of a table-full of French people. They shrieked with laughter and kissed each other and even infected *Madame la patrone* with their hilarity until she went round the table kissing the men amid squeaks of laughter from the girls. They are jolly people the French and refreshingly light-hearted and childlike.

Yesterday I went up to the Hospital to see our latest casualties, a Pilot and a Mechanic who while trying a new machine had the misfortune to crash heavily. The machine was a 'write-off' as indeed almost were the occupants. The Pilot broke his collarbone & his ankle, and cut his face to ribbons, while the AM broke his shoulder, cut his forehead to the bone and generally smashed himself up.

In the evening we had our great boxing show, the most ambitious we have ever tried – all professionals collected from all round the countryside. The hangar in which the meeting took place was converted into a miniature NSC. A raised ring in the centre with electric arc lights above, and all round banks of seats improvised from all sorts of odd timber and boxes. Hours beforehand a margarine queue was waiting to get in. Officers we charged five francs, NCO's one franc fifty, and men half a franc. When the show started at six o'clock there must have been nearly 2000 souls packed round the ring. Moreover all smoking hard so you can imagine the atmosphere was fairly solid!

The first three bouts were 3-round contests between local heroes, which produced good sport and whetted our appetite for the big events. I was one of the judges and you can picture what sort of fun we had when I tell you that only in one event did I have to give a decision.

The six-round contest went three rounds at such a pace that the leader on points collapsed through sheer fatigue and had to be carried out of the ring. Then followed some excellent catch-as-catch-can wrestling in which two RFC men took on two champions, one the featherweight champion of England, and the other unbeaten welterweight champion of Europe. Needless to say the RFC men hadn't much chance. The next item on the programme was an exhibition bout between Bandsman Rice and Trooper Wood of New Zealand. Wood however failed to turn up and who do you think helped to deputise? None other than your young hopeful. Rice asked me if I would spar two rounds with him and seemed mighty keen to get me in the ring. I told him I was no aspirer either for championship honours or an early grave, but on his promise to let me down lightly agreed.

As a matter of fact I wouldn't have missed it for words, for you have to get into the ring with one of those fellows to realise how immeasurably they are above the ordinary mortal. His footwork was marvellous and despite his size and weight he was as light as a feather. My first three attempts to hit him were ludicrous. I never saw him move but I was at least a foot short each time. Having sized me up he let me hit him and smothered me in return with taps which wouldn't have killed a fly; duck and slip as I would he always touched me and never heavily.

25 March 1918. It is so long since I wrote that I think I can best give you my news in diary form.

Friday 15th. Masters, the Assistant Chaplain General of this Army came to lunch with me, and together we tootled around a bit and called on Irwin the Corps Chaplain who is an extraordinarily good fellow and has collected a DSO, a Military Cross and a bar! In the afternoon we distributed the prize money to the boxers, and sent the surplus, some £20, to St Dunstan's Hostel for Blinded Soldiers. A Confirmation class and a couple of rubbers of auction filled in the evening. The next day was normal, a little shelling of the back areas, & for me a tour of my parish arranging Services for the morrow.

Sunday 17th. Services as usual, eight in all, and in the afternoon tea with the Sisters at the CCS. The tea party was greatly enlivened by one of the convalescent officers – a Pilot from one of my Squadrons – who borrowed the necessary clothes from the Matron and camouflaged himself as a Sister. Only one or two were in the know, and you would have roared to see the Sisters and visitors being introduced to the New Sister who wisely sat with his back to the light and said very little. Everybody was spoofed. One of the Sisters – a broadminded woman I reckon – even went so far as to whisper to the Matron that at last the hospital could boast a pretty nurse! Certainly his disguise was excellent, and though he must have been suffering acute torture from the tightness of his clothes and his inability to smoke he smiled sweetly the whole time. I wish you could have seen the faces of the assembly when as the dénouement he suddenly took off his veil and cap and asked for a cigarette.

The next day we started early to salve a machine which had crashed last August in no man's land. During the fighting the wreck had been buried by shell fire, but was washed to light again by the winter rains. Since August the tide of battle has flowed onwards and so it was possible to get up to the crash by daylight. I went off by lorry with the breakdown party taking with us a derrick and necessary tackle. When at last we succeeded in hoisting the engine and wreckage we found the poor Pilot still in his seat with his hand on the controls. He had evidently been killed in the air and so had been spared the mental agony of falling 'out of control'.

Eventually we managed with the help of strong tobacco to get him away and into the lorry which was waiting some distance back. Leaving the party to complete the work of salvage I went off with the body to the nearest cemetery. On our way down we were stopped by a young sub who asked me to give a lift to his party of ten men. I told him I had a six-month-old corpse on board, but apparently with the noise going on he didn't hear what I said so thanked me profusely and started to get his men embarked. Apparently he saw me still trying to explain, for he came along and said 'what did you say you had on board?' – 'A six month old corpse' I shouted in his ear. 'Oh' he said and wilted away.

After burying the poor fellow and seeing about his cross, I called in at a Divisional Headquarters to give the Senior Chaplain a message from one of his flock whom I had happened to talk to in the CCS on one of my visits round the wards. To my surprise I found the Senior Chaplain was none other than your old friend Willie Crosse to whom I introduced myself as your son. He sent all sorts of messages of greetings to you, and wanted to know how and where you were. I saw him again the following day at a Quiet Day which Irwin had arranged for all the Padres of his Corps. The said Quiet Day was somewhat of a misnomer for our meditations were sadly interrupted by the arrival of 15 inch shells in the same quarter of the town in which we were congregated. I don't know if all the Padres were as windy as I was, but personally I found the spasmodic arrival of a ton

196

of potential death with appropriate noises highly detrimental to my powers of concentration and to my peace of mind. The nearest one fell in the house across the road killing a woman and rattling down on the roof of Talbot House a perfect storm of half bricks and debris.

The next day we had a Confirmation in a Church Army Hut near the line, to which I took two boys of the Flying Corps. Our tender broke down on the way up and we just managed to arrive as the Bishop was processing up the aisle. Again meditations were somewhat interrupted by the unreasonableness of the Bosch gunners, but once again no harm was done.

Friday last Major Sutton took me for a joyride. I have long wanted to see the trenches from the air, but have always felt it was hardly fair to ask a pilot to take me for a joyride there when he has to go so often as a matter of duty. However the Major isn't in the same category, as he hasn't to aviate except when the spirit moves him.

Of all my flights this was by far the best. Before I had only seen green fields and farms and rest billets below me. This time we went over the war zone flying over parts I knew only too well when with the Infantry, including dear old Wipers. It was absolutely entrancing. Wipers from the air is even more imposing than from the ground, for the completeness of her destruction is more apparent. The ground each side of the trenches is indescribable, every natural feature is effaced, and the earth pockmarked with shell holes.

From the air the ground looks like one vast dirty brown sponge, in which only a trained observer can make out trenches and gun emplacements. As we were not carrying a machine gun, we had to play at Tom Tiddlers ground, and just for one minute did we actually cross the line and fly over Hunland.

While up there I saw six of our Scouts dive past us at a German plane a thousand feet below. It was a wonderfully beautiful sight. From the ground aeroplanes looked like birds, but from the air they look for all the world like fishes. The Scouts reminded me irresistibly of a shoal of minnows.

Unfortunately they were too late to get the Hun, for as soon as he saw them coming he put his nose down for home. The Hun in the air, up here at any rate, is very tame and always runs away unless he outnumbers us three or four to one. The same is true I think of his Infantry, but as he generally does outnumber us, this failing is not so apparent.

197

Of the war down south I don't intend to speak. So far very few details have come through; but what has is not very reassuring. To a mere onlooker he seems to have scored a goal, but whether he will maintain his lead remains to be seen. Personally I don't think he will, and am still quite optimistic about the ultimate score. What fills me chiefly with wonder is the uncanny skill of his meteorological experts. We never seem able to foretell the weather more than two days ahead and then are generally wrong; the Bosch makes no such mistake, which has given rise I think to the expressed idea that the weather always favours the Hun.

1 April 1918. While up at the CCS the other day I was inveigled into sitting for my caricature. The artist, who is at the moment convalescing in hospital after trench fever, has done it awfully well. I'm trying to get hold of it; at present it adorns the wall of the little sitting-room of the ward, and all attempts to purloin it have failed.

Another honour has been conferred upon me. I am the subject of a nonsense rhyme, words by Major Sutton & 'the Pig' – Commander of Ack Flight, and illustrations by a pilot named Darnley. It too is awfully well done and is to be produced in book form – for private circulation only be it noted.

In the afternoon I went up to the CCS to see Wedgwood, the wounded Observer. He got a bullet in his chest while doing a flight over the line. He was wearing one of those steel body shields but the bullet went through as clean as a whistle and is now in his lung. The Doctors held out very little hope of saving his life, but he is so much better that I believe he will pull through. While up there, at the CCS I mean, I had tea in the Sisters' Mess, and afterwards saw an operation. A man had come in with a very acute appendicitis, and an immediate operation was necessary. Several of the officer patients wanted to be present so I helped to form the mob of onlookers.

Contrary to expectation it didn't make me feel a bit sick, nor did I feel at all like fainting. In the operation itself I wasn't very interested, but in the group round the table I found much to amuse me. The poor patient was so covered with blankets that I hardly noticed him, but the surgeon, the nurses & the orderlies looked like a lot of priests round an altar. All in long white robes, with linen masks round their heads and faces, and India rubber gloves. The vesting and preparations beforehand really took longer than the actual removal of the offending appendix. What struck me as so remarkable was the entire absence of blood. Each little vein as it was cut was nibbed with a pair of tweezers until the poor patient's tummy looked like a jeweller's shop – instruments everywhere. I had had enough before the wound was finally sewn up so I shall be anxious to hear today when I go up to see Wedgwood if any of the tweezers or swabs are missing.

4 April 1918. You will have received the note I scribbled at [brother] Hal's bedside at the bottom of his letter; so here follows the full details which I then promised.

A letter from [sister] Gladys on Tuesday was the first news I had, and a great weight it took off my mind as until then I had quite made up my mind that Hal was scuppered or at best a wounded prisoner in Bosch hands. That evening I bustled round trying to find a car going to Boulogne. For about an hour I had all the wires in the Corps telephone system working overtime, and at last managed to get permission for an ambulance to take me down.

Next morning – yesterday – I started off after breakfast and in three hours made Boulogne. A good run for seventy-five miles of not too perfect roads. I arrived just as Hal was giving vent to his feelings. He was sucking an old Briar and singing a duet with the fellow in the next bed, while waiting for his lunch – and what a lunch the young man ate! To look at him one would never think that he was seriously wounded. He looks the picture of health, his respiration and his temperature are normal, his spirits are unbounded, he smokes umph cigarettes, and enjoys his vittals. If it wasn't for the heavy bandages round the top part of his body, you would never think he was wounded at all. I stayed with him until eight o'clock in the evening and during that time he had three handsome meals. The sister in charge who is a sweet woman very kindly gave me tea and dinner in the ward and told me how fond they all are of Hal. Certainly he rags them all unmercifully, asks when they are going to wash his feet again, demands whisky and sodas and has to be content with lemon squash, informs them all that he is married so there's no good them setting their caps at him, and all that sort of rot. I've never seen such a cheery ward. There are the two other boys in his room – all chest cases – he has the bed nearest the window with the daffodils in a vase on his little table surrounded by cigarettes, ashtrays, writing pads, books and everything a man could want.

I think the poor old kid has a certain amount of pain, but his chief enemy is boredom at having to stay in bed, and worst of all has to lie in the same position all the time. His left arm is completely dud – no feeling or use in it at all; he calls it his flipper and demands that it should be powdered every time he sees a nurse standing still for a minute!

The doctor told me that he hoped in time to be able to join up the two ends of the severed nerve, which will give him back full use.

I didn't see his wounds but apparently one bullet entered just below his shoulder blade – he was walking back from an Advanced Machine Gun Post when he was hit – smashed his collarbone and came out bringing with it about an inch of bone and the nerve centre of his arm. The other bullet is still embedded in the muscle of his back. Luckily his lungs don't seem to be affected though the bullet must have passed through the top part of them. He talks and sings without the slightest effort and, as I told you, is allowed to smoke as much as he likes.

As yet the surgeons haven't operated or attempted to remove the bullet, nor will it be possible to move him for about another fortnight, in which case I hope to be able to get a day off again later on and run down for a last peep at him before he crosses to England.

The chief impression I've carried away is the stupendous losses of the Huns. He is full of admiration of the way they came on, wave after wave, despite the immense execution which our machine guns and rifle fire did on them. He is certain that on his sector anyway the Bosch lost more men than we had all told to withstand the onslaught. And that it was simply weight of numbers which carried them over us.

8 April 1918. The day after I saw Hal, the weather being delightfully 'dud', fine but heavy ground mist and low clouds, we played a game of rugger. It was a trial match with a view to choosing a team to represent our Wing. It was a good game despite the fact that I was on the losing side. By one of the tragic fates of war I am burying this afternoon the fellow who led our pack that afternoon. He was an old Observer, nearly due for a period of rest in England. He had been up with a newly joined Pilot, showing him the line and pointing out landmarks and places of interest to him, and was coming into the aerodrome again when the Pilot lost control and nosedived into the ground – both were instantly killed. The same day an exactly similar accident happened at No. 9 but in this case they both got off with broken legs. I don't envy the job of an experienced Observer taking up some of the new Pilots. The Pilots are really not to blame but the system which sends them out apparently insufficiently trained, or at any rate with insufficient self-confidence. It so often happens that new Pilots kill themselves before they have been out here long enough to do any war flying at all.

In the evening we had another concert of a very different order. A Belgian Regimental string band gave a Concert in the spare hangar and wonderfully fine it was. In particular their first violin gave three solos which simply enraptured the whole audience. The Belgian may have his drawbacks, but he certainly can play. Afterwards the Belgian Officers came in to dinner, and after Mess joined heartily in the 'rough house'. I wish you could have seen their stately nanny-goat-bearded Colonel dancing with our CO.

Between the concerts I had another flip with Major Sutton. Ten machines took to the air to practise flying in close formation. I was thankful that we were leading, for not only did I have an excellent view of the others, but also there was less chance of being run into. As it was we just avoided a collision when we dived together on an imaginary Bosch convoy.

Chapter 11

The Measure of the Bosch

The turning point when the German thrust to Hazebrouck and northern France is halted

13 April 1918. As you know I had the afternoon and evening with Hal last Tuesday and found him going on steadily and cheerfully towards recovery. I was lucky enough to get a seat in a tender which was taking a Pilot of ours down to a special Hospital at Etaples.

As we were making our way into the Hotel Meurice I was hailed by an Army Sister – to my surprise I found she was one from the CCS here who had gone off at a moment's notice with an operating team to help in the work down south. The story of her experiences, her escapes as the Bosch came on, and the tending of the wounded in open fields, and the way the Orderly carried all the instruments on his back when their Ambulance broke down was quite thrilling. She is now back here again, and it rather looks as if she may be doing the same sort of thing again before long.

On Thursday my old Squadron at last got marching orders. I was very unhappy saying goodbye to them for I don't know when or if I shall ever see them again. It was a fine sight to see them taking to the air as a Squadron, for as a rule they work all on their own, and only three or four machines are in the air at once. They flew away with their buses packed so full of their spare kit etc that I never expected they would be able to get off the ground. The same day I said goodbye to another of my Squadrons, and yesterday the Squadron to whom you have been sending my letters flew away, so my little parish is fast flitting away. I am staying and moving with No. 7 Squadron which is now my address.

Yesterday we had rather a bad day; a machine coming back from the line on a bombing expedition smashed on landing and with a fearful bang blew up. Both the Pilot and Observer were killed, and practically nothing was left of the machine so we have no idea how this accident occurred, but we suppose that they failed to drop one of their bombs which in addition must have been defective, and that it exploded through the jar of a bad landing. Anyway it was very sad and cast quite a gloom over us all. They were both such nice fellows and only out a short time [Lieutenant Hughes and Lieutenant King].

17 April 1918. The past week has been full of rumours and alarms. Our hopes and fears have been in a continual state of ebb & flow as reports have filtered through of the progress or otherwise of the German thrust towards Hazebrouck.

All last night the air throbbed with the barking of the 75's, and this morning we heard of the success of our counter-attack. It seems pretty certain now that we have succeeded in holding up the Bosch's very brave bid for Northern France. We have had some anxious moments – the further one is behind the line the more apprehensive one becomes, I find – and altho' we are by no means out of the wood yet, still I think our ultimate victory has been made more certain and the end brought perceptibly nearer.

After standing by all Friday and most of Saturday we finally moved late in the afternoon to another aerodrome a few miles away. It was a purely precautionary measure and as events have turned out quite unnecessary. However it broke up our delightful little home and we are now living in less comfort and luxury.

As our transport is somewhat limited and the distance short, the lorries and tenders made a double journey and thus the whole Squadron lock-stock-and-barrel with all its accumulated kit was successfully moved.

While waiting for the second half of the exodus the pangs of hunger assailed me; the Mess was naturally all of a 'no how' being partly here and partly there, so off I went to the nearest Belgian cottage and in my very best French asked the good lady of the house if she could give me '*quelque chose à manger*'. I was doubly hurt and disappointed when in broken English she replied '*I no sprechen Englisch*'. Smiling bravely to hide my aching pride and tummy I withdrew to the local estaminet where I demolished an excellent omelette and salved my lacerated feelings in a beaker of native vinegar.

I hurried back after my meal expecting to find the transport waiting for me, but my hopes were too optimistic and it was not until dark that the tender to which I and my baggage were allotted was ready to start. I got inside at the back while waiting in order to shelter from the cold and wintry wind which was blowing and which incidentally has blown ever since.

After a weary wait in the dark, too cold & lazy to get out again to find how much longer we were going to hang about, I heard the welcome sound of the driver winding up the engine, and could scarce forbear to cheer. At the precise moment the car started a fellow hurled himself in behind – a regular leap in the dark – and caught me fair and square on the bridge of my nose with his hoof.

Roused from a state of coma I asked him what the blankety-blank he thought he was doing. In the dark he couldn't see me and in fact until I spoke was ignorant of the presence of a fellow passenger. 'Who the blank are you anyway?' he asked, after which we relapsed into silence and it wasn't until we both got into the light of our headlights at the end of the journey that I discovered that he was the Sergeant Major, and he discovered that I was the Padre.

24 April 1918. After the first mad minute of the German onslaught when nobody knew anything and feared the worst, things have quietened down considerably.

The Bosch of course has a pretty hefty kick or two still left and will probably get his head down again before long for another wild charge, but I hope and think we have got the measure of him and whatever he can do will only be a useless butting of his head against our boundary wall. Which same is a very costly business so that whatever we may have lost in prestige, morale, territory or material, we seem likely to get its full equivalent in the Bosch casualty lists. Both sides inevitably exaggerate the losses of the other, not necessarily of malice aforethought, but because dead men always look more numerous than they are.

If you see twenty dead men in a deserted trench you would be prepared to swear that the whole Company had been wiped out until you begin to count them. All the same, allowing for unintentional exaggeration, I believe the Bosch casualties have been abnormally high, and when all is said and done, killing Huns is the only way to end the war & bring Germany to her senses.

I have taken the opportunity of having two or three joyrides. Flying is really a very fascinating game. You clamber into your seat muffled in leather coats & helmets feeling no end of a dog and wait half expectantly, half apprehensively, while the Pilot and Mechanic go through a weird but inevitable piece of back chat. 'Switch off' says the Mechanic, 'Switch off' replies the Pilot, switching off the electricity. 'Suck in' says the Mechanic and proceeds to turn the propeller backwards. Being no engineer I'm uncertain who or what does the sucking in, but eventually the sucking-in process is complete. 'Contact' says the ack emma, 'Contact' replies the Pilot, and the Mechanic with a 'one, two, three' gives a heave & a swing to the old prop. Generally nothing happens. 'Switch off' says the Mechanic, 'Switch off' echoes the Pilot, 'Contact' bleats the Mechanic, 'Contact' retorts the Pilot, and so the merry game goes on until with a roar the engine starts and the prop buzzes round with such a whine that everything and everybody is nearly blown away. In the summer it must be very nice and refreshing, but on a cold day I'm always sorry for the poor Mechanics who hold the bus back while the Pilot races his engine to see that all is well.

Everything loose is whirled away in a welter of dust and cinders. Then comes the mad rush across the aerodrome with an uneasy feeling that you are bound to hit the sheds at the other end, which changes into a wonderful feeling of elation and exhilaration as you soar into the air, and see miles below you the tops of the sheds which a moment before you thought would contain your mangled remains.

I'm an awful coward at heart and always have terrific wind up in the air, but at the same time enjoy it immensely. It's very fascinating to see the world from above & to pick out well-known roads or to see your own little wooden hut looking so small and insignificant below. It gives you a wonderful feeling of security when you are inside that same little hut, and hear the Bosch circling around above preparatory to laying his eggs on top of you.

Last Saturday the Hun was particularly offensive, and we who cowered in his target were correspondingly apprehensive. The German engines have a distinctive pulsing throbbing purr, and we lay and quaked while one after the other of the blighters circled round the aerodrome and loosed off his pills. No harm was done, but I know we all wished our beds didn't stand up so high above the ground. One man, preferring the certainty of pneumonia to the chance of getting a bomb splinter even went so far as to get under his bed!

Yesterday the Pig (Glenny), who is by the way a Flight Commander and an excellent fellow, flew me over to an aerodrome which we both knew very well to call on a French Squadron who have come there. As the papers have told you, the French have come up here to help us; and blue & khaki mingle everywhere.

In the evening three of their Pilots came over to dinner and we had a Mark-1 binge in their honour. Extraordinarily nice fellows they were, and entered wholeheartedly into the ragging after Mess.

Yesterday the Squadron who now share our aerodrome [70] brought down a Hun two-seater – an unusual feat for an Artillery Observation machine for they are armed only for defence. In high glee they brought the remains back here so we all had a chance of inspecting its internal workings & fittings.

From the noise that has just broken out & is going on now, I rather think the Bosch head-butting process has started again. God bless all the poor fellows in that hell tonight.

27 April 1918. Yesterday, I think, gave me a better insight into the tragedy of war than all the shells at Delville Wood or the loathsome mud at Serre, or the machine guns at Monchy, or the lice and filth of any old part of the line, or even the ruins of Wipers and the devastated villages of the Somme.

I was coming back from a very famous town up in these parts when I overtook a family trudging along the road – refugees from one of the villages destroyed during the recent German push – all dressed up and nowhere to go. Father, mother, two or three daughters, an aunt or two, some little kiddies all in their Sunday best, and carrying in their hands and on their backs the few family treasures they had been able to carry away. Having a tender to myself I was able to give them a lift a few miles further into safety but where they were going or what they were going to do, they had no idea. It was the Sunday finery which was so pathetic.

All day long a stream of country carts piled high with bedding and furniture followed by refugees is passing back away from the scene of the fighting. At the tail of most carts are tied two or three calves and a cow, all that remains of a flourishing little farm. Often a family not owning a cart go past with all their belongings piled on a wheelbarrow, which they take turns to push. It's so sad to see some poor old girl, who ought to be sitting by her fireside, staggering along harnessed by a broad band over her shoulders to a handcart or wheelbarrow.

However our turn will come. Fighting a defensive battle is the hardest of all tests, but and if we stick it now – no despair or grousing or pessimism – we'll win in the end, have no fear.

2 May 1918. A wire from the ACG has just arrived with instructions that I shall forthwith report myself to No. 4 Squadron RAF so tomorrow morning I pack up my kit once more and remove myself elsewhere. I am so awfully happy here and shall be very sad to leave No. 7. However there's not to reason why, there's not to make reply, there's but to say goodbye.

7 May 1918. By ringing up the ACG I managed to put off the evil day for twenty-four hours. This gave me time to pack up and to say goodbye in comfort; it also let me in for a farewell speech after Mess in reply to the toast of my health and happiness.

On Friday I made the move – a long dusty journey by road. Major Sutton was going to fly me over but at the last minute the machine was wanted for some other job, so I accompanied my kit, my dog, and my servant in the tender.

I hated leaving No. 7 and dreaded beginning all over again with new Squadrons. It was with the same feeling that I had when I went to Rossall for my first term that I reported myself for duty here. I still feel very much like a new boy but I hope in time I will like my new parish as much as I did my old one.

I find I have four Squadrons to look after, one two-seater Squadron [4] with whom I live, and three Scout Squadrons [23, 29 & 210]. Two of these I discovered with joy were old friends, one is the same Squadron which I found had gone south on my return from leave, and the other is the one which came in their place.

In the former not a single officer remains except the CO and old Pye the Recording Officer. All the Flying Officers have either been knocked out or gone to Home Establishment.

In the afternoon we had a funeral. Just before I arrived four members of the Squadron were killed in a collision in the air. One was a member of the Church of England, two were RC's, and one a

Wesleyan. So three Padres turned up each to bury their own. It was rather an impressive Service for every officer & man of the Squadron who was not on duty came to the cemetery.

I have an excellent billet here, a room to myself in a block of Officers' Quarters – a great improvement on my last where I shared a draughty hut of the same size with four others. However creature comfort is far from being everything, though it's a great help to letter-writing and quiet reading.

12 May 1918. I was very interested to find that one of the Flight Commanders here, known to all as Steve, was none other than the gallant fellow who used to cheer us all so much at Monchy by flying low over the trenches, machine-gunning the Bosch and waving his hand to us. I think I told you about him at the time. He made a great impression on us all, he was our sort of ideal airman. The King's Own – if there are any left – will be awfully interested to know that I have met him. He now wears a DSO, and a bar to his Military Cross, and right well he's earned them I know [Capt W.J.C.K. 'Steve' Cochran-Patrick].

The other day the Doctor was over here and was going back to No. 7 so I got him to give me a lift in his tender. It was like going home, the relief of being among friends after the strain of being on my best behaviour here was delicious. No. 7 made me spend the night with them, promising to send me back by air the following morning. Accordingly after a joyride with Bertie Sutton, who wanted to take some photographs from the air, I flew back here in the old Quirk, piloted by Flight Commander Watts.

The Quirk has a strange history, which I must tell you. One day one of the Pilots had to make a forced landing on a disused Belgian aerodrome, and while wandering about waiting for his Mechanic to come over to put his engine right, he discovered in an old hangar a strange-looking machine. On closer examination it proved to be of a make which was very popular two or three years ago. How long it had been there nobody knew, but for ten francs, the only Belgian who was anywhere about, said he would look the other way while they removed it. Though old it proved to be perfectly sound and good, so now after a thorough overhauling it is used as the Squadron taxi. If anybody wants to go anywhere out comes the old Quirk and away you fly. The strange thing about the business is that neither the Army nor the Navy have any record of it. All engines and aeroplanes of course are numbered and records are kept. The Navy say they had such a number but it was a complete write-off at the end of 1915. The only explanation is that some enterprising spy got hold of the wreckage of two or three crashes, and made one complete machine. The fact that it had certain gadgets and instruments on it unlike any issued by the government rather bears out this idea.

Anyhow the old Quirk, bought for ten francs, is a great acquisition and the source of amazement to all who see her stately progress across the sky.

From one of Mother's letters I rather gather that she thinks I spend my whole time in the air. As a matter of fact all told I have only had eleven flights, and seven hours is my total flying time. In the flying world a pilot doesn't talk about how long he has been out here, but how many hours flying he has to his credit. At first it is rather amazing to hear a fellow say with a ring of pride in his voice that he has done fifty hours or a hundred hours as the case may be. It sounds so little, but into those hundred hours are crowded a thousand thrills and fears and hopes. In the long summer days a man may do six hours flying a day for a week on end, but on the average a pilot who has been out here for twelve months will rarely have more than 350 hours to his credit – in other words you will average an hour a day.

The aerodrome here rather lends itself to golf, so on 'dud' days the CO and one or two more ardent golfers knock a ball about. Yesterday I had a game with Steve. The entire stock of clubs consists of about half a dozen irons, mostly cleeks and mashies, putters are unnecessary as we have no greens, or holes for that matter. We beat around hitting little wooden pegs in lieu of holing out. It was quite a joy to swing a club again, and greatly to my surprise I hit one or two good balls.

17 May 1918. The other evening as we were settling down to our after-dinner game of bridge came the report that one of our machines had made a forced landing a mile or two behind our front line. It was one of Steve's flight so he asked me to go with him in the car to bring back the Pilot and Observer. The CO very kindly lent us his touring Crossley into which we crowded two men and their blankets who were to be left on guard over the machine, picketing ropes and other tackle to keep the aeroplane from being blown away, and our two selves.

We had been given a pinpoint map reference of where the old machine was, but in the dark it took us some time to find it. It had come down in a field near a Battalion in rest, and the Pilot and Observer we discovered going to bed after having been royally entertained by the Infantry. I don't think they were at all pleased to see us, and to be hauled off. After we had seen the machine pegged down safely and the guard installed, we climbed on board the car and started our return journey. It was now midnight, beautifully fine and starlit with sufficient moon to tempt the Bosch night-bombers. We were about half way home when the racket started, and a beautiful show it was. The sky was a trelliswork of light. I counted seventeen searchlights stretching their long greedy fingers up into the sky. You could almost imagine that they were some live things feeling for their prey.

Suddenly one of them found a Bosch plane, high up in the heavens, and at once they all clustered on to the unhappy Hun, making him look like a silver moth while from all sides archies and machine guns opened up with terrific noise and energy. Little stabs of light showed where the shells were bursting, while streams of luminous bullets streaked across the sky like the tail of a comet.

The Bosch however seemed quite unconcerned and coolly pulled his string whenever he thought he was over a suitable target. They were heavy eggs he was laying, and the earth shook as they exploded in a fountain of yellow fire. Most of them seemed to be falling between us and home so we stopped the car and watched the show which out Brocked Brock at his best. When things were quiet again we pushed on and found in one place the road covered with earth and clods and telegraph wires. A bomb had dropped a few yards away in a ploughed field and had done no harm. It is a really remarkable thing how often bombs drop in the only open space possible for them to fall without doing any harm.

A little further on we overtook a man wounded in the leg, not by a splinter of a bomb but by a great lump of earth that the bomb had thrown up. Him we carried to the nearest Hospital, and thence home to bed about 2 am.

Next morning there was great energy displayed in sandbagging our huts. Fortunately it was a 'dud' day so all the officers turned out in the drizzle and like the Balbus of old we built a wall round our quarters.

21 May 1918. Despite the ideal weather, the Bosch makes no move, each day we expect to hear that he has begun again to battle his way through, but the hours of daylight pass with a marked absence of alarms and excursions without.

Two nights ago he came over in shoals all night long and dropped bombs all over the countryside. Some were uncomfortably near, near enough to make us all very frightened, but not near enough to do any damage to persons or property.

27 May 1918. I have quite got over the new-boy-at-school feeling and am very much at home with my new Squadron. Active service is a wonderful school for friendships, and you get as forr'ad in a few days out here as you do in the same number of years at home. My parish now consists of three Stations, more or less in a straight line, each about ten miles distant from the next one. I live at one end where I have three Squadrons [4, 85 & 29], the middle Station consists of an Air Park – a sort of glorified Quartermaster's stores where spare parts are kept and where crashed machines are repaired, while the furthest station consists of dear old No. 7 and one other Squadron [70].

I had a long crack with everybody, did a tour of inspection through the repairing sheds, watched the nimble-fingered sailmakers stitching the fabric over the frames of the planes with envious eyes. Sewing always has a great fascination for me. Then to the Officers' Mess for tea where with my bread and butter I swallowed the dust which had accumulated in my teeth and throat. Feeling better, I pushed off amid a cloud of dust like a sandstorm in the Sahara, through which with the half eye still serviceable I saw a vision of white veils, and waving hands, and above the noise of the engine heard shrill cries and hellos.

Realising that the white veils wanted me to stop, I obediently stopped, removed the obstruction from my eyes and discovered three Sisters from the Hospital which used to be near us at No. 9. It was a great meeting and we had a long talk of old times. They had gone off into the blue and at short notice when the German advance threatened to engulf them, and I had often wondered where the tide of war had washed them.

29 May 1918. I seem to have been running about a good deal this week. Monday was spent visiting the sick, the wounded, and the crashed. Most of the Flying Corps casualties in my parish go to the Duchess of Sunderland's Hospital not a hundred miles away. The Hospital is in the grounds of a Chateau, the tents and huts dotted here and there in the shade of the trees – a beautiful site in every way, which must seem like heaven to the poor fellows straight from the fringe of hell in the front-line trenches. I took Spot down with me the other day and put him through his tricks before an admiring audience. He's a frightfully keen little beast, and climbs trees or the side of huts in an amazing fashion to get at the stone which he drops on your toe as an invitation to you to throw it for him.

No sooner had the performing dog made his final bow than an airman appeared overhead and proceeded to enthral everybody with hair-raising stunting above the tops of the trees. Loops and rolls and sideslips, and contortions which nobody else ever tried or even thought of, followed each other in breathless rapidity. Every man who could leave his bed or persuade his pals to carry him crowded outside and gazed upwards open-mouthed. Even the wounded Pilots in the Hospital were thrilled, so you can imagine that it was some show.

On Tuesday I went down into the Town to do some shopping and to buy tobacco and cigarettes, and to do other small commissions for fellows in Hospital. In the afternoon I went off lorry jumping to a village eight or nine miles away where the CCS which used to be near my first aerodrome is now installed. The Hospital is not working at the moment, the marquees and Orderlies being in one place and the Sisters in another. I found the Sisters resting in a charming old Chateau. When I arrived they were all sitting in little groups among the trees, having a well-earned rest and sun bathing. I sat and talked with them for a time, and then in order to escape the ordeal of having tea with them en masse, I took the matron and two others to a little cottage nearby where we repasted very handsomely on omelettes and coffee. It was a very happy interlude in our bachelor existence out here.

Yesterday I had another joyride. Two pilots, Steve and another, were going on leave, so Hodge and I went with them in the tender as far as Boulogne – an hour's run from here through very English-looking scenery. We arrived at half past six – too early for dinner – so after booking a table at the Mony, and beds for the travellers at the Folkestone, we sat in one of the open-air cafés, drinking cordials and watching the world flow past.

What a cosmopolitan place Boulogne is nowadays, endless streams of soldiers of all nationalities, English and Welsh in their sober khaki, kilted Jocks, slouch-hatted colonials from Australia and New Zealand, who stroll along with an air of truculent independence, multitudes of French Officers and poilus in their different shades of blue, heavily bemedalled and much-married, and dark-skinned Portuguese in German Field grey, Belgians in tasselled caps, Americans looking very clean and strong, Chinamen in tight black silk and straw hats. These are the woof in the tapestry of life; short-skirted WAACS, frail-looking French nurses in clinging blue and nun-like caps, healthy English FANYs who have left their cars and ambulances in the garage for the time being, white-booted and powdered French beauties, VADs in sober blue, Army Sisters in red capes and flowing veils, these form the weft, and all hustle and jostle along the narrow roads on their several lawful occasions.

3 June 1918. The fine weather still continues and the Flying Corps work prodigiously – from 3:45 am to 9:30 pm they ride and rule the air. They do the same thing during the hours of darkness too, but as I have no night-flying Squadrons in my parish I don't know very much about their activity. Before it is light the first machine leaves the ground in order to be on the line at dawn, to watch for German attacks. All day long in regular reliefs, machines patrol the front, ranging guns, taking photographs, spotting and locating German gun positions, taking notes of road and railway traffic, and getting our guns on to favourable targets as they appear. There they stay all the live-long day, and twilight has changed to darkness as the last of the birds fly home to roost.

Thursday and Friday last week I spent with No. 7, arriving about teatime after a long and dusty journey by road. I found them all playing tennis on the cinder court which through neglect had grown a very handsome crop of weeds all over it. I played a few sets in the cool of the evening, and registered a vow to have them all out in the sma' wee hours to weed and roll the court. Accordingly next morning I got all those who were not flying to join the Tennis Court Improvement Society, and in our pyjamas we did a couple of hours solid work removing the fungus and levelling off the molehills. While so engaged we saw a strange-looking machine trying to land on the aerodrome. Judge our surprise when we suddenly saw the black crosses on the tail and fuselage. It was a Hun two-seater lost to the wide. Unfortunately as he was about to land he saw the markings on one or two of our machines which were standing outside the hangar. That put the wind up him, and with a roar he opened up his engine and beetled off like stink. So utterly surprised were we that not a shot was fired at him, and he got away with it.

On Sunday I did the double journey again, breaking it going to have a Service for my Air Park. My sixth and last Service was in the Ante-Room here after Mess for the Officers of the Squadron which use this aerodrome. Rather an awe-inspiring ordeal to preach to one's pals and Mess mates, but a very nice little Service all the same. To the Service came a Gunner Major attached to No. 4 for a few days' liaison. After the close he told me that he was a Presbyterian Minister who had been called up at the beginning of the war. He now wears the Mons medal and a DSO.

8 June 1918. On Monday I called on the new Squadron [No. 54] who have lately come in on our aerodrome. Having introduced myself I proceeded to take lunch off them. At the same table was a young Canadian who had received by the day's mail a letter from his people, written on receipt of a report that he had been wounded. He was much amused, never having been or felt better in his life, and immediately after lunch sat down and wrote a letter to that effect. An hour later he went up on a patrol and was shot down with a bullet through his back. I saw him in Hospital later, not very bad luckily, but wasn't it an extraordinary coincidence?

The manner of his wound was rather strange too, as apparently he was shot down by five of our machines who evidently mistook him for a Hun. I say apparently because despite exhaustive enquiries we have been unable to saddle the responsibility, and whoever they were, they have discreetly remained dumb.

It was in order to try to get evidence that I went with the Major next day to the scene of the affair, and questioned the Gunners and Archie people who witnessed the scrap. The final proof and most conclusive of all that he was shot down by our own machines, was provided by the bullet which wounded him. It was a day or two before it could be extracted. Great excitement as it was removed from the unfortunate man's body and proved to be of English make!

As far as I was concerned the most interesting part of the trip round the Batteries was due to the fact that it was through country which I knew well in the days when it was used as a rest area by the

Infantry before the German push transformed it into the battle zone. On two separate occasions we went back to there to 'rest' and refit when I was with the King's Own, and in those days the war seemed miles away, we could hardly hear the guns and all was so peaceful and restful. My billet was a little cottage at the bottom of the hill under the shadow of the church, and my hostess a motherly old soul with one arm [Eecke].

I went through that same village the other day with the Major. Now every second house is in ruins, and hardly one has escaped the marks of shells or bombs.

For auld lang syne I asked the Major to stop the car while I ran down the hill to see my old billet. It was intact, with only a few scars from splinters. As I ran down the hill the door opened and out came my old one-armed billet keeper. She had seen me through the window and gave me an almost embarrassing welcome.

Poor old thing, how she talked – so fast that I was half a sentence behind the whole time and couldn't understand half she said. The cottage on each side was knocked in, but she meant to stick it to the end. It was her own house and *le bon Dieu* would protect her, the *Curé* had persuaded her to take the precaution of moving most of her furniture to a place of safety, but for herself, no, she would stay there. Would I have an omelette or some coffee, and how was my servant and 'Spottie', and when did I think the war would end?

Before I could frame an answer she had started again on a long story of how her dog had died, poor little Mimis, and I could do nothing but hold her hand and nod sympathetically. Eventually I said goodbye and tried to go, but it wasn't until I had promoted the Major into a General, and endued him with a hasty temper and a horror of being kept waiting, that I was able to tear myself away.

Poor old thing. It's that which brings the pathos and tragedy of war home, and stiffens our resolution to see it through to the bitter end.

12 June 1918. The past week has been one of changes; all my Squadrons have lost their leading lights – packed off to a Home Establishment for a few months' rest, while yesterday two of my Squadrons went off at short notice to another sector. In the evening a new Squadron [85] came in to take their place, commanded by a very famous airman Major. The Censor won't allow me to mention his name [Mannock], but it was very interesting meeting a public lion of his reputation. After seeing all his machines safely landed he came into our Mess for tea, as indeed did all his Pilots – their own Mess being still on the road with the transport.

On my way back the following day I broke my journey at my Air Park and stayed to dinner. The meal was interrupted by the news that a Bosch was bringing down one of our balloons in flames. Out we all dashed into the road and there sure enough was the balloon coming down, but not in flames, and not through the action of any Hun. The rope holding it to earth had broken and it was drifting slowly with the wind toward Bosch-land so one of our machines went up and put a few bullets into it to let the gas escape and so hasten its descent on our side of the line. The Observers meanwhile had launched themselves out and had come down by parachute. Incidentally what an awful moment that must be – diving into space with the ever-present possibility that the parachute may not open.

Only the other day near No. 7 one failed to work and the Observer was killed. On this occasion however both landed safely and unharmed.

16 June 1918. Strange to say nearly the whole of the BEF is prostrated with flu. The epidemic is said to have found its way from Spain, but how introduced I don't know. Certainly it is a very virulent kind of flu, short and sharp. High temperature, sore throat, heavy head and breaking back – the same old symptoms only intensified.

19 June 1918. On Monday I got up to go over to No. 7's aerodrome to bury a Flight Commander of the Squadron across the way. He was an old Pilot of No. 7 who migrated across the aerodrome to take promotion. Poor fellow. He killed himself in a new machine in an accident which with his experience and his known steadiness seems absolutely incredible. Either he fainted in the air or his controls jammed, for he dived into the ground with full engine on.

A strange incident which in the old days would have been regarded as an omen happened shortly before he was killed. Saying he wanted a cross for a friend's grave, he went across the aerodrome to get an old four-bladed propeller, and returned half carrying half dragging it over his shoulder. Curiously nobody has any idea who the friend can be of whom he spoke, and so the prop which he carried is now the cross which marks his own grave.

I've never told you very much about the Squadron [70], to which he belonged – the Squadron who share the aerodrome with No. 7. They are a very interesting crowd, commanded by a Major who by nature and profession is an artist of no mean ability.

One of their Observers until a short time ago was leading boy in Lincoln Cathedral. His voice is still unbroken, and he sings as only leading boys can. It's a perfect joy to listen to him. A visitor to the Mess – an old Colonel – hearing this clear sweet voice warbling away, thought there must be a lady in camp, and refused to believe otherwise until the fellow was produced and made to sing in his presence.

More famous even than their soloist however is their tame ram Buchanan. 'Butch' as they call him affectionately is the result of a bet. At Mess one night, for some unknown reason two fellows wagered that one would produce a black lamb before the other could produce five sucking pigs. The rest of the Mess took little interest until next morning they found the two parties to the bet nursing the results of their midnight foraging. There sure enough was a black lamb, and there sure enough were the sucking pigs, three only however instead of five, which caused the finder of the lamb to crow until the pig-fancier in his turn insisted on washing the face of the lamb. Good for him that he did, for under the camouflage of dirt was a nice white face – hence the name. How they divided the stakes is of no interest, but the pigs they ate, and the lamb they kept. Buchanan is now a youth of distinctive personality. He quite owns the Mess, and butts his way through life quite merrily, eating chocolate with avidity and looking less like a sheep than most of his family.

I took Spot over with me one day. It was the first time Spot had seen Butch and the meeting was historic. We all lay around under the canvas awning outside the mess and roared with laughter.

Spot with ears cocked back in a very stiff and jerky way interviewed Buchanan, who was quite unperturbed and, feeling his position as host, wished to be friendly. Spot couldn't make him out at all, but took a fancy to his ears which he kept on trying to lick, jumping back every now and then in a jerky way as if expecting Butch to bite him or do something equally extraordinary. The look of mystification on Spot's face was irresistibly funny. Apparently he could think of nothing else to do but to lick one ear in a tentative way, then hop round to the other side and lick the other ear. Butch stood it for some time, but eventually growing weary of having his ears washed so often, gave Spot a gentle butt while he wasn't looking. The pained surprise with which Spot looked round as if to ask what had hit him, and Buchanan's unassumed look of innocence set us off into roars of laughter again.

For an hour or two they played together, Butch doing a discreet gambol from time to time, and Spot trying to wrestle with him. The last we saw was of them trotting off together to the kitchen to look for food, Butch I suppose ever mindful of the laws of hospitality having invited Spot to have a 'spot of something'.

24 June 1918. Today is a glorious day – raining cats and dogs and looks like going on forever. Glorious weather from the Flying Corps' point of view as it gives them a holiday, and after so much fine weather they badly need a breather. Yesterday after my Services for No. 7 and the other Squadron on the aerodrome [70] I was having lunch with Major Sutton and the Pig when a man came into the Mess in a pair of canvas overalls. I thought it was an Ack Emma (Air Mechanic, *anglice*) to see about the electric light, and imagined that the other two had gone dotty when they jumped up and hurled themselves at the poor unfortunate man. Having nearly strangled him with their protestations of joy, they pulled him out of his overalls. The grub became a butterfly. He turned out to be an old fellow Pilot who had just flown out from England – some Pilot too to judge by his ribbons – a DSO and bar, a Military Cross and two bars, a White Eagle of Serbia, and a *Croix de Guerre avec palme*. Funnily enough that very morning I had seen a photograph of him with his wife and kiddy in one of the illustrated daily rags [Major G.D. Murlis-Green].

I heard a strange story a day or two ago – told me by a Squadron Commander and therefore of unimpeachable authority. A Hun plane was brought down on our side of the line by some of our Scouts. The pilot was wearing a civilian morning coat & trousers of fashionable cut, with a very old pair of dancing pumps. Unfortunately the poor fellow, having sixty bullet holes through him, was dead, and therefore unable to explain his unconventional garb, and we are left in doubt whether the Bosch supplies of uniform material are giving out or whether he was going 'in cog and mufti' to a Tango Tea when he had finished his job on the line. Anyway it is only one more strange incident in an exceedingly strange war.

The Austrian offensive has not altogether been the success that they must have hoped for and expected. I'm beginning to think that perhaps the longed-for peace will come, when it does come, through Austria. Accounts rather lead one to believe that all is not well with the Austrians, and that in fact they are nearly ripe for an internal debacle. Germany's loan of food to her allies is significant, and her suggestion of sending twelve Divisions to her assistance gives one to think furiously.

A captured Hun airman on being told that but for Russia's defection, Germany would have been already beaten, replied that the Allies weren't the only people who had useless allies, but that Germany too had her difficulties; and admitted that they were afraid Austria might let them down. Let's hope they will. Anyway I remain an optimist, and believe the war will be over by November, with the Allies on top.

Chapter 12

'Three Cheers for the Armistice!'

All involved in the Big Show in August and October with huge bombing raids; villages being liberated around Menin but fierce fighting until 11 November

30 June 1918. On my return across the aerodrome to my bed in the Pig's hut, I found the Pig waiting up to tell me that he had arranged for us to be called at 2:15 am as he was going to take me up to see a small battle which was billed for an hour before dawn.

By 3 am we were in the machine, running up the engine, while Mechanics did what was necessary by the light of the paling moon reinforced with electric torches.

In the still night air the engine ran as sweetly as could be, and it wasn't long before we were doing that mad rush across the aerodrome and soaring into the starry night. Beneath me I could trace the network of roads which looked surprisingly white, but the rest of the earth was simply black nothingness stabbed here and there by solitary lights. We circled round once or twice to get height and then off we flew towards the line. Below me I could see our lighthouse flashing out its dots and dashes, pointing the way to night-bombing machines coming home after their work was done.

When we got near the line our Artillery was already at work putting down a barrage on the Hun trenches. The roar of our engine drowned the noise of the guns, but the bright flashes as the gun is fired, and the dull red glow as the shells burst made a wonderful picture.

Our job was to locate the positions of the Hun batteries that were expected to retaliate, but as far as I could see they seemed to take our barrage lying down. Presumably they didn't want to give their positions away before they were ready to launch their own offensive; anyway the fact remains that they made very little reply to our artillery preparation.

It was only a small raid, and in the dark it was impossible to see our fellows going over the top. As the firing died down, the Pig took advantage of the darkness to fly well over the Hun lines, then dived down firing his front guns at Bosch trenches and at the roads used by his transport. It was a wonderful experience, the steep dive, the double rat-a-tat of the two machine guns firing together, followed by the zoom and climbing turn as we got into position for another dive. Having exhausted our ammunition we turned our nose for home. Dawn was just beginning to break and a long pink slit in the black clouds heralded the new day.

Coming home we followed the most historic road of the war, flying low over the shell-pocked fields, zooming over the trees, then down again so low that I felt I could have plucked the cap off Tommy Atkins if he had been astir. 'Contour chasing' as the Flying Corps call it, is the most exciting form of flying, for it is the only time that you get any idea of the speed you are going. Up in the air the absence of any fixed points makes the realisation of speed impossible. It is only the rush of air that convinces you that you are moving at all; and the higher you are the slower you seem to be going.

On this occasion the Pig wanted to drop a message at the Headquarters of the Division concerned, so we circled round the dropping station, firing lights to attract their attention. Nobody however appeared to be awake, so there was nothing else to be done but land the machine and deliver the message by hand.

Down we came, did an excellent landing, just missing a reserve trench which has been dug across the middle of this old aerodrome. Incidentally it was an aerodrome used by one of my Squadrons before the Bosch advance brought it too near the line to be safe. For about ten days I lived on that aerodrome just after Christmas. Now all the hangars are gone, and the place is hardly recognizable. The Pig woke up an Orderly, delivered his report of the raid, and off we set again for home. It was quite light by the time we got home, so instead of going back to bed at once we played a set of tennis. By the time I had beaten him it was nearly 6 o'clock, but we turned in for an hour or two and appeared as the last bell was going, in excellent form and appetite for breakfast.

In the evening it cleared up and I saw a most wonderful crash – a machine taking off hit the wing tip of a machine standing on the ground that swung it off its course into some sheds. Hitting the roof of one shed it bounced through a thick hedge leaving its undercarriage behind it, then did a complete somersault, tried to get inside an Armstrong hut used as a bedroom by one of the Flight Commanders, succeeded in forcing its way half-in, then turned round and ended right way up, a total wreck but both Pilot and Observer were untouched. They were sitting there surrounded by the debris of their triumphant progress, broken woodwork, torn fabric, corrugated iron from the roof of the shed, twisted wire, branches of hedge and splintered planks, all splashed with thick black oil from the burst oil tank, and with earth from the hole they'd ploughed up, and yet not a scratch or a mark on either of them.

7 July 1918. The other day I had to go to a distant Cemetery to take some roses which a mother had sent out with the request that I would put them on her boy's grave – the Flight Commander who was killed in a crash of whom I'd told you in a recent letter. Spot watched the sidecar which was to carry me to the Cemetery, with longing eyes but I sternly ordered him to stay behind and look after my kit, and off I went. Two miles later we had to slow up for the traffic, and there *ventre à terre* with heaving sides and about a square foot of panting tongue was Master Spot, who in spite of orders had decided to follow me. I hadn't the heart to send him back and anyway his beam of delight when I told him to jump in fully repaid me from my loss of dignity in going back on my word.

For the rest of the journey he stood bolt upright with his hind feet on my lap and his front on the front of the sidecar, sniffing the air and vainly trying to keep his balance as the sidecar bumped its way over the unholy holes and ruts. However with his tail firmly anchored in my hand he managed to maintain his position much to the evident delight of the gamins in the villages we passed through.

While I was busy with the grave, Spot found a delightfully filthy duck pond in which he disported himself with great abandon unbeknown to me. The dénouement came when we were setting off again. He bounded into his old position and drowned me with liquid slime. The next mile or two he had to run behind and cover his wetness under a coat of dust.

A day or two later I took him to see Butch while I paid a pastoral visit to the Squadron who owned him [70]. On this occasion there was another dog on the premises, a little terrier bitch to whom Spot took a great fancy and Butch was rather left in the cold. The two dogs tore about the grass rolling each other over and chasing madly round in circles. Butch watched for sometime, until piqued by their obvious indifference to him, and feeling it was time to put a period to their neglect, tried to join in.

As they dashed wildly round the Mess and across the grass, Butch tried to cut them off, but failing badly, trailed in behind. Picture the absurd trio, the two terriers entirely absorbed in their own company and absolutely indifferent to Butch's attempts to fraternise, racing madly about with this preposterous black ram lumbering after them, and trying to butt his way into their notice every time they started wrestling. With a supreme air of not noticing his presence they continued to ignore his pathetic efforts, until the poor beast was almost frantic. As a final attempt to impress them that he was quite as active as they, he cut a series of ridiculous gambols which reduced us all to a state of flabby and painful laughter. He was just preparing to make his presence felt by jumping on them as they lay on the ground scrapping for an opening, when one of the fellows called him off with an offer of chocolate, over which he is a perfect food hog. In the enjoyment of his chocolate he found a solace for his wounded pride and feelings.

A few days ago a new Pilot coming back to the aerodrome in the early morning mist hit the top of a tree and crashed into the ground. The poor fellow was instantly killed, in fact so badly smashed that we had to bury him where he fell. Last Friday I went off with one of the photographic section to take a photo of the grave and to erect a cross made as usual out of a broken propeller. The crash occurred in the home paddock of a farm in which a Battalion late from Palestine were billeted. The fellows of course crowded round watching as we turfed the grave, erected the cross, and generally made it ready for the photograph. It pleased me immensely to get among the Infantry boys again and to listen to their quaint stories of the Holy Land. What wouldn't I give to have been where they have and seen what they have seen!

In one of my letters I told you about the obsolete old aeroplane which one of my Squadrons found. They have now had it fitted up with dual-control as an instructional machine partly in order to prepare Observers to be able to take command if their Pilots get killed in the air, but chiefly in order to teach me to fly. Last Thursday I had my first two lessons. The instructor really flies the machine but when he gets up to a safe height he takes his hands and feet off the controls and tells the pupil to carry on. At my first attempt of course I was all of 'no-how' and couldn't even fly straight, but the second lesson found me much more confident, and I did a few turns very gingerly, and flew straight without much difficulty.

I hope this won't worry you. I'm rather afraid it may however, because I know you think flying is very dangerous. War flying has a certain danger of course – in fact it is probably only less risky than being in the trenches, but flying qua flying is really safer than riding a motorbike. And in any case I am too much of a coward to do anything dangerous.

Besides it all helps on the good work, in addition to amusing me to learn, and them to teach me, the graceful art of being a Sky Pilot. So please don't be angry.

13 July 1918. A long spell of dry weather came to a sudden end last Monday evening. I had had a headache all day and knew that thunder was in the air, but the storm when it came took everybody by surprise. The sky was full of machines at the time, and as the first drops began to fall, they all came beetling home as fast as they could hoping to beat the storm and get under cover before it burst. You can imagine what a scrum there was as they all tried to land together. In the excitement one fellow overshot the aerodrome and crashed into the far side ditch and hedge and turned turtle, out he jumped unharmed and the next minute the machine went up in a huge flame and smoke. His petrol tank had apparently burst open and running over the hot engine the petrol burst into fire and wrote-off the machine.

No. 7 have got rather an amusing device for teaching Pilots to get a quick aim on enemy aircraft which they happen to encounter in the atmosphere. It consists of an old fuselage so balanced on a sort of stand that by working the controls in the ordinary way you can turn it to the right or to the left and raise or depress its nose. On the fuselage is fixed a machine gun, again quite in the ordinary way, for in every aeroplane the front gun is fixed and to aim your gun you have to aim your machine at the target.

Accordingly this contraption is placed in front of the butts in which they have a number of disappearing targets. As soon as the target appears, the game is to swing your gun on to it by working the rudder and joystick and then press the trigger. Generally by the time you have pointed the machine successfully at the target and are about to loose off a nice little burst, the beastly thing vanishes, and another appears at the other end of the butts. It is a most amusing and instructive game, and I thoroughly enjoyed myself in it one afternoon.

On Tuesday I went over to a neighbouring town [Aire] for the tail end of a Quiet Day. I had meant to go there for the whole day, feeling much in need of a spiritual tonic, but so many things cropped up that although I got up early it wasn't until after lunch that I could get away. Ted Talbot was giving the addresses, the third and last of which I heard, and quite a lot of old friends were there – Big Neville, and Arthur Longden, and Dick Dugdale, and a heap more of padres I knew before the war or met since.

Yesterday we had a Conference of all the RAF Chaplains with Bishop Gwynne, the Deputy Chaplain General, in the chair. The Conference lasted all day with a break for lunch, and we discussed everything connected with our work, pooled our experience & shared our sorrows and disappointments, and came away feeling all the better for it. At least I speak for myself.

C of E are now a distinct branch of the ACD with our own senior man and our own organisation. One day – but not during the war – we will sever our connection altogether with the Army and become pukka members of the RAF.

Apart from the usefulness of the Conference I enjoyed my day because I met a lot of old friends, and really out here it is a relief to get into the atmosphere of religion and among people who understand.

The Padre really is a lonely sort of soul, despite his many pagan friends. He has to make and keep his own atmosphere, which isn't always easy in the ultra-material world which war creates.

17 July 1918. I am living for the present in a hole in the ground – a very delectable hole, mark you, but a hole none the less. From outside you would say it was an ordinary bell tent, and you would be right, but open the flap and you gaze into a young artesian well, some five feet deep, at the bottom of which repose my bed, writing table, armchair and washstand, all made on the premises by the wizards of the Air Park with whom I am spending a few days [Arneke].

I've been staying here since Monday, and am very happy. The Air Park is a mobile halfway house between the Air Depôts and the Squadrons. Here damaged planes are repaired, and every conceivable spare part of an aeroplane is kept ready to be issued to a Squadron at a moment's notice. At the moment they are not very busy – proof conclusive of our air supremacy – so that it is an excellent opportunity to visit this particular corner of my parish, of which I have seen far too little in the past. They are an exceedingly nice set of fellows here, very friendly and hospitable.

23 July 1918. I am still living in my hole to which I have become quite attached. At the moment it is raining hard out of a leaden sky and my tent leaks in three or four places, which keeps me busy moving my bed & myself about to find a dry spot. However I'm glad to see the rain as it gives the overworked Mechanics a chance of getting a little rest, and the overstrained Airmen an opportunity of seeing life on the ground.

On my way home in the tender we were stopped by a crowd of Australians who had been dining – perhaps not wisely – in the city of Mother's schooldays [St. Omer]. They wanted to go south-east while I wanted to go more or less north-east. The tender having been boarded, I half expected that I should either be thrown off, or taken south willy-nilly. However we went east as a sort of compromise, and finally parted good friends, with me still in possession of the tender.

The Australians are great fellows to fight and I take my hat off to them every time, but when you get eleven of them giving off whisky vapours like so many carburettors, anything may happen.

28 July 1918. I have moved my home yet again and am now back with my old friends No. 7. I find the only feasible plan with so scattered a parish is to make one Squadron my headquarters from which I go off for a day or two at a time to stay with the others. Like a wandering friar I meander around, returning to my headquarters to change my shirt and get my mail.

On Tuesday evening we had a farewell dinner for Doctor Frazer who has gone to another Wing. He is a big fat man and his description as a 'kindly old gentleman', while it riled him, hit him off to a T.

After the dinner and speeches we adjourned to a hangar which had been fitted up for a Concert. The Concert was given by a party of Yanks from the American Division in the neighbourhood. It was the most refreshing show I've seen from many a long day – all the performers were professionals and really excellent. The accompaniment was supplied by a small orchestra, a fiddle, a piano, a banjo and a ukulele. Perfectly priceless they were, especially when they played typical American ragtimes. Then the banjo and ukulele got intoxicated with their own music, and carried the audience away to the limit of enthusiasm.

The show was of the usual song, dance and recitation variety, and yet 'usual' is the one word which couldn't be applied to it for it never once got onto the beaten track, but from start to finish was absolutely original and unusual. For example the first item was a dance – a *pas de seul* – by an accomplished tango expert. Then came a fellow who told stories in a typically American way. Then a female impersonator who was perfect, and so on – and nobody ever sang more than one verse of the song, or worried the audience to sing the chorus against their will.

The more I see of the Americans, the more convinced I am that it has been part of the German propaganda over the last decade or more to misrepresent intentionally the American character to us, and our national character to the Americans. Both armies are being agreeably surprised to find that their preconceived notions were hopelessly wrong, and I believe one of the greatest blessings of the war will prove to be the drawing together of our two nations.

On Friday we lost one of the very best pilots in France. By the time this arrives you will have seen in the papers the death of Major Mannock. He was CO of one of my Squadrons [85], a most charming cheery fellow, and the best leader the Air Force has ever seen. We had a Memorial Service for him this afternoon to which practically the whole Squadron came. He was so unassuming that perhaps you have never even heard of him. He studiously refused to be boosted by the press, and yet his record is second only to Major Bishop, with something like seventy Huns to his credit [Major Edward 'Mick' Mannock VC DSO** MC**].

227

2 August 1918. I've been out all day in the rain, paying pastoral visits and making arrangements for special Services for next Sunday to commemorate our entry into the War. Now changed and replete I am sitting in the Armstrong hut I share with Ned Kelly – the Recording Officer.

The first two days of the week I stayed with No. 4, and buzzed around that end of my parish. As I was getting into my tender to come back with my servant, my dog, and my kit, a machine landed on the aerodrome from the Squadron who own Butch and who share this so-called aerodrome with No. 7. The Pilot suggested that I should fly back with him. I jumped at the offer, for the journey by air saves at least an hour and all the dust and bumps and monotony of the journey by road.

It was a two-seater machine, but as he had brought his Observer with him I made the third and I was more than a little doubtful of the ability of the machine either to hold or carry a second passenger. However by standing sideways we both managed to fit into the Observer's cockpit. Even when sitting and sheltered by the Pilot in front, the draught is so great that it is almost impossible to face the wind without goggles, but standing up you get the full force of the rush of the wind and the slipstream from the propeller. Standing up too makes you feel terrifically insecure and liable to fall out – a complete delusion incidentally – and altogether intensifies the thrill of flying. However we did the journey without adventure or mishap and made a perfect landing at this aerodrome to the no little astonishment of the bystanders who, seeing two figures in the observer's cockpit, rubbed their eyes and wondered if the vintage was after all more crimson than they had imagined.

The next day I borrowed Happie's motorbike and hied me off to see my one-armed old friend at Eecke. All went well, I arrived safely and spent an hour with the old girl, who to eke out a living has opened her spotless kitchen to the world and sells coffee to the troops at *trois sous* the cup. The place was full when I arrived, and the constant stream of Tommies came and went the whole time.

I met an old friend down at the CCS where I had dinner – one of the Doctors looked very hard at me and said 'We've met before haven't we?' I didn't know that we had, for I've got a memory like a sieve. However he seemed to know and said after a little thought 'Weren't you at The Bluff in March '16?' Was I not indeed, and then I recognized him. He was the MO of the next Battalion to us and he shared our Aid Post after his own was knocked out. Incidentally he got a MC out of the show, and apparently lost his hair, for it was the absence of this which made me fail to recognize him.

8 August 1918. On Sunday and Monday I was busy with Services; being the fourth anniversary of our entry into the War, we had special Services to which goodly numbers came.

Personally it goes against my grain, but on such occasions cheap heroics are expected and appreciated. So we sang warlike hymns and I gave them a sermon in which 'honour' and 'duty' and 'trustees of the dead' and 'cost what it may' were conspicuously present.

One of my Squadrons [29] have moved a few miles away to another aerodrome [Hooghuys], so though my numbers are not increased, the bounds of my parish enlarged and I had to carry on the good work on Monday. They are in a delightful little spot now, and I enjoyed my Service and meal with them very much. During the two days I had ten Services and travelled eighty-five miles to hold them.

14 August 1918. On Sunday I got over to one of my Scout Squadrons to hold a Service only to find that they were all away on the big show, so the Service fell through. Later I heard the details. Five Squadrons took part, roughly some fifty or sixty machines, in a big daylight bombing raid on a large German town. Each machine carried four bombs and a full supply of ammunition. You can imagine what the Germans felt like when they saw that aerial armada arriving. Among other things they shot up a Hun aerodrome, and chased the panic-stricken Mechanics all over the country, firing and bombing them to extinction. They all came home, full of buck, having never seen a Hun plane or received a single scratch. As the objective was a long way over, many of the Pilots took their shaving kit and a big supply of cigarettes in case they were forced to land through engine trouble, but luckily all the engines behaved well and brought everybody home safely.

Yesterday I had my first flip this month. Wilberforce Fletcher – one of the Flight Commanders – had to test his engine so took me up. It was a cloudy misty day so our hope of snatching a sight of Blighty was not fulfilled. We went up to the sea however and flew along the coast watching the shipping and filling our lungs with ozone. It was a most enjoyable flight and the sea looked delightful.

We seemed to be flying in the middle of a big saucer. All round was a solid bank of clouds so that the joint between sea and sky, and the earth and sky was indistinguishable. Everything sloped up to a clear-cut line where the clouds came to an abrupt end, over which was the perfect blue of heaven.

The sight of the sea and the white horses breaking on the sand so inflamed me that in the afternoon I took the Major and the Doc off to the nearest reservoir, and had a most delightful bathe. Spot went too and enjoyed himself as much as the perspiring mortals. It was a gorgeously hot day and the water was almost tepid, and we bathed *au naturel* to our great content.

Today I am busy with a scheme to raise money for the RAF Widows and Orphans, and the Prisoners of War fund. I am trying to get every officer and man to give one day's pay, so far with good success.

18 August 1918. The outstanding event of the last few days has been the tennis party which was a great success. All the morning those who were not flying were busy on the court sweeping, rolling and marking, mending the netting, and erecting a very fine canvas pavilion as we say in France. By the time we had finished, the court was hardly recognizable, and I went off to fetch the guests confident and happy in the knowledge that all was well.

Ten Sisters came in all the glory of their caps and capes and we played strenuous sets of tennis while the official photographer took snaps. The Mess President excelled himself and gave us a fruit-salad tea, while the photographer took us sitting round the little tables on the lawn [sic]. Those who couldn't play tennis wandered round the hangars inspecting the machines and having their internal workings explained by enthusiastic Pilots. I don't suppose that the dear things understood a tenth of the technical jargon which for ever flows from the mouths of flying men, but everybody seemed to be thoroughly happy and the Sisters went away at seven o'clock enthusiastic about their little outing.

The next day I did a tour of my parish, had a meeting of RAF Chaplains, whereat our areas were rearranged with the result that some of my distant parishioners have been transferred from my care to a less distant Padre, while I have a new Squadron nearer at home to look after.

22 August 1918. The last few days have been extraordinarily full, and today seems likely to prove no exception, so I have roused myself early and am sitting in my pyjamas writing this before the heat of the day makes writing too much of an effort. It is going to be another scorcher, already my Armstrong hut is becoming an oven, so I must hurry along.

As I told you in my last letter, my parish has been somewhat altered, and I have a new Squadron [79] and Wing HQ [at Watou] to look after in exchange for No. 4. Accordingly on Monday I set off to pay a parochial visit on the Wing Commander, but finding all but the Wireless Officer out, I amused myself and Spot for half an hour by punting about on the artificial stream which flows through the grounds of the Chateau where Wing HQ are housed. Spot loves the water and was highly delighted when I shoved him off by himself in a leaky canoe. He dashed up and down from stem to stern barking furiously until the water in the canoe was up to his flanks. Then he decided to abandon ship, flopped overboard and tried to come on board my wherry-punt. Not wanting a shower bath I played the Hun and drove him from me, but he had his own back by getting in at the other end and soaking me. I stopped to tea – a tea ever memorable for the strawberry jam and toast on which apparently Wing HQ regularly regale themselves.

From there I drove to the Canadian CCS to see Davies, the wounded Scout Pilot who I feared would lose his arm. All the bone in his elbow has been removed, but he is making a wonderful recovery and is to keep his arm, but has what the surgeon calls a flail-joint. On Tuesday to get away from the sweltering heat the Pig took me up for an engine test. Spot seeing me clamber into the back seat jumped on to the wing and scrambled in after me, and off we went. Armed with goggles and helmet the rush of wind is bearable, but poor Spottie was nearly blown away so I had to turn round with my back to the wind to shelter him. For some time he sat still on my knees, but when the Pig began stunting, Spot grew restive and once in the middle of an Immelman turn, when he suddenly caught sight of the ground above him, he got such wind up that he tried to jump out. I held him in by the skin of his back, but for the rest of the flip he was evidently unhappy, and was pathetically pleased and effusively relieved when we were safe once more on *terra firma*.

In the afternoon I went to the Wing again and had more strawberry jam and saw most of the Headquarters and arranged for

Services and so on. Then on to see my new Scout Squadron to whom I introduced myself. I found them all building a little paddle boat for the moat round the farm in which they live. An extraordinary cute piece of work, with a one-manpower engine to turn the paddles consisting of a bicycle chain and pedals.

3 October 1918. I sent off a FPC as soon as I arrived, just to let you know that I was safely back in harness after a most delightful holiday. Tuesday morning when I got to Victoria to catch the leave train, who should be standing there but Hal who had travelled up to Town the day before. I can't tell you how pleased I was to see the dear old boy, looking very smart and soldierly in his uniform and medal ribbons. It was a fitting close to a very perfect leave.

Luckily the sea was smooth and a rich deep blue and equally luckily I met two pals on board so had an excellent crossing and successfully got over the nasty feeling of leaving Blighty for frenzied foetid Flanders.

I am now back with No. 7 and funnily enough we are on the same aerodrome as I was on when I first joined the RFC last winter [at Proven], and in the same Armstrong hut. Everybody is very excited about the War news. It certainly is splendid. We are expecting to move forward soon across the old belt of devastated country and occupy an abandoned German aerodrome!

I've come back to practically a new parish for there have been a lot of changes during my month's leave and every Squadron has moved somewhere else. However I'll soon settle down and get to grips with my new parishioners.

15 October 1918. We've been battling all this week as the papers will have told you. At least my Squadrons have been taking part in the Big Show on our Front, while I have been anxiously waiting for news, and writing what sympathy I can to the relatives of those who have not come back.

It's been rather a black week for us, though the gloom of sadness has been pierced by the splendid news of our progress. Victory is sweet, but the price of victory is only less bitter than the cost of defeat. So many good fellows have gone west, though luckily as we pushed forward we have been able to recover their bodies, and lay them to rest in the little Cemetery near our aerodrome.

Today I've been up over some of the recaptured ground trying to find the body of a boy who was brought down yesterday. After the war he was hoping to be ordained – such a nice fellow. He came to the Service which I had for his Squadron on Sunday evening and stayed to the Celebration afterwards. Next morning he was brought down in flames. His father is a parson in Lincolnshire and he is the second son they have lost.

However the news is good. Everywhere the line is in motion and the Bosch seem to be intent on beating it while the beating's good.

Did I tell you that the Pig has been given an Independent Command? I went over to see him on Friday and to congratulate him on winning the Distinguished Flying Cross – that in addition to an MC and bar which he already possesses. While there I had my first flight in a Bristol Fighter which is I suppose the finest aeroplane in the air.

Yesterday I spent most of the afternoon trying to obey a vague wire which I received from my Senior Padre bidding me to meet him at a very indefinite place that afternoon. No details as to time or exact place of meeting. However eventually we found each other and had a chinwag. He is Keymer, late Vicar of Eastleigh, and one of the authors of 'The Church in the Furnace'.

On my way back by tender we ran into a Belgian gendarme. It was just getting dark and the moon was half up and our lights were only feeble enough to make the slight ground mist visible – altogether a most deceptive light. Anyway he was standing on our side of the road making love to a girl standing in the doorway of her house. Neither the driver nor I saw him until we were on him, and the swerve was too late to miss him. Our mudguard caught him on the shoulder and sent him reeling into the arms of his lady love. I jumped down and ran back to see the extent of the damage. He was more surprised than hurt, but I was much tickled by the girl taking our part, and roundly slating the unfortunate man for being in the way. I rather expected to have my face scratched by her. Love is indeed a strange possession.

20 October 1918. Sunday evening, a good day's work behind me, to wit four Celebrations, two Matins and two Evensongs, to say nothing of three hours on the road in a bumpy tender; a nice tired feeling. Outside a deluge of rain pattering on my canvas roof, inside a crackling fire in my little Queenie stove and a nice bright light – what more could mortal man desire? Except it be, as an incentive to enjoy the present, the knowledge that in forty-eight hours time we shall be dumped homeless and roofless in the middle of a lately abandoned German aerodrome.

What do you think of the news lately, isn't it rather magnificent? Ostend, Lille and Douai in one day is more than encouraging, and if we can only keep the pace going, another few weeks ought to see us throwing pontoons across the Rhine.

I had a trip up to the war on Thursday. I went up to bury two of our fellows who had come down behind the Hun line, but whose machine had been recaptured as our line advanced.

It was inexpressibly strange to ride along across the belt of devastated country through which the old no man's land used to run, and to see, from a rational viewpoint, the well-known places.

The roads across this dreary shell-torn wilderness are of course atrocious, and the pack of transport moving forward was so great that we were reduced to a snail's pace. Getting along wouldn't be so bad if it weren't for the transport of our gallant allies. The Belgians especially seem to tie their lorries together with string. You never saw such ramshackle affairs. The ditches each side are strewn with wrecks, which have either petered out or become bogged. Of the remainder one half tows the other half. Certainly at any given moment I should be prepared to swear that of the lorries on the road, not more than a third are capable of moving under their own steam.

However this is a digression. I wish I could make you see the dismal waste each side of the road, one unending sea of brown mud littered with the debris of war, bits of decaying wood, old and twisted strands of barbed wire, broken rifles, torn and mildewing sandbags, and a thousand and one other relics of four years of war – more like a glorified rubbish dump than a smiling countryside. And then at intervals, notices bearing the names of villages unknowable as such except for an extra big heap of rubble marking the site of the village church.

Once through this nightmare of beastliness we got out into the country the other side, which until a fortnight ago was the Hun back area. It was amazingly interesting to see his notices everywhere and all the other signs of his recent occupation. Of course the advance has gone forward so quickly that the country is practically undamaged except for an occasional shell hole, and a dead horse or cow in the fields. The villages are a little more knocked about where street fighting took place, but a few new tiles and a pane or two of glass will soon put them to rights again.

As we went through in our car the liberated civilians were frightfully bucked to see us, waved their hands, and smiled from ear to ear. At that particular moment we held one half of a certain big town and the Bosch the other half, and between were huddled a mass of civilians who were filtering through our lines and streaming back along the roads to safety. Very pathetic to see the poor creatures trudging along, humping bundles of bedding and treasured possessions, but all wonderfully satisfied apparently to see friendly faces again. A party of six nuns, all splattered with mud, were stomping along among the crowd looking rather forlorn and homeless. Goodness knows where they would eventually find a home.

It was rather significant how thin and pale they all looked compared with the civilians our side. I think that the food shortage must be quite as bad as rumour would have us believe, certainly they looked as if they had been living on substitutes for some time, and not too abundant a supply at that.

Anyway I'm very optimistic about the end of the war coming soon. I hear that in some places at home they had it that peace was declared, and had a great flag-wagging night on the strength of it!

24 October 1918. We are now occupying an old German aerodrome [Bisseghem] about thirty miles east of where we were when last I wrote. We pulled out our roots early Tuesday morning, and with lorries laden to the skies the pilgrimage to the new home started. Being wise I bribed the CO of one of my Squadrons to take me as his Observer and so was spared the long weary hours on the road. The aerodrome qua aerodrome is good, but the Hun in his retreat destroyed all the huts and billets which he used and we have had to find a temporary home in ruined houses about a mile away. Ruined perhaps is a strong word. The glass in the windows is certainly ruined, not a pane anywhere, and most of the tiles are napoo, but the four walls stand and afford a shelter from the weather if not from the cold wind. However we must never forget that there is a war on, which is just what we are apt to do in the Flying Corps.

The pathetic exodus of civilians continues; all day long a steady stream of them meanders towards the rear pushing wheelbarrows piled high with bedding and the inevitable kitchen stove; those without handcarts carry huge bundles slung across their shoulders, occasionally a bullock is harnessed in to do the work of hauling. More often than not they are without stockings and very few have leather boots. Carpet slippers or sabots for the most part.

One poor woman who had trudged all day behind a handcart found shelter for the night in the cottage where our Squadron Office is installed, and there gave birth to a daughter – and *mirabile dictu*, both are alive and doing well.

Today I walked into a big city [Menin] about two miles in front of where we are. It is the selfsame city which two months ago was the target of a daylight bombing raid about which I told you. The Bosch frightened perhaps by the Daily Mail 'town for a town' campaign had evacuated it without doing any more damage than the demolition of all the bridges. The tide of war has however left it a little bruised and weary. A good deal of glass is broken and a few houses have been hit by shells, while several walls bear the scar of street fighting and machine-gun bullets. The civilians however remain, and the ordinary life goes on. I went in to get my haircut ostensibly, but I combined with business the open-mouthed enjoyment of a tourist. The town is *en fête*, from every house flutter Belgian flags, and the broad grins of the civilians testify to their joy at seeing the last of the Huns. While walking down one street a little girl, nine or ten years old, ran across the road and shook hands with us, and showed her pleasure at seeing us by saying the only word of English she knew which rather inappropriately was 'goodbye'.

30 October 1918. For the last few days I've been staying with the Pig who, as I think I told you, has been given an Independent Command and runs a Flight of very superior battle planes. I return to No. 7 in a day or two. Meanwhile I am living in a hut built by the Bosch in his usual thorough manner. The only fear is that he may have left a mine underneath it, in the pleasant way which is all his own, but so far nothing has gone up and expert search has revealed no sign of a booby-trap.

4 November 1918. We live in stirring times, and the line moves so quickly that front areas today are back areas tomorrow. Everything is consequently in a state of unsettledom and we live from hand to mouth mentally even more than physically.

The news that Turkey has thrown her hand in, and that Austria has accepted our terms of an Armistice is very encouraging and has pleased us all immensely, though there has been no joybells and no extravagant demonstrations. We all feel that victory and peace are a stage nearer, possibly well in sight, but nobody seems prepared to do any shouting just yet.

During the middle of last week the Bosch was very active at night bombing – over every night laying eggs but did no real damage apart from putting up a dump of his own abandoned ammunition. As generally happens it's the poor civilians who catch it. One of his bombs I heard killed an elderly Belgian rentier, whose wife and family had been killed two months ago by one of our bombs – so between us and the Bosch the entire family has been wiped out.

Today there passed our billet a farm cart laden with furniture, drawn by a horse and a cow yoked together. The horse, strange as it may sound, didn't resent apparently the indignity, but ambled along quite happily with its unusual stable companion. An even stranger sight was to be seen the other day. A very smart phaeton, beautifully polished, containing four *belles dames* delightfully gowned, complete with furs and *Maison Lewis* hats came down the street driven by the family coachman in livery and cockade, and between the shafts a fiery high-stepping dun cow!

I find now that a good deal of my sympathy has been squandered unnecessarily on the poor Belgians laboriously dragging or pushing carts loaded high with furniture. In the innocency of my heart I thought they were trying to rescue their household goods from war's engulfing tide. Apparently in most cases it is somebody else's, and the frenzied hurry is not due to the fear of shells, but to the fear of being caught by the rightful owner before they can get away with their loot.

Today I did my first loop, or rather I was looped for the first time. I always thought that it must be a very thrilling experience and was rather disappointed to find that there is practically no sensation in it at all. It is all over so quickly that you hardly realise that for an instant of time you are upside down in the air.

The air is full of wild rumours; the wildest perhaps is that all the U-boats are sailing the high seas flying white flags, waiting to surrender to the first trawler on the horizon.

11 November 1918. This is the last letter I shall write during the war, for hostilities cease in ten minutes time. Now that it has come my mind refuses to comprehend the wonderful fact that the war is over and that the long strain and anxiety is removed.

We were all in Mess last night, waiting for dinner to be served when the news came. I was over with one of my Squadrons. We had just had a Service, and had adjourned to their ante-room which was a German Flying Corps Mess until about a month ago [Menin].

While waiting for dinner we were discussing a German flying song which the Bosch had painted on the wall over the mantelpiece. It was the usual hot air about fearing neither death nor foe; and how when the wind did blow that was the time they particularly liked to cleave the air with their wings. I had got as far as Tod and Teufel when the telephone rang. Nobody stopped talking while the Wireless Officer went to answer the phone, then he turned round and said 'the German government has advised the plenipotentiaries to accept the terms of the Armistice' – 'Three cheers for the Armistice'. And you can imagine that they were the loudest and heartiest three cheers ever given.

Everybody came dashing in to see what the matter was, and learning the good news likewise gave tongue until the whole country-side was cheering. The first to realise the import of the message dashed off to the aerodrome and fired the whole stock of Very lights into the air. Everybody must have had the message about the same time, for within five minutes lights were going up in all directions, flares, Very lights of every colour, red & green & white, star shells, bonfires – everything in fact that would give a light or make a noise was used to express our joy. Even the searchlights went mad, and dashed wildly backwards and forwards across the sky. Never have I seen such a sight or heard such a din. Curiously I felt quite unmoved. My dinner didn't seem to taste any sweeter. I suppose one's mind can't conceive what peace means all at once.

Hostilities have now ceased, but back here the world seems to be going on much as usual. I suppose tonight however we shall have an organised celebration and then perhaps the truth will begin to dawn on us.

Later. Your letter has just arrived with the two for me enclosed. The very dirty torn envelope contained a copy of the sporting paper in which the account of my two rounds with Bandsman Rice appeared. It makes me smile: 'Sgt Bandsman Rice, the famous boxer, gave some good exhibitions of boxing. First he gave 2 rounds with Rev.

M.P.G. Leonard DSO, the Padre, a veritable fighting parson. In this Rice showed what a master he is at footwork, and the Padre showed he was quite used to the "mits".'

I have moved back to No. 7 and am living in a workman's cottage which I have to myself. All this quarter of Menin – no harm in mentioning where I am now the war is over – is deserted, and we each have a house to ourselves.

I have chalked 'Vicarage' on my front door, and live in the room which was once the parlour. I stick to one room because my furniture looks lost if I don't keep it all together. I've got an excellent little stove, and a good supply of brickets, kindly left by the Bosch when he went away. At the moment the stove is functioning hard, and 'all is lovely in the garden'.

16 November 1918. I can hardly yet realise that the war is over. Every night since the signing of the Armistice has been beautifully clear and moonlit, ideal nights for bombing. The fact that there hasn't been any, and that we've slept quietly and peacefully in our beds, has helped to bring the meaning of peace home to me: all the same I can hardly realise what a wonderful time we are living in.

Epilogue

For decades after the Great War, in many parts of the world, the names of 'Tubby' Clayton and Pat Leonard meant 'Toc H'. This was the army signallers' version of 'T H' – standing for Talbot House in Poperinghe. It became the name of an organisation with branches springing up in Britain and then the Dominions, involving huge numbers of ex-servicemen and the younger brothers of men who had died in the First World War.

Talbot House had been a focus of hope and relief for men of all ranks. Under the inspired leadership of Padre 'Tubby' Clayton, Toc H developed an outreach with specific aims: 'to preserve that depth of comradeship, to honour the fallen, and to train boys and young men for future leadership and commitment to service'. It exists to this day.

Pat Leonard was deeply involved for over ten years as it grew in importance – the Prince of Wales regularly attended meetings, and in their week in Boston during the 1925 World Tour, over 1,000 came to each midday Service held by Tubby and Pat in the Cathedral. Branches sprang up from there to Atlanta, from Quebec to Vancouver, in Ceylon and India, Australia and New Zealand. They were welcomed by bishops and archbishops, by Lord Forster in Australia, by General Plumer in Jerusalem ... and by masses of ex-servicemen.

To an Australian journalist Tubby described Toc H as 'a series of teams of men, mostly in their 20's and 30's, who undertake to give a proportion of their time to social service, particularly in boys' work. A quarter of a million of the boys of Great Britain are under our charge, either through the Scout movement, Brigade work, Newsboys' clubs, Juvenile Offenders or Children's Courts, sometimes through the most down-and-out clubs one could imagine.'

Hostels were set up by Toc H for men seeking work in the cities and Pat Leonard was Chaplain to 'Mark IV' in Manchester.

In 1933 he married Kathleen Knights-Smith, then Head of St Mildred's Settlement on the Isle of Dogs, and they had four children: twins Mary and John, Elizabeth and Andrew.

Pat Leonard hated the pretence, the hypocrisy, the clichés and uninspiring Services which put so many men off God. He believed that faith must be seen to be real, relevant, personal and caring, and this conviction coloured his approach to all his jobs – at Toc H headquarters, as curate of All Hallows' Church on London's Tower Hill, from 1936 as the Rector of Hatfield, with all its Second World War de Havilland connections, from 1944 as Provost of St Mary's Cathedral, Glasgow, and finally from 1953 to his death in 1963, based in Norwich as Suffragan Bishop of Thetford, ministering throughout Norfolk.

'Within a matter of months,' wrote the Editor of the *Norwich Churchman*, 'he had become one of the best loved figures in the Diocese.' 'A real man of God,' said the *Church Times*, 'much in demand for retreats and quiet days.'

He was hoping to retire at seventy-five but 'this cancer business has rather upset my plans ... I've been fairly busy with Confirmations and a couple of Institutions but I'm taking life pretty easily and not going out of my way to look for work.'

At Leiston Abbey, in Suffolk, where he was leading his last Retreat, a participant wrote: 'He was clearly in agony and could only speak and swallow with difficulty. In spite of this, or maybe because of it, every one there was caught up by his words. There seemed to be a living urgency of prayer on all our parts, to provide his valiant spirit with the strength to complete this task. His humour, his love, his joy in believing penetrated through all he said. I don't need to refer to my notes for his opening words: "It is an abiding comfort that God knows us through and through." These words spoken in agony of body but with such shining peace of mind.'

'I am so very thankful that I knew him.'

Index